PFITZ
PALES

The 'Musical Legend'
and its Background

PFITZNER'S
PALESTRINA

The 'Musical Legend'
and its Background

OWEN TOLLER

With a Preface by
DIETRICH FISCHER-DIESKAU

Other Operas
No. 1

TOCCATA
PRESS

To the memory of
Harold Truscott

First published in 1997 by Toccata Press.
© Owen Toller, 1997.
Music examples set by Jiří Kub

British Library Cataloguing in Publication Data
Toller, Owen
    Pfitzner's 'Palestrina'. - (Other Operas
    Series, ISSN 0960-0108; v.1)
    I. Title II. Series
    782.1092.

ISBN 0 907689 24 8
ISBN 0 907689 25 6 (pbk)
ISSN 0960-0108

Typeset in 11/12pt Plantin by York House Typographic Ltd
Printed and bound by SRP Ltd, Exeter

Contents

List of Illustrations

PREFACE

Dietrich Fischer-Dieskau

The ancient Greek myth of Amphion tells of how a man is called upon to complete a work, although he is deeply hesitant and mistrusts his own abilities, of how he experiences a moment of superhuman inspiration, awoken in him by a higher power, and of how, shortly afterwards, he finds himself old, disappointed and – above all – alone. A man from whom, his duty done, Apollo has wrenched the lyre and led away; there is nothing left for him to do but disappear.

But in him we also recognise Palestrina, whom Pfitzner made the central character of his most important opera, with a subject that, in some noteworthy aspects, offers analogies with Wagner's *Meistersinger*. The difference is that Wagner has his Sachs defend new ideas and a free approach to creativity, whereas Pfitzner insists that only the traditions of the old masters are valid.

Thomas Mann and his friend Bruno Walter, who conducted the premiere, were not the only ones to admire the judgement with which Pfitzner shaped the work, never letting the massive, highly polyphonic orchestral writing obscure the singing voice. The leitmotifs are clearly distinguishable and can easily be followed. All this points, above all, to Wagner's principles, which indeed govern Pfitzner's tonal language unopposed, although the manner in which that language is used and its colouring are fundamentally different. It is not so easy to make the proportionality work: the longish address of Morone, say, or the extended declaration of Borromeo in the First Act (both of which I have sung). In contrast, the shortness of the scene in which the Mass is composed seems to leave the central meaning underexposed, after an extended exposition which appears to be leading to something else.

7

Again as with Wagner, both libretto and score are by the
composer himself. This music drama about the earthly shell
of a composer constitutes both the loftiest and deepest –
indeed, the most important – creation in German music since
Parsifal. But it is less the history of Catholic church music
against a backdrop of Renaissance cardinals that we admire
than an entirely unique self-confession, the story of an old
master whose pupil Silla wants to go over to the monodists of
Florence and whom no threat of Carlo Borromeo can force to
compose the *Missa Papae Marcelli* – until the masters of old
and the angels more or less dictate it to him. We must see it as
a fascinating allegory of Pfitzner himself, in the creative
compulsion of his masterly late-Romanticism, confronted
with the atonalists of the Schoenberg school. The colossal,
sweeping scherzo in the Council Act shows, with deep irony,
how the outside world holds art in contempt, seeing church
music as, at best, a brief hindrance or a cog in the machinery
of political intrigue. The radiance of the resignation-filled
final act, by contrast, transplants the wistful dream of recognition entirely to the inner world.

That recognition has been widely accorded to *Palestrina*
ever since its first performance in Munich. But even apart
from the difficulties of casting – which is always apposite and
justified – this work places heavy demands on any company
open to the German language, demands which Pfitzner's
exclusive German-ness can compound in other countries.

In conversation, Pfitzner would often throw back his head
and cover his forehead with his hand. He would seem with-
drawn, as if into some distant suffering. But that same Hans
Pfitzner also allowed a glimpse of a genius that was destined
to surpass the commonplace – a genius the core of which is
hidden from the rest of us.

I

PFITZNER'S *PALESTRINA*:
AN INTRODUCTION

Hans Pfitzner's 'musical legend' *Palestrina* is considered in German-speaking countries to be one of the supreme masterpieces of music, and yet it is all but unknown elsewhere. The opera, first performed in 1917, tells the story of the composer Palestrina, his struggle to compose following the death of his wife and in the face of the threat of anti-musical decrees of the Church, and his eventual composition of the *Missa Papae Marcelli*, which, so legend has it, was dictated to him by angels and reconciled the Church to contrapuntal music. The story, set against the historical background of the Council of Trent, is also an allegory of the individual artist in society as well as a statement of Pfitzner's own beliefs about the musical climate of his time. The music is of profound nobility, constructed with enormous subtlety and skill.

Pfitzner was born in 1869 and died in 1949; he was conductor, pianist, critic and – I have no doubt – one of the great composers. He and Richard Strauss were Germany's two leading musicians between the 1890s and the rise of Hindemith's generation. The original plan of this book was to provide an exposition of all the different aspects of *Palestrina* – the music, the drama, the historical and philosophical aspects; and, as Pfitzner's music in general is still little known, I have taken the opportunity of giving brief descriptions of some of his other compositions.

Pfitzner is a particularly difficult composer to study, for a variety of reasons. His musical language, though in no way

9

obscure, makes few concessions; some of his biggest orchestral and instrumental works are stubbornly hard to bring into focus, hiding innovation and experimentation behind conventional exteriors. Pfitzner's melody, though copious, varied and beautiful, takes some assimilation. As a man Pfitzner was curmudgeonly, alternating bitterly dogmatic criticism with almost paranoid complaints about the neglect of the recognition he saw as his due. Above all, his life and political morality are bound up in his works to so complex a degree that it is hard to discuss his music in some circles without violent controversy. For some, the name of Hans Pfitzner is blackened by his relationship with the Third Reich; indeed, to many this 'reputation' is far better known than the music. It is invariably based on the most superficial acquaintance with the facts, if that; the facts are very confusing, but that is no excuse for condemning Pfitzner without investigating them. Much recent writing has focussed on Pfitzner's life, political beliefs, personality or place in the context of musical, literary or philosophical history. In an era when the ability to listen to pure music is being steadily eroded, Pfitzner the pure musician has not been allowed the opportunities he deserves – opportunities granted to lesser composers who happen to be more politically correct, or who offer more handles to non-musical discussion.

Pfitzner's operas, and *Palestrina* in particular, are allegorical and cannot be fully understood without knowledge of the underlying allegory. But Pfitzner is above all a pure musician. For a just appreciation of his qualities it is necessary to remember that all extra-musical factors are subservient to the music itself.

The literature in English on Pfitzner is tiny, but it has recently been vastly enriched by John Williamson's *The Music of Hans Pfitzner*.[1] Williamson presupposes some acquaintance with Pfitzner's life and works, but readers of this book are strongly recommended to continue to his.

It would take an extraordinary polymath to do justice to all the sides of *Palestrina*. For 'a mere musician, a chorister' to attempt to add significantly to the body of Pfitzner scholar-

---

[1] Clarendon Press, Oxford, 1992.

ship represented by such apostles as Adamy, Osthoff, Rectanus and Williamson, especially when aware that he is a layman in many respects, would be presumptuous in the extreme. Rather, this book is written for the intelligent non-specialist – in the hope that more will find their way to one of the greatest of all operas; and in the conviction that *Palestrina* demands to be heard, known and appreciated by a wide international audience, and that it amply repays the efforts it requires.

ACKNOWLEDGEMENTS

It is pleasant to acknowledge the help of numerous friends, acquaintances and others in this study. My thanks to Chris de Souza and Antony Shelley, for first staging *Palestrina* in London and enabling me to catch their enthusiasm for the work, and to the former as well for his time and knowledge in discussing it with me; to the late Harold Rosenthal for supplying information about performance history; to Jenny Ball, Elisabeth Barrington, Dorrit Dunn, Daniel Franklin and Jim Lambert, for helping, in the form of translations, to conceal some of the many cracks in my German; to Peter King, for translating the Latin extracts; to David Fallows, Annelore Habs, Erik Levi, Peter Maudsley, Julia Price, John Williamson, Stephen Willink and Gerd Ueckermann for help in reference-chasing and useful suggestions; to Angela Escott, Hazel Morgan, Hazel Wedderburn, Simon Bainbridge, Leo Black, Charles Hollander, Leslie Howard, the Rev. Hugh Mead, James Murray, Peter Toye, Jonathan Varcoe and John Williamson, for obtaining material for me, on loan or otherwise; to Eric Sneddon, Charles Stewart and, again, Hugh Mead for reading drafts of certain sections and giving advice; to John Wagstaff for help in compiling the bibliography; to Martin Anderson, for numerous valuable suggestions leading to improvements in content and style; to the staff of Harold Moore's Records, London W1, for obtaining a number of obscure recordings; to the staffs of the British Library, the Cambridge University Library, the library of the Royal Academy of Music, the Goethe Institute and Hammersmith Public Libraries. Special thanks to Kate Caffrey, for some of the translations and a good deal of typing; and to all my former colleagues at St Paul's, but particularly those in the music department, for having put up with rather a lot. Help with the proof-reading was provided by David Brown, Guy Rickards and Richard Whitehouse.

Above all, my gratitude is due to the late Harold Truscott. His suggestions and advice after reading the typescript in an earlier draft were responsible for this study being significantly less inadequate than it would otherwise have been; he gave freely of his time and his enormous knowledge of and enthusiasm for the music of Pfitzner and his contemporaries, not only enabling me to learn far more about Pfitzner but also opening doors to vast regions of hitherto unfamiliar music. Many ideas were triggered off by his comments; the footnotes do not do justice to his contribution. Sadly, he died before this book could reach print. It is only right that it should be dedicated to his memory.

In spite of such welcome assistance from so many different quarters, the errors and inadequacies which remain are entirely my own responsibility. I am grateful to the following for permission to reproduce copyright material: Langen Müller Herbig (Walter Abendroth, *Hans Pfitzner*, 1935); Faber & Faber Ltd (Antony Beaumont, *Busoni, The Composer*, 1985; Robert Donington, *The Rise of Opera*, 1983); *The Observer* ('Sayings of the Week'); Thames & Hudson Ltd (Kurt Blaukopf, *Mahler*, 1973; Arthur G. Dickens, *The Counter-Reformation*, 1968); The Hogarth Press (Fritz Busch, *Pages from a Musician's Life*, 1953, translated by Margaret Strachey); Breitkopf & Härtel, Wiesbaden, for permission to quote from the libretto of Busoni's *Doktor Faust*; Oxford University Press (Ernest J. Dent, 'Hans Pfitzner', *Music and Letters*, 1923; Knud Jeppesen, *The Style of Palestrina and the Dissonance*, 1946; Arthur Schopenhauer, *Parerga und Paralipomena*, translated by E. F. J. Payne, 1974; John Williamson, *The Music of Hans Pfitzner*, 1992); Fontana Library, for adapting a map in Geoffrey Elton, *Reformation Europe 1517–1559* (1963); *Gramophone* (Edward Greenfield's review of *Palestrina*, February 1974); Thomas Nelson & Sons Ltd (Hubert Jedin, *The History of the Council of Trent*, translated by Otto Graf, 1957); Sheed & Ward Ltd (Hubert Jedin, *Crisis and Closure of the Council of Trent*, 1967); Dr Hubert Kriss (Rudolf Kriss, *Die Darstellung des Konzils von Trient in Hans Pfitzners musikalische Legende 'Palestrina'*, 1962); The Earl of Harewood and The Bodley Head (*Kobbé's Complete Opera Book*); Secker & Warburg Ltd (Thomas Mann, *Doctor Faustus*, translated by H. T. Lowe-Porter, 1949; Robert Gutman, *Richard Wagner: The Man, His Mind and His Music*, 1968); from *Reflections of a Nonpolitical Man*, by Thomas Mann, copyright 1983 by Frederick Ungar Publishing Co., Inc., reprinted by permission of the Ungar Publishing Company; from the libretto of *Taverner*, by Peter Maxwell Davies, reprinted by kind permission of Boosey & Hawkes Music Publishers Ltd; Verlag Waldemar Kramer, Frankfurt-am-Main (Joseph Müller-Blattau, *Hans Pfitzner*, 1969); Associated Book Publishers (UK) Ltd/ Routledge & Kegan Paul (Ludwig Pastor, *History of the Popes*, translated Kerr, 1928); Hamburg State Opera (Hans Pfitzner, 'Mein Hauptwerk', a contribution to the new Hamburg production of 1937, quoted from the programme book of the premiere of the production of *Palestrina* of 18 November 1979); Gustav Bosse Verlag, Regensburg (H. Rectanus, 'Pfitzner als Dramatiker', from *Beiträge zur Geschichte der Oper*, 1969); Prof. Dr. Hans Rectanus and Konrad Triltsch Verlag, Würzburg (Hans Rectanus, *Leitmotivik und Form in den musikdramatischen Werken Hans Pfitzners*, 1967); J. M. Dent & Sons, Ltd., and Everyman's Library (Rousseau, *The Social Contract*, translated by G. D. H. Cole, 1973); Atlantis Musikbuch-Verlag, Zurich (Ludwig Schrott, *Die Persönlichkeit Hans Pfitzners*, 1959); The Society of Authors on behalf of the Bernard Shaw Estate (Bernard Shaw, *The Perfect Wagnerite*).

Music quotations: from Pfitzner's *Palestrina*, © 1916 by Fürstner, Ltd., © assigned 1951 to Schott and Co., Ltd., London. Examples reproduced by permission of Schott and Co., Ltd.; C. F. Kahnt (Pfitzner, 'Herbstbild', Op. 27, No. 2). From Giovanni Pierluigi da Palestrina, *Pope Marcellus Mass*, A Norton Critical Score, ed. Lewis Lockwood, © 1975 by W. W. Norton & Co., Inc., used by permission of W. W. Norton & Co., Inc.

Illustrations: Fratelli Alinari, Florence (D. Crespi, *The Dinner of S. Carlo Borromeo*); the Historical Archive of the Vienna Philharmonic Orchestra (manuscript of *Palestrina*); Collection Meseu de Arte de São Paulo, Brazil (Tiziano Vecellio (Pieve di Cadore), Belluno, 1488–Venezia, 1576), *Portrait of Cardinal Cristoforo Madruzzo*, oil on canvas, 210x109cm; photo by Luiz Hossaka); BBC Hulton Picture Library (C. Laudy, *The Council of Trent*, engraving, 1565; *Giovanni Pierluigi Palestrina*, engraving after an original in the archives of the Vatican Museum); Service Photographique de la Réunion des Musées Nationaux, Paris (Titian, *The Council of Trent*, Museé du Louvre, Musées Nationaux).

Every effort has been made to secure the necessary permissions, but in a few cases it has proved impossible to trace the copyright holders. I apologise for any apparent negligence.

Owen Toller,
Northwood, 1996

II

DRAMATIS PERSONAE

I *Singers*

Pope Pius IV	basso profundo
Giovanni Morone, Cardinal Legate of the Pope	baritone
Bernardo Novagerio, Cardinal Legate of the Pope	tenor
Cardinal Christoph Madruscht, Prince-Bishop of Trent	basso profundo
Carlo Borromeo, Roman Cardinal	baritone
The Cardinal of Lorraine	bass
Abdisu, Patriarch of Assyria	high tenor
Anton Brus von Müglitz, Archbishop of Prague	bass
Count Luna, spokesman of the King of Spain	high baritone
The Bishop of Budoja, Italian Bishop	tenor
Theophilus, Bishop of Imola, Italian Bishop	tenor
Avosmediano, Bishop of Cadix, Spanish Bishop	bass-baritone
Giovanni Pierluigi Palestrina, Kapellmeister at the Church of Sta. Maria Maggiore in Rome	tenor
Ighino, his son, fifteen years old	soprano
Silla, his pupil, seventeen years old	mezzo-soprano

14

Bishop Ercole Severolus, Master of
    Ceremonies of the Council of Trent[1]   bass-baritone
Chapel singers of Sta. Maria Maggiore
    in Rome • Singers of the Papal
    Chapel • Archbishops, Bishops,
    Abbots, Orders General, Envoys,
    Procurators of sacred and spiritual
    leaders, Theologians, Doctors of all
    Christian nations • Servants • Town
    soldiers • People of the streets

II *Silent roles*

Two papal nuncios • Lainez, Salmeron,
    Jesuit generals
Massarelli, Bishop of Thelesia,
    Secretary to the Council
Giuseppe, Palestrina's old servant

III *Singing Apparitions*

The spirit of Lucrezia, Palestrina's
    dead wife   alto
The spirits of nine dead Masters
    of Music
Three angel voices   high soprano

---

[1] Pfitzner's order of precedence places Severolus after Silla. I have no idea why this should be the case, unless it underlines the fact that the real Severolus was not a bishop but a layman; *cf.* pp. 270–71, below.

III

SYNOPSIS

After the orchestral Introduction, the curtain rises on a room in Palestrina's house in Rome. Silla is playing over to himself a song that he has written, but he repeatedly breaks off to look forward to the chance of going to Florence to join the circle of the Camerata; he is tired of the conventionality of life in Rome. Ighino enters, and the two boys discuss the question of fame. Ighino says that his father has been much saddened and has given up composing since the death of his wife Lucrezia. Silla shrugs this off and goes back to his song.

He is interrupted by the entrance of Palestrina and his friend Cardinal Borromeo. Borromeo criticises the song they have overheard as being sinful in its modernity. After the boys have gone, he tells Palestrina that the Council of Trent, directed by the Pope, has been threatening to destroy all polyphonic church music, but that the Holy Roman Emperor Ferdinand opposes this extreme measure. Borromeo suggests that Palestrina write a setting of the Mass to show that the Council's objections to polyphonic music can be overcome, but Palestrina refuses the commission, saying that his muse cannot produce such things to order. Borromeo leaves angrily, and left alone in the night Palestrina contemplates the futility of life. There now appear to him the spirits of nine great composers of the past. They tell Palestrina that it is his duty to God to continue to compose and that he must fulfil the purpose for which he has been placed on earth. They disappear, to be replaced by a host of angels which dictate to Palestrina the work known as the 'Missa Papae Marcellae'.

The spirit of Lucrezia adds her inspiration. Palestrina has thus achieved an inward peace, and he falls asleep exhausted. As dawn breaks Silla and Ighino run in and find him sleeping amid the completed pages of manuscript.

There is a substantial Prelude to Act Two, which is a depiction of the Council of Trent in General Congregation. The Master of Ceremonies is directing the arrangement of the hall by the servants. Cardinal Novagerio warns them that there must be no repetition of their recent brawling and that Cardinal Madruscht will not stand for it. The delegates begin to arrive. Among them is Borromeo, and he and Novagerio discuss some of the important issues to be raised during the Congregation, including church music. Borromeo cannot report progress of Palestrina's composition. Other arrivals include the Cardinal of Lorraine, unyielding figurehead of the French, the 'German Bear' Madruscht, the Archbishop of Prague, the Bishop of Budoja who represents all the worst sides of the Italians (in the view of the Spanish contingent), and the strange and primitive Patriarch of Assyria. The Congregation is given a magnificent formal opening, and Morone, President of the Council, begins his address. Soon points of order and precedence are raised; the Italians wish to bring the Council to a conclusion as quickly as possible, but the other nationalities want more time for discussion. The conflict between Italians and Spaniards, not helped by the attitude of the Cardinal of Lorraine, simmers beneath the surface and sporadically flames up. Budoja makes several attempts to be funny. The question of church music is coolly and easily negotiated by Borromeo, but at last the Count of Luna, spokesman of the King of Spain, succeeds in provoking Lorraine and pandemonium breaks out. Morone manages to restore a semblance of order and closes the session for an early lunch. Most leave, but Novagerio remains and effects a reconciliation between Morone and Lorraine as well as dismissing Budoja, who is preoccupied with travel expenses. On to the empty stage now emerge the servants of the various nationalities. They have seen the arguments between their masters and now a full-scale battle develops. Madruscht appears at the head of a troop of soldiers and the rioters are shot down, as was threatened at the beginning of the Act.

Act Three begins with a quiet orchestral Introduction. We
are again in Palestrina's study in Rome, and the composer is
seated in a chair, Ighino alongside him. A group of singers
from Santa Maria Maggiore are in the room, anxiously awaiting the outcome of the performance of the Mass before the
Pope. They comment to one another that Palestrina has aged,
and he himself seems scarcely aware of where he is. Ighino
explains how the Mass was handed over to release him from
prison. Suddenly cries of 'Evviva' are heard from the street,
and a group of papal singers bursts into the room with the
news that the performance has been highly successful and
that the Pope is delighted. A further group brings the astonishing news that the Pope himself is coming to express his
appreciation. When he arrives, his words of praise are those
attributed to Pius IV at a later performance of the Mass.

When all the others have left, Borromeo remains. He too is
won over by the beauty of the Mass and he tries to express his
contrition to Palestrina. The two men embrace, and Borromeo leaves. Ighino comes forward and tell his father that Silla,
his head still full of new theories, has gone to Florence; but
when renewed cries of 'Evviva' are heard Ighino runs off to
join the celebrations. Alone, Palestrina goes to the organ and
plays a few notes. Cries from the street can still be heard, but
Palestrina is deaf to them, contemplating the fulfillment of his
task as the curtain falls.

IV

PFITZNER AND THE WRITING OF *PALESTRINA*

In the earlier years of the twentieth century the major German and Austrian opera houses were run by a succession of highly gifted all-round musicians, many of whom were noted composers. Richard Strauss and Gustav Mahler are the two most famous; Hans Erich Pfitzner was one of their number. A few years younger than those great men, he was born in Moscow on 5 May 1869. His father was a professional violinist who had gone to Moscow from Würzburg, returning to become music director of the Stadttheater Frankfurt in June 1872. Pfitzner's grandfather had been a musician too, a choirmaster in Frohberg. As Joseph Müller-Blattau writes, 'Music was not only much heard in the family, it was an element of life'.[1] So it is not surprising that when Hans left school at the end of March 1886 he went straight to the Frankfurt Conservatory. There he attended the theory classes of Iwan Knorr and studied the piano with James Kwast. He became a fine pianist, regularly appearing as an accompanist in public until late in his life.

At the Conservatory he wrote his first works and made a number of important acquaintances. One of these was James Grun, an Anglo-German who was to become the librettist of his first two operas. Another was Paul Nikolaus Cossmann, subsequently a leading journalist, apostate Jew, trenchant right-winger and prisoner of the Nazis. Cossman gave Pfitzner much financial and other practical help, and strongly

---

[1] *Hans Pfitzner*, Kramer, Frankfurt, 1969, p. 5.

19

influenced his political thinking.[2] Knorr's pupils also included Percy Grainger, Norman O'Neill, Balfour Gardiner, Roger Quilter and Cyril Scott, the so-called 'Frankfurt School'. After graduating, Pfitzner moved in 1892 to Koblenz to teach piano and theory at the Conservatory there, and in May 1893 he conducted a concert of his own music in Berlin, the first event to put him on the musical map. The programme included part of his incidental music to Ibsen's *The Feast at Solhaug*, the Cello Sonata, Op. 1, 'Dietrich's Narration' from his first opera *Der arme Heinrich* (an excerpt that became popular), a Scherzo for orchestra and some songs. The Scherzo, intended as part of a symphony, is Pfitzner's first surviving orchestral work; it shows competence in handling the orchestra, but its energy is facile, derived from plain repeated rhythms. The Cello Sonata is an immediately attractive work, demonstrating the young composer's lyrical gift.

The music for *Das Fest auf Solhaug* was Pfitzner's first work for the stage. It consists of three orchestral preludes vividly evoking contrasting atmospheres, together with solo and choral songs and melodramas. Begun while he was still studying at Frankfurt, it was the first work he completed after graduating. This substantial score meant a considerable amount to Pfitzner, and its failure to reach performance was a source of considerable frustration and disillusionment. The exclusive rights to the use of the standard German translation had been assigned to a Danish composer, Peter Lange-Müller. Pfitzner visited Ibsen himself in Munich in an attempt to resolve the problem, but he was unsuccessful; nor would Hans von Bülow take up the cause of the young and then unknown composer. Pfitzner naturally felt that providence was against him; he made this claim quite often during the rest of his life, though rarely with such good cause as now.[3]

[2] *Cf.* John Williamson, *op. cit.*, p. 16.

[3] *Cf.* Hans Pfitzner, *Reden, Schriften, Briefen*, ed. Walter Abendroth, Luchterhand, Berlin, 1955, pp. 193 *et seq.* I am indebted to Dr John Williamson for sending me a copy of his article 'Pfitzner and Ibsen' from *Music and Letters*, Vol. 67, No. 2, April 1986, pp. 127 *et seq.*, which describes the

Much the most impressive of the early instrumental works
is the D minor String Quartet of 1886. The themes are
characteristic and pregnant. The first subject of the first
movement takes on many different shapes while retaining its
own identity, a characteristic of Pfitzner's, as is the anticipation in the Scherzo of the dominant trill in the first trio. The
Scherzo itself has an irresistible lilt and the finale's major-key
theme droops with a sort of post-Classical knowingness. The
influences of late Beethoven and Brahms are present – here is
a young man hoping to write like an old one – but the
assurance of the work is astonishing and it is full of fingerprints which the later music leads one to call Pfitznerian.
   Der arme Heinrich was first produced in Frankfurt in January 1897. The story, based on a narrative poem by Hartmann
von Aue (*c.* 1200), is similar to that of Sullivan's *The Golden
Legend.* Sir Henry (Heinrich) lies ill, with a sickness that no
doctor can cure. His servant Dietrich journeys to the abbey of
Salerno, where he learns that Sir Henry can be cured 'only by
the willing sacrifice of a virgin'. (The events of this journey
form the substance of Dietrich's Narration.) Dietrich's
daughter Agnes volunteers herself. At Salerno the sacrifice is
about to take place when Heinrich's fervent prayers for the
return of his strength are granted and he saves Agnes at the
last possible moment. (In Longfellow/Sullivan the doctor is
Lucifer disguised as a friar; Grun and Pfitzner dispense with
this detail.) Considering Pfitzner's lack of orchestral experience, and that this was his first work on a really large scale, *Der
arme Heinrich* is a most impressive achievement. Wagner's
influence, though clear in the *Tannhäuser*-like music of
Dietrich's entrance, in some *Parsifal*-like passages and in the
generally extremely slow pace of the declamation, is nothing
like as all-pervading as might be expected, and for much of

episode in detail and to which those interested in the *Fest auf Solhaug* music
are referred. Dr Williamson also points out that the Hoch'sche
Conservatoire under Bernhard Scholz was a singularly reactionary establishment in terms of musical style; it may be wondered whether the
conservative atmosphere contributed directly to Pfitzner's artistic tendencies or merely encouraged his existing inclinations.

the score Pfitzner's own personality is dominant. The writing
for orchestra is exceptionally assured and there is much music
of power and beauty; in addition it is magnificently constructed, showing an approach to tonal and dramatic
architecture that alone would be sufficient to mark its composer as an important figure. Its initial success (Humperdinck
was among many who praised it) is easy to understand,
although the comparatively static nature of Act II and the fact
that its originalities are less obvious than its derivations probably help explain its failure to gain a place in the repertoire.

Pfitzner's teaching and his efforts to stage *Heinrich* took up
most of the next few years, and his next large work was the
F major Piano Trio, Op. 8, of 1896. This is an intriguing but
difficult piece. The nominal major key is misleading; for
much of the time the work evokes the stormy temper of
Brahms' F minor Piano Quintet, and Pfitzner ends unequivo-
cally in that key. The second subject of the first movement, at
first given no more than a mention, is recapitulated simultaneously with the first subject and it is only given full stature in
a long nostalgic interlude at the end of the finale just before
the final F minor outburst.

In September 1897 Pfitzner took up a new post at the Stern
Conservatory in Berlin. There, between 1905 and 1907, his
pupils included the young Otto Klemperer, who described
him as an erratic and unorthodox, but fascinating, teacher.[4]
In the next few years Pfitzner became Kapellmeister at the
Theater des Westens in Berlin, before moving to Mainz and
Munich. In 1899 came one of the more unlikely events of
musical history. Pfitzner had fallen in love with Mimi, the
daughter of his former teacher Kwast, but as her parents
refused permission for a marriage the couple decided to
elope. Leaving Germany they travelled through Switzerland,
Italy and France to England, all in order to avoid the possible
pursuit of Percy Grainger, who also had his eye on Mimi. The

---

[4] *Cf.* Peter Heyworth, *Otto Klemperer: His Life and Times*, Vol. 1, Cambridge University Press, Cambridge, 1983, p. 20; and Martin Anderson
(ed.), *Klemperer on Music*, Toccata Press, London, 1986, pp. 166–68 and
171.

marriage took place in Canterbury Cathedral, and they began
their honeymoon at the resort of Herne Bay.[5]
By now Pfitzner's career was beginning to develop in earnest, and particularly as a composer of lieder. His songs form a
significant contribution to the German lied and display a
personality which, though less obviously striking than that of
Wolf or even Strauss, is nevertheless at its best strongly
individual. (The lesser examples sound like watered-down
Schumann.) As with Strauss, the majority of the songs are
early works and it is in them rather than in the instrumental
works that a true Pfitznerian character first appears. The fine
set of five songs after Eichendorff, Op. 9, reveals many
characteristics. The first song, 'Der Gärtner', consists of a
simple chorale-like melody, growing with an easy mastery
into several contrapuntal lines for the second verse. From
E flat it finds its way to E before returning with mysterious
suddenness to the former key. 'Die Einsame' and 'Im
Herbst', second and third of the set, show Pfitzner's gift for
passionately ranging but classically balanced melody. The
most individual of Pfitzner's songs are generally those of a
darkly melancholic or even tortured character, the melodic
lines twisting back on themselves and often being subject to
unexpected but expressive chromatic inflections. The chorale
which is so prominent a feature of both *Palestrina* and the later
Eichendorff cantata *Von deutscher Seele* is transfigured in two
magnificent songs. In 'Hussens Kerker' (Op. 32, No. 1) it is
modified in subtle and complex ways by variations of texture.
'In Danzig' (Op. 22, No. 1) uses an omnipresent one-bar
figure in the deepest octaves of the piano to evoke the noise-
less town at night. This ostinato becomes identified with the
distant roar of the sea, but it is no piece of onomatopoeia;
rather, the image of the poem gives rise to a musical idea from
which the whole song is built up.[6]
'An die Mark' (Op. 15, No. 3) is a remarkable evocation of
a landscape without any recourse to that word-painting which

[5] Walter Abendroth, *Hans Pfitzner*, Langen-Müller, Munich, 1935; *cf.* also
John Bird, *Percy Grainger*, Elek, London, 1976/Faber, London, 1982,
pp. 38 *et seq.*

[6] Williamson, *op cit.*, pp. 42–46.

Pfitzner so despised. At first such things as the unexpected cadence to F minor instead of A minor at the eighteenth bar sound self-conscious, but their rightness soon becomes plain. John Williamson, in his essential chapter on Pfitzner's lieder, points out how the effect of this song is built up from spare contrapuntal lines which collide to produce diatonic dissonances over a very slowly moving harmonic background.[7] The implacable spareness of texture contributes to the bleak but ultimately consoling atmosphere. Among the later songs, those written after *Palestrina*, 'Abbitte' (Op.29, No.1) startles by its 'progressive' harmonies; the opening chords sound like nothing so much as Scriabin. John Williamson has demonstrated how these extreme chromatics are used within the thinking of the Germanic tradition while at the same time demonstrating Pfitzner's ability to respond to the language of his more extreme contemporaries.[8] Similar examples are the cat's cradle of arpeggiated counterpoint in the interlude before verse three of 'In Danzig', held in thrall by the ostinato in the bass, and the whole of the Goethe setting, *An den Mond* (Op. 18). This song is dominated by a whole-tone scale, but Pfitzner treats the scale not atonally but as an elaboration of the augmented fifth chord in various contexts.[9] The crucial thing, though, is that in all these songs the harmonies are not merely effects; they are completely subservient to the creation of an overall mood and atmosphere, a single coherent inspiration. The results are among the most intense and impressive in the repertoire. But the range of his songs is considerable from the Schubertian pathos of the gently undulating $\frac{6}{8}$ of 'Sehnsucht' (Op. 10, No. 1) and the heart-easing simplicity of 'Schön Suschen' (Op. 22, No. 3)[10]and 'An die Bienen' (Op. 22, No. 5) which combines this mood with Pfitzner's own sidestep modulations, to the inwardly rapturous 'Mailied' (Op. 26, No. 5), 'Sonst' (Op. 15, No. 4), and a

---

[7] *Ibid.*, pp. 228–33.

[8] *Ibid.*, pp. 238–40.

[9] *Cf. ibid.*, pp. 234–37.

[10] John Williamson points out how the simplicity is an example of art concealing art: *op. cit.*, p. 250.

*Pfitzner in 1900, in a Christmas photograph inscribed to his parents
(courtesy of Annelore Habs and the Hans Pfitzner-Gesellschaft)*

group allied to German folksong: 'Gretel' (Op. 11, No. 5),
'Untreu und Trost' (1903, no opus number). In *An den
Mond*, Op. 18, Pfitzner unexpectedly makes use of a whole-
tone scale. The accompaniments show unceasing variety of
keyboard figuration and expression.

Pfitzner's next major work was *Die Rose vom Liebesgarten*,
an opera which was first produced at Elbersfeld on 9 November 1901. James Grun again wrote the libretto, his

starting-point being a painting by Hans Thoma (a close friend of Grun's sister).[11] The opera is an elaborate allegory concerning the Guardianship of the Garden of Love. The hero, rejoicing in the name of Siegnot, is Spring-Guardian of the Garden, of which the everlasting rose is a symbol. In his quest to find a woman with whom to share the Guardianship he meets the Fountain-Elf Minneleide (i.e., love's sorrow). She enchants Siegnot, but she is afraid to give up the world she knows for the Garden. As she hesitates, the gate of the Garden closes and the pair, left outside, fall into the hands of the villainous Nachtwunderer. Siegnot is wounded and Minneleide imprisoned in a mountain. Siegnot prays for help, whereupon he gains miraculous strength and throws down the mountain. All, including Siegnot, are killed – apart from Minneleide, thanks to the magic power of the Rose. Through her sorrow she finds the virtue she had previously lacked. She brings his body back to the Garden and, within, Siegnot awakes to a new life.

The escapist nature of this plot is a good deal more obvious than its symbolism, a fact which is worth bearing in mind when considering the relevance of the 'ivory tower' in *Palestrina*. But the music of *Die Rose* marks an expansion in Pfitzner's range – this is the first large-scale work in which a light, celebratory mood dominates. The simply diatonic nature of the opening Spring Festival scene in particular is delightful without being trite and the humour of the grotesque Moorman, inhabitant of the Forest, is delicately captured. The harmonic language is essentially diatonic, coloured not by chromaticisms but by such devices as inversions of secondary sevenths and multiple suspensions. Long orchestral interludes are a prominent feature of the score; the prelude to Act II, depicting drops of water falling in underground caverns, is a remarkable piece of pointillist scoring, while the Funeral March is magnificent in its intensity. Wagner's influence is much less obvious than in *Heinrich*, apart from the names of the characters and the general symbolic nature of the opera. As in *Heinrich* the vocal line is often stolid, not helped by the persistent squareness of James

[11] *Ibid.*, pp. 13 and 99.

Grun's rhyming couplets, and there are still some longueurs; but the main obstacle to the success of *Die Rose* today, despite much superb music, is the impossibility of the preposterous plot. Yet if in the subsequent neglect of these two operas no major injustice has been done, it is still possible to feel that *Heinrich* is at least as good an opera as Strauss' *Guntram* and to see why it was to Pfitzner rather than to Strauss that those concerned with the future of German opera looked, until the first performance of *Salome*. Mahler conducted the Viennese premiere of *Die Rose* and apparently considered it a masterpiece.[12]

The major-key simplicity of *Die Rose* is probably connected with the composer's expressed interest in Marschner and, to a lesser extent, Weber, but Pfitzner makes it his own – certainly it is hard to find any more definite links between the music of *Die Rose* and, say, *Hans Heiling* and the style recurs in several works, notably the D major String Quartet, Op. 13, and *Das Christelflein*, his next opera.

The Quartet, written in 1902–3, much impressed Gustav Mahler, although its apparent simplicity can be disconcerting. In the opening *moderato* (the actual heading is 'In mässig gehender Bewegung') Pfitzner seems to eschew rhythmic variety in favour of the plainest of homophonic styles or note-against-note counterpoint, yet the result is mysteriously impressive. It has a rigorous intensity that seems to anticipate the Shostakovich of, say, the Fourth and Fifth Quartets. The rondo theme of the finale sounds like an eighteenth-century dance-tune, but its treatment is thoroughly Pfitznerian and its style looks forward to his last string quartet, in C minor, Op. 50, of forty years later.

In 1905 Pfitzner wrote incidental music for a production of Kleist's play *Das Käthchen von Heilbronn* (Pfitzner's score drops Kleist's definite article), the overture to which probably remains his most familiar purely orchestral composition. Opening and closing with virile energy in the 'knightly' spirit of the play, the E major melody of the second subject, representing Käthchen herself, is one of Pfitzner's loveliest, and the development section is particularly dramatic and

---

[12] *Cf. Klemperer on Music*, p. 148.

intense. The remainder of the *Käthchen* music consists of a
Prelude to Act Three, a postlude to the Eldertree scene (with
a stirringly Elgarian march), and a melodrama, intermezzo
and march for the end of the play, using parts of the Overture
and culminating in a rousing C major conclusion, in the
concert ending, clearly by the composer of *Die Rose*.
Käthchen was followed by *Das Christelflein*, first given by
Felix Mottl in Munich in 1906. In its first version Pfitzner was
merely supplying incidental music to Ilse von Stach's play,
but in 1917 he turned it into a full *Spieloper*.[13] The plot, which
this time really is a 'fairy story', concerns the arrival of the
little elf of the title in the Forest on Christmas Day. She meets
a group of humans and learns human sorrow through witness-
ing the death of a young girl. The Christchild appears and
brings the girl back to life. Her family celebrate Christmas,
and now that the elf has gained a soul through what she has
seen, the Christchild takes her to heaven, defeating the
attempts of the Firman (a huge fir tree) to keep her on earth.
While angels sing a Gloria, she enters the gates of heaven and
becomes the Christelflein. The opera is composed as a Sing-
spiel – that is, with some spoken dialogue separating the
'numbers', which range in length from substantial scenas to
mere songs. The overture is absolutely delightful and was a
favourite of Otto Klemperer's, whose opinion of the music of
his former teacher was not always high.[14] The music for the
Elflein and the Christchild requires a particular kind of high,
boyish soprano of a type which must have been familiar to
Pfitzner; several of the songs, such as the irresistible 'Gretel',
call for the same type of voice. Without giving any impression
of 'writing down', Pfitzner adapts the idiom of *Die Rose* by
simplifying the phrase structure (through symmetry is often
avoided in subtle ways) and by ensuring that the emotional
temperature remains in check, with, for example, the sweep of
strings at the end of Act One. But despite the light touch and
the charm of much of the music I find it difficult to reconcile the operatic sophistication to the subject-matter. *Das*

[13] Williamson, *op. cit.*, pp. 119–20.

[14] *Cf.* Peter Heyworth, *Conversations with Klemperer*, Gollancz, London,
1973/Faber, London, 1985, p. 53.

*Pfitzner during his Strassburg period (courtest of Annelore Habs
and the Hans Pfitzner-Gesellschaft)*

Christelflein is not for the diabetic, although it would make a
good occasional alternative to Humperdinck at Christmas
time.

The most significant change in Pfitzner's life was his
appointment in October 1907 as director of the Conservatory
and conductor of the symphony orchestra in Strassburg.
Rudolf Schwander, Oberburgermeister of the city, invited
him there with a view to his taking virtually complete control
of the city's musical life, and when three years later he also
became director of the opera at the Stadttheater this goal was
more or less achieved. In Strassburg he was to stay throughout the war years until 1918, despite a series of disputes with
other influential musicians, administrators and critics, and it
was during these years that *Palestrina* was written, composed
and produced.[15] Müller-Blattau writes:

> In his Strassburg domesticity, living among his friends, his
> wife and his children, it was noticeable that he no longer
> seemed complex and over-nervous but entirely healthy, pure
> and naive, full of wit and humour [. . .] In his heart there was
> a deep love for the spoken stage, and when one heard him

[15] Heyworth, *Otto Klemperer: His Life and Times*, Vol. I, pp. 88 *et seq.*

reciting poetry or declaiming drama, one realised his suppressed acting talent. Sprinkled in him was something of a Strassburg Beckmesser, later to appear as Novagerio in *Palestrina*. This devotion to the theatre [...] led to his great performances as an opera conductor.[16]

One of the difficulties caused by the composer who writes his own libretto is that the student is deprived of the often vitally fascinating correspondence between composer and librettist; one thinks, for example, of the Verdi-Boito or Strauss-Hoffmansthal letters. One is driven back, therefore, to the composer's own explanations, whether in his contemporary private letters or his own later published observations. The idea of *Palestrina* first seems to have entered Pfitzner's head in about 1894 or 1895:

> The plan of making a great Roman church composer the hero of a drama led to a very fruitful period of my life. It had already come to me when I was a minor Kapellmeister at the Stadttheater at Mainz in the 'nineties of the last century. I had sought to fill the gap in my knowledge of music history in my Mainz days, and become a student of the musical history of Palestrina's life.[17]

In an important letter of 14 November 1910 to his close friend Arthur Eloesser, critic and literary researcher, and author of a standard history of German literature, he speaks of 'a vision that has been floating in my mind for more than fifteen years'.[18] The idea sprang from his reading of volume IV of August Wilhelm Ambros' *History of Music* (1878); some of it is quoted by Lewis Lockwood in his edition of the *Missa Papae Marcellae*.[19]

The only substantial work that Pfitzner wrote between *Das Christelflein* and *Palestrina* was the Piano Quintet of 1908, one

---

[16] *Op. cit.,* p. 171.

[17] 'Mein Hauptwerk', first published in the programme for the Hamburg State Opera production of *Palestrina* in 1979.

[18] Quoted by Abendroth, *op. cit.,* p. 166; *cf.* below, p. 38.

[19] *Cf. Palestrina: Pope Marcellus Mass*, Norton Critical Scores, New York, 1975, pp. 138 *et seq.*

of his most highly regarded works. The strongly constructed first movement has fine, serious themes; the whimsical second movement is followed by a deeply felt *Adagio*. Just as with Wagner, there was then a pause in his creative output while he contemplated the theory of opera. In this case the principal result of his thinking was the extended essay 'Zur Grundfrage der Operndichtung' (1909), which defines some of his ideas on the nature of composition and offers a critique of the plotting and realisation of opera, with many examples from Wagner and others. Pfitzner's own account of the conception of *Palestrina* appears with minor variations in several different forms. I follow here the manuscript of a lecture given in 1932:

When hardly out of the conservatory, I had begun to steep myself in the study of the history of music more than I had been able to do as a student, and, for the first time, I was looking more thoroughly at this period of the development of music – then the vision of Palestrina appeared to me in a particularly mysterious, peculiar light. I saw immediately that an artistic drama of the first class was contained in the life of this man, even if it was not a drama in the usual sense or of a traditional form. My vision was roughly was follows: a man sits in Rome throughout almost the whole of the 16th century in one and the same place, his whole life long he does not leave his place of work. He does nothing more than serve his art, develop his gifts to the highest degree, just working and working, making the most of the talent that God has given him. Treated sometimes favourably, sometimes unfavourably according to the mood of the Pope who reigned at any particular moment, this genius lives quietly and unostentatiously, rewarded with nothing other than the feeling of his value, in obscurity. And then all of a sudden a blinding light falls on him, he stands, so to speak, in the illumination of world history. The following occurrence thrusts him into it: the polyphonic style of music, which for several centuries the greatest artists of a cultured world had built up together, one after another, this whole development is threatened with destruction. The unartistic world, those who occupy themselves outside in the bustle of human interests and passions, has it in mind to trample upon the countless masterpieces which have appeared in the course of time as if born of one spirit, to commit them to eternal oblivion. And then the cry went out to him, Palestrina, save music! It seemed to him as if his predecessors, who lived, worked, struggled and acted just like him, as if these were reaching out their hands from their graves and were shouting to him: You, who are of our spirit, save our works! And lo and behold, his life is worthwhile now, his constant work in the silence: he is ready! He is found to be great in the hour of need, he writes the work that brings salvation. A spiritual Herculean task is accomplished, he had succeeded in doing the most difficult of all things: to create beauty to a forceful command. From the outset it was clear to me that there would be, so to speak, two worlds coming into play against each other as agents, in the plot. The first one external, with its loud and wild bustle, which rolls along in the temporal sphere and which is simply called the 'world'; and the other inner, quiet one, which seeks eternity in the heart of the creative man. The latter produces its spiritual work not with the other world, at its bidding; nor is it against it, against its will; rather, it does so over and above the other world, without it, subject to quite different laws to those which operate in that world.[20]

These two worlds also had to be expressed in the form of the work. They constituted the actual plot. And so I saw, before I actually realised it precisely, what had to happen in the individual acts, a kind of triptych as form: a first and third act for the actual world of Palestrina, and in the middle the picture of the hurly-burly of the external world, which is forever hostile to the quiet work of the genius. This could only be the Council, the starting-point for decrees hostile to art.[21]

After the shape of the work had become gradually clearer to me during these studies, and I could see its contours and shadings ever more clearly before me, one day I wrote as the first words of the libretto the four lines which conclude the entire work:

Nun schmiede mich, den letzten stein
An einer Deiner tausend Ringe,
Du Gott; und ich will guter Dinge
Und friedvoll sein.[22]

---

[20] This sentence is a paraphrase of Schopenhauer; *cf.* p. 69, below.

[21] *Reden, Schriften, Briefen*, pp. 26 *et seq.* (translation by Daniel Franklin).

[22] *Ibid.*, p. 27; translated by Veronica Slater (*cf.* note 106 on p. 213, below) in the notes for the Deutsche Grammophon recording (2711 013), 1973.

According to Abendroth, these lines were written towards the end of 1909.[23] But the major task still lay ahead:

> But I wanted to put no History of Music into verses or scenes. The legend of the Saviour of Music [...] seemed to me to contain a great dramatic kernel and, above that, a concept of the philosophy of art which had never been put forward in any other artist's drama. [...]
> Then I felt myself to be no poet and I had never ventured the slightest distance into this territory, whatever name it might be given. Therefore I entrusted my plan, even in its merely sketched state, to some of my poetical acquaintances: two ladies and a dramatist who was at that time very well known. The two ladies were at once ready and supplied me in the shortest time moderately practicable sketches, but these shared with what I had recited and entrusted to them only the vulgar externals, without having anything in the least to do with my true conception. It is indicative that one of the ladies had, as it were, made Palestrina's wife the chief character; while the other had made Palestrina's daughter and her wedding to one of the master's pupils the principal events. Whereas the dramatist explained my plan as an expert to the listeners: this subject-matter is above all undramatic in form.[24]

This paragraph is perhaps disingenuous. According to Hans Rectanus,[25] Pfitzner had shown a one-act sketch of the libretto to James Grun, and that the 'two ladies' were Ilse von Stach (later the librettist of *Das Christelflein*) and L. Andro, the pen-name of Therese Rie, though elsewhere Pfitzner said that a fourth poet, Richard Voss, had been consulted and that it was he who had 'wrecked Pfitzner's original idea'.[26] Both Voss and Grun focussed on the performance of the Mass

[23] *Op. cit.*, p. 162.

[24] *Reden, Schriften, Briefen*, p. 27.

[25] *Leitmotivik und Form in den musikdramatischen Werken Hans Pfitzners*, Konrad Triltsch Verlag, Wurzburg, 1967, p. 104.

[26] From Victor Junk's diary, quoted in Elisabeth Wamlek-Junk, *Hans Pfitzner und Wien*, Schneider, Tutzing, 1986, p. 153; translation here by Julia Price. *Cf.* also Bernhard Adamy, *Hans Pfitzner, Literatur, Philosophie und Zeitgeschehen in seinem Weltbild und Werk*, Schneider, Tutzing, 1980, pp. 25–26.

rather the moment of its conception; they had not appreciated that the *Einfall* – the inspiration – had to stand at the heart of Pfitzner's opera, just as it stood at the heart of Pfitzner's theory of composition.[27] Therese Rie later claimed that she herself was responsible for several important elements of the final scenario, if not parts of the libretto itself, and that Pfitzner had failed to acknowledge her contribution. According to her,[28] she came into contact with Pfitzner when she sent him a libretto on an entirely different subject, in 1900 or soon after. Her sketch for the *Palestrina* libretto is dated July 1909, and it begins with an outline of Palestrina's emotional state after the death of his wife: complete indifference even in the face of the news, brought to him by his pupils, of the Council's threat to condemn music. He is left alone, and the figure of the dead Lucrezia appears to him. It speaks tenderly, even sentimentally, to him and introduces the Masters of the Past, who plead with Palestrina along lines vaguely similar to the completed libretto. They in turn introduce the angels, who encourage him further and tell him to listen to 'the music of the spheres' before leaving him asleep and disappearing, whereupon two pupils (called Gino and Claudio) enter and find their master asleep.

Act Two, set in the palace of Cardinal Vitelli, introduces Borromeo as well as the epicurean Cardinal Vitellozzo and the zealous Geronimo, who wishes to see the fires burn,

Destroying the decadence of mankind,
The poison of their senses and
The damnation of their souls, their shame: music.

Borromeo opposes him. Palestrina enters, with his pupils; he refuses to argue with Geronimo but obtains permission to perform his Mass, at which Geronimo falls in tears at mankind's perdition and Borromeo claims that beauty is not evil but 'a bridge to carry the pious soul to Heaven'. The sketch ends with a monologue for Palestrina.[29]

[27] *Cf.* Williamson, *op. cit.*, pp. 132–35. The concept of the *Einfall* is discussed below, pp. 91–94.

[28] In a typescript first published in Wamlek-Junk, *op. cit.*, pp. 154–68.

[29] *Cf. ibid.*, pp. 169–81.

It is easy to identify the repetitive and sentimental elements in this draft, to contrast this obvious plan for Act Two with Pfitzner's own, wholly unconventional version, and to admire the comparative historical accuracy of the final product; indeed, Pfitzner reverses the idea of having the Mass music performed in Act Two by making that act so explicitly 'antimusical'. Nor does Rie provide a satisfactory plan for a third act, as Pfitzner himself pointed out in a letter of 4 August 1909.[30] He also disliked the 'Savonarola-like figure' of Geronimo and the introduction of the Angels. But he did retain the angels, though he reduced their words to those of the Mass they are dictating; and if Rie is to be believed, the appearance of Lucrezia was entirely her idea. She said that the whole concept of Act One came to her at once.[31] Pfitzner later told a friend that 'the fundamental idea of *Palestrina* is the appearance of the Masters. This scene corresponds to a yearning from my childhood and youth',[32] but Rie told their mutual friend Victor Junk that Pfitzner hadn't gone into such details but 'merely indicated his intentions'.[33] She also claimed that the idea of the Masters appearing to Palestrina and insisting that he carry out his appointed task '*had not yet occurred to Pfitzner*'.[34] It is difficult, therefore, to be dogmatic about how much of the final scenario was Rie's invention, although she gave particular emphasis to Lucrezia being hers and she was outraged at Pfitzner's lack of acknowledgement. On the other hand, even if she invented the idea of the pupils' scene at the end of Act One, the use Pfitzner made of it was particularly significant and original, as will be seen later.[35]

In any case Pfitzner had at last realised that the final libretto to be his own.

[30] *Ibid.*, p. 159.

[31] *Ibid.*, p. 154n.

[32] From the diary of Margaritta Fischer, recorded on a visit to Munich in April 1925; *ibid.*, p. 153.

[33] *Ibid.*, p. 154.

[34] *Ibid.*, p. 158, translated by Williamson (*op. cit.*, p. 133); italics in original.

[35] *Cf.* pp. 171–74, below.

What emerged was so negative that my vision had diminished to the point where I said to myself: 'When Nature has implanted an idea so deeply into me, I will become a instrument to bring this idea to the surface. I shall set myself to work earnestly'. From then on I studied for two whole years all I could get hold of concerning the Counter-Reformation, and above all the two great Council histories by Sarpi and Pallavicini [. . .]. The first scene I wrote was that of the spirits in the First Act. It was, so to speak, the egg from which the whole work was hatched.[36]

By this time his major compositions had begun to decline in favour; there were no productions of *Der arme Heinrich* or *Das Rose*, and in Munich internal arguments surrounding Pfitzner increased, culminating in a boycott of him in April 1910. This reduction in his day-to-day work came, therefore, at an ideal time for him to concentrate his efforts in *Palestrina*, in much the same way that Mahler could only compose during his summer breaks from the Vienna Opera. A draft of the first act was completed during the summer of 1910, as the following letter to Eloesser makes clear:

[28 July 1910]

I have yesterday finished the first act of a great stage-work [. . .]. It is a plan which has occupied me for about fifteen years and to this poetical end I have struggled vainly to become ever more of a poet. Now in the highest need, for this huge work, have I brought myself to forge Notung. It is a deeply personal business. The material is itself more historical than anything I have done hitherto [. . .].[37]

On 4 August he went to Baden-Baden to recover from his exertions, Mimi following him two days later. There he stayed until 21 August, returning to Strassburg for a performance of *Käthchen von Heilbronn*, play and music together. Some idea of Pfitzner's doubts and worries and the strain under which he was writing – a state of mind which finds its memorable expression in Act One of the opera itself – can be gained from the following letter to Eloesser of 14 November 1910, already mentioned.

[36] *Mein Hauptwerk, loc. cit.*

[37] Quoted in Abendroth, *op. cit.*, p. 166.

Act One, Scene One: first orchestral draft
(courtesy of the Sammlung S. Kohler)

[. . .] Please read what follows alone and treat it as highly confidential. You ask me what has become of my Palestrina. You see, this part of my letter – and perhaps the next part of my life – will be concerned with this question. 'The mention of the word P. gave me a kind of pang of conscience.' [. . .] It is most important to me that no man should know, above all, the name P., that the title of the work hanging in the air should not be named as such; you see, only the first step has seriously been taken in this matter. You no doubt know what my view is on opera composition and artistic writing in general; and you no doubt know that it is no frivolous view and how I despise people who, without being artists, set about writing 'texts', which they consider to be works of art, like X . . . etc. What you do not know about, though, is my personal artistic misery, my stagnation as a composer, which has been caused by very complicated or very simple reasons, with their origins both outside and within myself. In order to make the confession that follows, I must indeed use the word 'despair', despite my very tranquil, sober mood this morning. Well then: after I had approached several lady writers and had even in vain let two writers know of my concept (if one can so call a vision that has been floating in my mind for more than fifteen years), I finally realised that I must either fashion it into shape myself or forever leave it be; and this summer I completed the writing of the first act of my 'musical legend' *Palestrina*. [. . .] I do not yet know whether I can bring it through to completion (by this I mean only the words) – 'I'm grappling with it'. I know that there are three acts; I know exactly what is to happen in the third, I know also where the second and third acts are to take place, and I am equally aware of what the whole mood, the 'branding' of contents is to be – but the real 'factual' content of the second act I do not as yet know.

I've had no ideas at all on this so far. Now I want to ask you whether you are willing to read this first act and give me your completely honest opinion of it. Whatever happens, it will not spoil our friendship, as you'll see when we drink our next glass of wine together [. . .]. Should I send you the act, then? [. . .][38]

Eloesser replied with 'detailed and clever objections and suggestions',[39] but Pfitzner wrote back on 4 April 1911:

[38] *Ibid.*, pp. 166 *et seq.*, translated by Daniel Franklin.

[39] Abendroth's words, *ibid.*, p. 186.

And now to your well-intentioned suggestion concerning
Palestrina: you must not think it amiss of me if I do not accept
it, if I do not even examine the drafts and suggestions [. . .].
You must believe that it is without any bitterness if I sum up
and answer you by saying that, judging objectively, you do not
think much of this piece of work at all; I was prepared for that
and do not go back upon what I said in my covering letter. I
ought rather to mention that you certainly don't seem to
realise fully what this artistic project means to me on a sub-
jective level. Such considerations can never by completely
separated from the positive evaluation of any piece of
work [. . .].[40]

This exchange tells us much about Pfitzner's lack of self-
confidence in this project which meant so much to him. But
for all that, the demands on him as conductor and producer
remained extensive. The letter to Eloesser ends with this
paragraph:

At present of course, I do not even have time to think, let alone
write; but neither would it be of any use to me even if I had
complete peace and quiet; but rather, also as a matter of
necessity, I must now work furiously and quickly catch up, as
it were, on my career; it is a matter of self-imposed rule that I
must pay these dues. If I can do it at all, I can also do it
alongside what I am doing at the moment; but when the words
are ready, I hope for quiet, to concentrate on the music, to
compose, something I have not done now for more than one-
and-a-half years; it remains to be seen whether, when I open
the chest, there is anything left in it [. . .].[41]

In 1911 the practical side of this career resumed its importance when he was appointed Operndirektor in Strassburg,
but he was able to complete the libretto of the second act on
28 July, a year and a day after that of the first act, and the
shorter third act ten days later. He had exhausted himself with
this work, and much of the last act was written in hospital with
the aid of his close friend Willy Levin. He gave a private
reading of the text to his own circle of family and friends on
19 September, and early the next year the whole libretto was

[40] *Ibid.*, p. 168; translated by Jim Lambert.

[41] *Ibid.*, p. 168; translated by Jim Lambert.

published in a private edition, even though composition of the music had scarcely begun.

On 1 January 1912 Pfitzner wrote the first notes of the score, its opening, the 'Ur-cell of the whole work'.[42] But he was constantly interrupted by other commitments. As opera director he was able to arrange productions of *Der arme Heinrich* and *Die Rose* in 1911 and 1913 respectively, and May and June 1913 saw him directing all the concerts and operas in the fourth Alsace-Lorraine Music Festival. He had by now made for himself a position of some eminence, but the situation was spoilt by the appointment of a new Intendant at the Opera House, one Anton Otto, whose views did not harmonise with those of Pfitzner, and the latter's artistic opportunities became more restricted. Yet during the busy winter season of 1913–14 Strassburg celebrated Pfitzner's presence with two Liederabends with Mientje Lauprecht von Lammen, the 'ideal singer of his soprano Lieder',[43] and a chamber-music concert including the Op. 13 String Quartet in D and the Piano Quintet. In all three concerts Pfitzner himself played the piano. What with all this and the usual routine opera work (a production of *Parsifal* was the far-from-routine crown of the season), he had little time for composition. Consequently he sought leave of absence from the Opera and the Conservatory for the season 1914–15 so as to further his work.[44] In his diary on 19 June 1914 he wrote: 'The real beginning of the work on *Palestrina*'.[45] The first act was finished at 9 p.m. on 27 July 1914.[46] Eight days later the War broke out.

In a remarkable parallel to Matthias Grünewald, as depicted by Hindemith in his opera *Mathis der Maler* of 1933–35, Pfitzner felt that it was his duty to serve his country

[42] *Ibid.*, p. 187.

[43] Müller-Blattau, *op. cit.*, p. 74.

[44] Otto Klemperer became his deputy at the opera house, where his successes encouraged those who resented Pfitzner's total power in the city to stir up strife (*cf.* Heyworth, *Otto Klemperer: His Life and Times*, Vol. 1, pp. 87, 92 and 96).

[45] Abendroth, *op. cit.*, p. 197.

[46] *Ibid.*

as a 'political' man; but his efforts to enrol himself on active service failed. He wrote to Felix Wolfes on 28 August 1914:

I am occupied with the second act, and have already in sketch the orchestral Prelude (very extended and weighty, 274 bars), the first scene with the servants, the songs of the Spaniards and the Italians [...]. But the voice is hard to sustain and preserve. Nevertheless, now even more than at first have I given myself up to the idea of helping in some way in the War, as far as can be done by a bungler like me. Even so I have also done much purely voluntary work, together with my wife, working as a station assistant, day and night.[47]

Three weeks later he was able to write:

My work makes great strides. [...] it is very easy and straight-forward for me and I have much pleasure in it. This style of the 'uncomposable' second act will certainly surprise and amaze some [...]. If *Palestrina* is completed before the war is over I will offer myself as a volunteer. But come what may I must complete this work.[48]

The second act was finished in sketch by the end of 1914, and in score on 12 April 1915. The third act was sketched between 26 April and 19 May; the instrumentation was begun on 31 May and the act completed on 17 June. A few final alterations were made and the entire score was complete on 24 June 1915.

Pfitzner had thought about the eventual staging of the work as early as 1911. He tried to arouse interest in Vienna, but his early champion Hans Gregor, Direktor of the Elbersfeld Stadttheater, where *Die Rose* had been first produced, was unable or unwilling to promise anything. More hopeful signs came from Munich where at the suggestion of Bruno Walter (who had first worked with Pfitzner at the time of the performances of *Der arme Heinrich* in 1895) the Intendant, Clemens von Franckenstein, seized on the chance of putting preparations in hand. Von Franckenstein, who had also stud-ied at Frankfurt, had a fine record of premieres. In March 1916 he was responsible for the first performance of the

---

[47] *Ibid.*, p. 198.

[48] Müller-Blattau, *op. cit.*, p. 75.

The autograph manuscript of Palestrina, *held in the Library*
of the Vienna Philharmonic Orchestra: the opening of Act Two
(photograph by Vouk, Vienna)

double bill of *Violanta* and *Der Ring des Polykrates* by the
19-year-old Erich Korngold, again with Bruno Walter conducting. Munich was holding a Pfitzner week in the summer
of 1916 and for a time there were hopes of staging the
premiere of *Palestrina* then, but they were frustrated. Instead,
all Pfitzner got was *Heinrich* and *Die Rose*, plus some
chamber-music and lieder recitals. Rumours had by this stage
begun to circulate, for instance, that the Berlin Hofoper was
to produce *Palestrina* as part of peace celebrations, but the war
inconsiderately dragged on. So Munich it was to be, but not
until June 1917.

The cast was strong: Karl Erb in the title-role, Fritz Fein-
hals as Borromeo, Friedrich Brodersen, Paul Kuhn, Gustav
Schützendorf, Paul Bender, Maria Ivogün, Emmi Kruger.
Bruno Walter conducted, and Pfitzner himself was in charge
of the production. Walter noted that during a rehearsal he
found one of the singers in tears and incapable of continuing
through emotion.[49]

The final rehearsal was held on Saturday, 9 June, the
Generalprobe[50] on the Monday, and the first night itself was
Tuesday, 12 June 1917. Practically all the country's leading
musicians were present, and several who would gladly have
been there were kept away by war commitments. It is
recorded that the audience was 'astonished and bewildered'[51]
by the Second Act, being 'cool and indifferent'[52] to it, and that
loud applause was not forthcoming. But there was a loud and
moving curtain-call for the composer at the end of the whole
work. The performance, as is now the usual practice, had only
one interval.

Afterwards there was a banquet in Pfitzner's honour. 'The
next morning during breakfast a theatre director made an
offer of staging the work – but only the first and third acts; the
second would be better kept for special occasions. [. . .] thus

---

[49] Abendroth, *op. cit.*, p. 212.

[50] A 'Generalprobe' is a full dress rehearsal to which the public is invited,
not unlike a preview.

[51] *Ibid.*

[52] *Ibid.*, p. 214.

began the comedy of the misunderstanding of the second act.'[53]

Pfitzner knew that in *Palestrina* he had given definitive statement to some of his most fundamental beliefs; later he spoke of it as 'the peak of my artistic life'.[54] In the years following its production, however, he wrote a number of his best compositions. The Violin Sonata of 1918 could be thought of as a reaction from the opera: its melodic warmth and energy within a traditional framework make it a thoroughly extrovert work, though it has its deeper side. With hindsight it may be significant that so positive a work could be composed at about the same time that Pfitzner was compelled by the military situation to leave Strassburg hastily for Munich; shortly afterwards Strasbourg became French once more. He returned to Berlin in 1920, to teach counterpoint at the Prussian Academy of Arts, and the next year he produced one of his most ambitious works, the 'Romantic Cantata on texts by Eichendorff, *Von deutscher Seele* (*Of the German Soul*). Written for four soloists, chorus, organ and large orchestra and lasting more than an hour and a half, it summarises Pfitzner's achievements in the setting of poetic texts in a large-scale synthesis in which the orchestra, in particular, is handled as memorably as in *Palestrina*. In it are found many of Pfitzner's hall-marks: soaring vocal lines, characteristic modulations, chorale melodies, and also a succession of orchestral interludes in which is found some of the most profound music he ever wrote. 'Tod als Postillon' has a wild sweep that nothing even in Act Two of *Palestrina* can manage, and the stillness and beauty of 'Abend/Nacht' is a memorable response to the experience of Nature. 'Ergebung' ('Dedication') is one of Pfitzner's most hauntingly individual passages. (These three interludes are sometimes given separately as a 'Symphonic Trilogy'.) Yet the twenty mostly short poems which form its textural basis do not add up to the sort of philosophical unity that the title implies, giving an unfortunate impression of

[53] *Ibid.*

[54] *Reden, Schriften, Briefen*, p. 35.

Bruno Walter and Hans Pfitzner during preparations
for the premiere of Palestrina *in Munich in 1917*
(courtesy of Annelore Habs and the Hans Pfitzner-Gesellschaft)

pretentiousness (in particular, I feel that the humorous elements are not well integrated), and the result is a work that I find more convincing when the poems are thought of, as Harold Truscott suggested to me, chiefly as a peg on which to hang the music.

The title of the work also causes problems. Its nationalist implications are as obvious as those of Elgar's *The Spirit of England*, though even a superficial examination of these two contrasting but profound works illustrates at once how unjustified those implications are. Yet it is typical of the difficulties and contradictions involved in the life and works of Hans Pfitzner that both the text and the music of *Von deutscher Seele* could not be more free of political content – with one exception. The penultimate poem of the cantata, 'Der Friedensbote', ends with the line

Schlaf ruhig, das Land ist ja frei![55]

[55] 'Sleep soundly, the land is indeed free!' *Cf.* Williamson, *op. cit.*, pp. 34–41, and his letter to *Gramophone*, Vol. 67, No. 7, December 1989, p. 1059.

Poster announcing the premiere of Palestrina *on 12 June 1917 (courtesy of the Bavarian State Opera)*

It is impossible to believe that in 1921 Pfitzner was not thinking of Alsace and Lorraine, anticipating a time when they might be 'freed' from the rule of a foreign power, and his setting of the line is too emphatic for it to be ignored. Subsequently the Nazis used the work for purposes of their own propaganda. Such associations are hardly relevant to discussions of the music today, but they do not make it easier to form an unprejudiced opinion.[56] But whereas the worst the England of 1915 can evoke is an unfashionable jingoism, over any suggestion of nationalism in the Weimar Republic falls the evil shadow of Adolf Hitler. It is necessary to give careful consideration to the question of Hans Pfitzner's relationship with the Third Reich.

Pfitzner was in many ways a difficult man, short-tempered, sometimes blunt to the point of rudeness and often unable to anticipate the results of his outbursts. He seemed to have the dual conviction that the world existed solely for his own benefit and that the same world devoted all its efforts to frustrating him. He took a delight in complaining, even in suffering.

We could approach such a personality with a benign tolerance and treat him as an escapee from a comic novel, were it not that, in the last two decades of his life, his destiny became increasingly involved with that of his country under the Third Reich. This is, needless to say, an extremely emotive subject and we are perhaps still too close to events to be able to arrive, not so much at the truth, as at a balanced view of the facts. Some writers[57] go out of their way to condemn Pfitzner as a Nazi; others,[58] with the difficult task of proving negative statements, claim that he was entirely blameless, even going

[56] I asked one of the world's most famous conductors if he had ever conducted any Pfitzner. His immediate response was: '*Von deutscher Seele?* Nazi music!'

[57] Such as Nicolas Slonimsky, *Baker's Biographical Dictionary of Musicians*, 7th edn., Oxford University Press, London/Schirmer, New York, 1984, pp. 1765–66.

[58] Such as Ludwig Schrott, *Die Persönlichkeit Hans Pfitzners*, Atlantis, Zurich, 1959, and Bernhard Adamy, *op. cit.*

to the length of suppressing evidence.[59] At least it may be possible to assemble some facts. That Pfitzner stayed in Germany throughout the period seems in itself a matter for instant condemnation by some writers. Fred K. Prieberg, in his thorough and carefully researched book *Musik im NS-Staat*,[60] has harsh words to say for practically every composer who stayed, Pfitzner being dealt with at length and even with venom. Few other writers today make much of Richard Strauss' relationship with the Nazi Party, despite the fact that he was President of the Reichsmusikkammer from November 1933 until his resignation in June 1935. Strauss had been suffering increasing disfavour during those two years, partly through his collaboration with the Jewish author Stefan Zweig, and the arbiters of Nazi cultural policy decided that Pfitzner should become their musical figurehead instead. Apart from Pfitzner's known nationalistic sympathies, his musical conservatism was thought to be more sound ideologically than Strauss' 'progressivism', though it had been a long time since Strauss' music could have been called progressive. Walter Abendroth wrote an 'official' biography of Pfitzner in 1935 which included a bitter and thinly veiled attack on Strauss[61] and which interpreted Pfitzner's life and art in terms of the party line. The book later did Pfitzner a good deal of damage and it has been gleefully quoted by his enemies. Peter Heyworth cites Abendroth's autobiography, written thirty years later, as saying that he had 'felt obliged to [give] more emphasis to Pfitzner the German patriot [...] and to emphasise certain

---

[59] Fred K. Prieberg, in *Musik im NS-Staat* (Fischer, Frankfurt, 1982, p. 223), says that Schrott was rather biased in selecting what passages of Pfitzner's letters and writings to quote.

[60] *Ibid.*

[61] This led to at least one amusing consequence. In reply Strauss set the poem 'Zugemessene Rhythmus' ('Measured Rhythm') from Goethe's *Westöstliche Divan*, a poem criticising talent at the expense of genius; to symbolise 'talent' Strauss quotes the C major theme from the finale of Brahms' First Symphony, and 'genius' the 'Richtige' theme from *Arabella*, the Ideology motif from *Tod und Verklärung*, and the opening of the *Meistersinger* Prelude (*cf.* Norman del Mar, *Richard Strauss*, Barrie & Jenkins, London, 1972, Vol. 3, pp. 389 *et seq.*).

The Pfitzner family in 1915
(courtesy of Annelore Habs and the Hans Pfitzner-Gesellschaft)

excerpts from Pfitzner's own writings that brought him the undeserved reputation of an anti-Semite'. Heyworth comments that 'it is hard to place complete confidence in a biographer who unabashedly confessed that he had loaded the evidence to make his book more palatable to the cultural arbiters of the Third Reich'.[62] This emphasis is doubly unfortunate because Abendroth's book also contains a vast amount of essential documentary and other source-material.

In fact, it is Pfitzner's prose writings that leave the widest scope for (mis)interpretation, though it is perhaps only in their unfortunate proximity to the atrocities of the 1930s and '40s that has brought from some commentators condemnation as passionate as that usually reserved for Wagner. Pfitzner had long been a fervent nationalist, even a xenophobe, despite his wide reading. As Peter Heyworth points out,[63] 'Since the early nineteenth century, romanticism in Germany had been identified with national revival'. Pfitzner

---

[62] *Otto Klemperer: His Life and Times*, Vol. 1, p. 109.

[63] *Ibid.*, p. 108.

A caricature of Pfitzner by Gerstenbrand
published in the Nazi newspaper Völkischer Beobachter
on 4 May 1939; it accompanied an article by Friedrich Bayer
celebrating Pfitzner's seventieth birthday on the following day

saw himself as defending the great and essentially German musical tradition against new, foreign influences; he would doubtless have subscribed to Hans Sachs' final speech in *Die Meistersinger.* The defeat of Germany in 1918 was a blow which intensified this nationalism; it must have been particularly hard to see his beloved Strassburg gallicised as Strasbourg and his opera post go to a Frenchman (Guy Ropartz, another neglected composer). When a political party arose which seemed able to restore German national pride lost in the humiliations of the Treaty of Versailles and the

French occupation of the Ruhr, it was hardly surprising that he embraced the movement with enthusiasm. The evil side of National Socialism emerged only later. Like the vast majority of the population of Germany, Pfitzner had shown enthusiasm for a cause without realising how bestial were to be its full consequences. Did the German people share a collective guilt for the Second World War and the events preceding it, as Thomas Mann argued in *Doktor Faustus* and elsewhere? In a letter to Bruno Walter[64] Pfitzner said that, on the contrary, to identify Germany with Hitler is 'morally infamous'; Germany had so much that is good and true notwithstanding Hitler's outrages, and 'to *this* land I shall remain true even to my last breath'.

Certainly Pfitzner gave hostages to fortune. Bernhard Adamy points out[65] that Pfitzner's artistic ideals reflecting the spiritual values of a people are often couched in the catchphrases of political jargon even while remaining apolitical. In his efforts to secure the recognition from the authorities that he felt due to his genius, he approached several musically inclined Nazi leaders, including Hans Frank, later Governer-General of Poland (this despite Frank's refusal in 1933 to help him concerning the withdrawal of an invitation to conduct a festival concert in Leipzig[66]). Also in 1933 he withdrew from an engagement at the Salzburg Festival, 'in accordance with Nazi policy concerning Austria'.[67] When Pfitzner's home was bombed in 1943, Frank invited him to Cracow, both to conduct a special concert and to stay with him indefinitely. Pfitzner gratefully wrote an overture, *Krakauer Begrüssung* (*Cracow Greeting*), for the occasion, and dedicated it to Frank. The visit took place towards the end of 1944 and the overture was duly performed, under the direction of Hans Swarowsky. It even includes a polonaise![68] Needless to say, the overture is

[64] Dated 5 October 1946, quoted in Hans Pfitzner, *Reden, Schriften, Briefe*, pp. 322 *et seq.*; cited by Adamy, *op. cit.*, pp. 267 *et seq.*

[65] Adamy, *op. cit.*, p. 308.

[66] Prieberg, *op. cit.*, p. 221.

[67] Williamson, *op. cit.*, p. 322.

[68] Prieberg, *op. cit.*, p. 225; Adamy, *op. cit.*, p. 337.

not mentioned in the standard list of Pfitzner's work, Op. 54 being 'without title', and his apologists are all too keen to ignore its existence.[69] (It would be interesting to know what happened to the score.) Pfitzner's friend Ludwig Schrott does not mention the overture; but he writes that '[Frank] angrily reported to him the inhumanity of the other NS leaders in the East. The Master was convinced that Frank exercised a comparatively gentle rule.'[70]

But all did not go Pfitzner's way. Frustrated in his attempts to obtain a state pension in 1934, when he was 65, he applied directly to Hermann Goering. Ludwig Schrott describes[71] the composer's own account of his subsequent summons to see the Minister. Goering believed that Pfitzner had exaggerated his financial hardship and started by criticising his musical achievements, and when Pfitzner replied that Goering should leave such matters of artistic opinion to him he was threatened with being sent to the Oranienberg labour camp. To which Pfitzner merely retorted: 'Do it if you dare!' The composer returned to his own world morally intact but with his faith in his country destroyed: 'For this Germany I do not exist'.[72]

Schrott goes on to say that this incident, together with Hitler's 'territorial adjustments', offended Pfitzner's sense of justice to such an extent that he no longer felt any patriotic fervour or sympathy with the Third Reich.[73] What could Pfitzner do in these circumstances? There was no one abroad to whom he could turn; he had been devoted to Germany for

[69] Erik Levi writes, in a letter to me dated 15 November 1988: 'In fact there are several other examples of works dedicated to party leaders that have mysteriously disappeared from work lists [. . .] e.g. Richard Trunk's *Feier der neuen Front*, a male voice cycle dedicated to Hitler and written in 1933, or Johann Nepomuk David's *Motet* on words by the Führer. Also you may have noticed that Richard Strauss's song *Das Bächlein* which he dedicated to Goebbels appears in the complete edition of his Lieder without a dedication'. Op. 54 has since been allocated to the second version of *Das Christelflein*; *cf.* Williamson, *op. cit.*, p. 124.

[70] *Op. cit.*, p. 49.

[71] *Ibid.*, pp. 54 *et seq.*

[72] *Ibid.*, p. 60.

[73] *Ibid.*, p. 49.

all his life. Emigration was simply not an option for him. Instead, he emulated Palestrina, the creation of his own imagination twenty years earlier; he withdrew into a world of pure music, ensuring the fulfilment of his own responsibilities as an artist while abdicating those as a citizen.

Is it possible to believe that an intelligent and cultured man could behave like this in all innocence? Prieberg is emphatic in his denial. Yet Pfitzner's behaviour is consistent with his fanatical self-centredness, his belief that the only thing that mattered in the world was his own music. Throughout his career he sought marks of official recognition, and believed himself fated to receive less than he deserved. Frank had helped him, so he was grateful and he maintained his attitude even when Frank had been condemned by the Nuremberg Tribunal: he sent Frank a telegram message of sympathy and comfort. There was courage in this principled action. The rise of the National Socialist party gave hope for his artistic ideals, so he supported them. The point is, I think, that Pfitzner's support for the regime and its leaders went exactly as far as, and no further than, the interests of his own compositions were served.

The issue of antisemitism is central to the problem of Pfitzner's beliefs and his conduct during the Nazi administration. Antisemitism was, it should be remembered, a firmly rooted idea long before the rise of Hitler, as any reader of Heinrich Mann's *Der Untertan* (1918), for example, will realise. Following Pfitzner's earlier frustrations, such as his 'defeat' by Klemperer at Strassburg in 1916,[74] he presumably saw the concept of antisemitism as another appropriate weapon in his repertoire of self-pity. He complained of 'international Jewish' activities, though he differentiated carefully between the idea of an international-Jewish conspiracy and individual Jews even when publishing some ill-judged outbursts.[75] But when it came to any direct action, theories gave way to decent and dignified behaviour. His first wife was not

[74] Heyworth, *op. cit.*, pp. 107 *et seq.*

[75] *Cf.* the preface to 'Die neue Ästhetik der musikalischen Impotenz', *Gesammelte Schriften*, Filser, Augsburg, 1926, Vol. II, p. 224; *cf.* also Prieberg, *op. cit.*, p. 35.

'racially pure', her maternal grandfather being the Jewish musician Ferdinand Hiller,[76] but that caused Pfitzner no qualms at all. In 1939 he refused to let concerts in honour of his seventieth birthday go ahead when the Nazis objected to Dorothea Braus, whose husband was a Jew, playing the Piano Concerto. In 1933 he wrote letters of support on behalf of his friends Cossmann, Eloesser and Felix Wolfes.[77] One of the Reich's more preposterous musical ideas was that Mendelssohn's incidental music for *A Midsummer Night's Dream* be replaced by the work of an Aryan composer, and several attempts were made (with musically predictable results); Pfitzner refused to have anything to do with the scheme, saying that he was not in the market to try to do better than Mendelssohn.[78] And despite his earlier argument with Klemperer, Pfitzner was generous in his praise when Klemperer conducted a 'consummate' performance of *Palestrina* at Cologne in 1920.[79] Bernhard Adamy says[80] that Pfitzner disliked the concept of 'Judentum', of a Jewish state or clique existing within another nation, and he felt that Jews should have no citizens' rights within Germany, though they were entitled to normal human rights. He tried to help Jewish acquaintances, especially when rumours of the persecution of Jews became increasingly insistent, but he still used the word 'Jew' as a term of collective opprobrium – as when *Das Herz* was badly received by the critics.[81] He feared the influence of the Jewish race on German culture, but remarked that the same would be true for any race.[82]

Pfitzner was never a party member, nor did he hold any post in the musical hierarchy of the Reich, though this was not altogether for want of trying. Most Party officials who had

[76] Abendroth, *op. cit.*, pp. 408–9.

[77] *Cf.* Williamson, *op. cit.*, p. 318.

[78] Among the composers who did attempt to improve on Mendelssohn was Rudolf Wagner-Régeny (Prieberg, *op. cit.*, pp. 216, 220–1).

[79] Heyworth, *op. cit.*, p. 150.

[80] *Ibid.*, pp. 275 *et seq.*

[81] *Ibid.*, p. 308.

[82] *Cf.* Williamson, *op. cit.*, p. 318.

anything to do with him obviously decided that he was not going to do any active work for the Party and in any case was a nuisance; he did not achieve his goal of taking charge of a state opera house, nor even of a state high school.[83] On being subjected in 1940 to an investigation into his official status and relationship to the Party, he gave flat negatives or 'don't know' to each question; nevertheless, the assessing official concluded that 'Pfitzner stands in agreement with National Socialism'.[84] This sort of evidence is typical of the bewildering contradictions that face the student of Pfitzner. He managed frequently to compromise himself with lip-service to the state, and Prieberg gleefully reproduces a letter in which Pfitzner quotes Adolf Hitler: 'I am a National Socialist and as such at once strike back against every attack'.[85] Prieberg implies that this is a complete self-condemnation. The last relevant fact is that Pfitzner appeared before a denazification tribunal at Munich and was exonerated on 31 March 1948.[86]

Such was the level of intrigue, censorship and their attendant attributes in the Third Reich that it is difficult to establish a picture with certainty from so many conflicting reports.[87] But Pfitzner's works of the period contain no trace of any political content[88] and I see no reason why they should suffer more on account of these difficulties than should, say, the

---

[83] Prieberg, *op. cit.*, p. 217.

[84] Joseph Wulf, *Musik im Dritten Reich. Eine Dokumentation*, Sigbert Mohn, Gütersloh, 1963, pp. 310–11. *Cf.* John Williamson's letter to *Gramophone* (*loc. cit.*).

[85] Prieberg, *op. cit.*, p. 224.

[86] *Cf.* Adamy, *op. cit.*, p. 276.

[87] Erik Levi's suggestion to me (*loc. cit.*) that frequency of orchestral performances might be an appropriate guideline to a composer's real standing is, unfortunately, less helpful than it might appear because of the small number of Pfitzner's orchestral works. The only purely orchestral mature compositions written before 1933 are the *Käthchen* music and the Piano and Violin Concertos. (*Cf.* Levi's *Music in the Third Reich*, Macmillan, London, 1994, pp. 217–18.) But Prieberg (*op. cit.*, p. 216) shows that there were about 18% fewer performances of the first four operas in the years 1933–38 than there had been in 1923–28.

[88] *Cf.* Adamy, p. 276.

music of Strauss or the music-making of Furtwängler, Karajan or Böhm.

Pfitzner's next important compositions after *Von deutscher Seele* were two concertos, for piano (1922) and for violin (1925). The former is of considerable technical difficulty, with a solo part of Brahmsian weight, although the scherzo and finale sparkle with wit and rhythmic energy. As a compendium of Pfitzner characteristics it could hardly be bettered, and it is a work to which I shall often refer. It also typifies the difficulty presented in Pfitzner's works in which the exterior masks a very different kernel. The assertive, 'Emperor'-like E flat opening gives a misleading impression of the first movement, much of which is introverted music at a slower tempo. Reconciling these disparate elements is not easy. The Violin Concerto has gained an element of notoriety through its having a 'slow movement in which the soloist is silent'. If these words send thoughts to Palestrina's absence from Act Two of his own opera, I think it is misleading; that 'slow movement' is an extended orchestral interlude in a single 35-minute structure in which the elements of different movements – exposition, variations, slow movement, finale/ recapitulation – are bound up together. (In this sense it is not unlike Schmidt's Fourth Symphony. Pfitzner tended to join the movements of his works together, and he actually calls his own C major Symphony, Op. 46, 'three movements in one movement', although in most such works the impression is of nothing more than asking for an *attacca*. The Violin Concerto is exceptional.) Indeed, I hear this section as in some ways corresponding to the orchestral *tutti* of a 'classical' concerto. It is true, however, that in some of his other slow movements the solo entry is substantially delayed, and Pfitzner was certainly not a composer to pander to a soloist's self-assertion. In any case, the whole work is among his warmest and most approachable, the 'fourth subject' or finale theme being among his most attractive ideas.

In the same year as the Violin Concerto he wrote what I think is his finest instrumental work, the String Quartet in C sharp minor. It can at first seem to be full of forbiddingly tortured chromaticism, but acquaintance confirms it as one of the outstanding quartets of its epoch. The unusual chordal juxtaposition of the opening leads to a quite magnificent development section, while the way in which the lyrical second subject emerges from a flickering texture is deeply poetic. The Scherzo is wild, headlong in pace; the quartet version calls for an almost Bartókian sonority, and similar imagination is revealed in the slow movement, whose traceries of sound build to a climax over massive *pizzicato* chords. The finale makes resourceful use of an off-beat tonic quaver; and the major-key coda reaches a wonderfully serene conclusion. The work gives the impression of a single unified inspiration and of an intensely personal inwardness of expression not unworthy of its great quartet predecessor by Beethoven in the same key. Pfitzner orchestrated the work in 1933, calling it his First Symphony, apparently in the hope of gaining it more hearings. Either version is valid, but although the string-quartet medium is at times strained in the original, I find the orchestral version makes the music sound a little cramped, demanding even more space.

In 1926 Mimi Pfitzner died, and just as with Palestrina in the opera (and with Elgar in real life) the event affected him so strongly as to bring about a fall – though not total cessation – in his creative output. In his essay *Mein Hauptwerk* he describes how during the writing of *Palestrina* he dreamt that some historian of the future was looking back over his works and deducing from them how much his wife meant to him. His diary of 1926 shows him in perplexity asking himself whether Christianity can bring him comfort in his distress – for instance: 'Follow Paul; he believes in a second coming [. . .]'.[89] At this period he concentrated on writing essays rather than music. His one published work of this year, a setting for baritone and orchestra of Meyer's *Lethe*, is a song of sorrow in personal loss and quotes the Lucrezia theme from *Palestrina* as well as other songs Pfitzner associated with Mimi. Nothing else appeared for three years; but then came two important works, the choral fantasy *Das dunkle Reich* (*The Dark Realm*) and his last opera, *Das Herz*.

Das dunkle Reich is a forty-minute cantata for soprano,

[89] *Ibid.*, p. 146.

baritone, chorus and orchestra, with an extended fugato for organ solo which anticipates the monumental interludes in Franz Schmidt's culminating masterpiece *Das Buch mit sieben Siegeln* of 1938. The poems Pfitzner sets are again commentaries on death and bereavement, starting with a pair of complementary texts by C. F. Meyer, 'Chorus of the Dead' and 'Chorus of the Living'. The former opens with a trudging triple-time choral unison, softening before it reaches an almost triumphant climax. Into this the Chorus of the Living breaks with noisy jubilation, an irony oddly Mahlerian. Eventually an orchestral 'Dance of Life' takes over, a waltz, though not so garish as those of Richard Strauss; there is a dark, pessimistic fear behind it. The ensuing 'Chorspruch' is halfway between recitative and chorale, the fermatas decorated with the orchestra. Goethe's song of Gretchen to the Mater Dolorosa moves from heavy chromatic inflections to the major-key sadness of innocent joy remembered; following the organ fugato Pfitzner sets Michelangelo's 'All Earthly Things End', once more in triple time. The climax of the work is 'Departure in the Light', Meyer's 'Hutten's Last Day', the hymn of a man who has struggled with Death welcoming the approach of release. Here are strong elements of *Palestrina* – the bass falling to prepare a modulation recalls the move to E flat minor in the Dictation Scene,[90] and angry rhythms briefly recall Borromeo. The agonised triumphant climax is magnificent, resolved in the musical language used earlier for Morone, the triple rhythms now affirmatively major. But it is with a reprise of the 'Chorus of the Dead' that the work ends. Significantly, Pfitzner wrote that he had composed no sacred works; rather, 'The close of the first act of *Palestrina* is my "High Mass" and *Das dunkle Reich* my "Requiem"'.[91]

The plot of *Das Herz* is equally significant. In this Faustian opera the famous Doctor Athanasius (i.e., 'immortal') binds himself to the wicked spirit Asmodi, Prince of 'malicious revenging Devils'.[92] In return for magical healing skills the

[90] *Cf.* pp. 165–66, below.

[91] *Reden, Schriften, Briefen*, p. 46.

[92] Robert Burton, *The Anatomy of Melancholy*, 6th edn. (1651), Part 1, Section 2, Member 1, Subsection 2.

doctor must pay with 'merely the heart of a human'. He obtains a heart magically and keeps it in pledge for Asmodi. But he does not realise until too late whose heart it is: that of his beloved wife Helge. Eventually Athanasius, condemned to death for the use of black arts, realises his sin and refuses to exchange the heart of an innocent for that of Helge. In this noble decision, like that of the Empress in *Die Frau ohne Schatten*, he and his wife are saved from eternal damnation. The outline of the plot was Pfitzner's own, and it is tempting to see in the Doctor's evil dealing with his wife's heart some expression of the guilt felt by a bereaved man, as well as the characteristic of the world towards the man of genius, as John Williamson points out.[93] The libretto was written by Pfitzner's pupil Hans Mahner-Mons, who wrote detective stories under the name of Hans Possendorf.[94]

Musically *Das Herz* shows Pfitzner at the height of his maturity. It is an opera of action and drama, not of reflection and ideas like *Palestrina*; but the language of the earlier opera is here adapted to create strong musical character and dramatic confrontation. Nor is the construction less subtle or impressive. The central conjuration scene in Act One crackles with energy, while the final anguish and aspiration of Athanasius relate the work to *Das dunkle Reich*. The evocation of the party atmosphere of 1700 is perhaps an anti-climax, but the well-known 'love theme' creates the love between Helge and Athanasius as something strong but chaste. For all Pfitzner's reputation as a 'ladies' man', his love music is always restrained, unlike that of Strauss.

Das Herz had the most auspicious of launchings, with simultaneous premieres in Munich and Berlin conducted by Hans Knappertsbuch and Wilhelm Furtwängler respectively.[95] But the unpropitious time of its creation and the somewhat clumsy occult details of the plot caused it to languish from 1955 until it was revived at Rudolstadt in 1993. This production showed, first, that the dramatic quality of the score is sufficient to make the occult element unimportant

[93] *Op. cit.*, p. 303.

[94] *Ibid.*, p. 302.

[95] Williamson, *op. cit.*, pp. 302 and 318.

and, second, that updating the context to that of modern heart transplants exaggerates rather than removes any absurdities.

Poor health again caught up with Pfitzner and in 1934 he was forced to give up his 'honorary life' post at Munich. But more terrible was the shadow caused by the rise of the Nazi Party. We have seen some of the problems Pfitzner faced under the new regime. On top of these, his sight weakened and his finances worsened. Approaching the age of seventy, with his health failing, he retreated into his own sphere of music, away from the harshnesses outside, for the second time in his life. In 1939 he remarried; his new wife was Mali Stoll. But after his home was destroyed in an air-raid and he had returned from his unfortunate visit to Cracow, he moved successively to Vienna, Garmisch-Partenkirchen and then, in 1946, to an old people's home in Munich. Here, with almost no possessions, not even a piano, he lived in misery until the Secretary of the Vienna Philharmonic, Rudolf Hanzl, arranged for him to be brought to Vienna and cared for at the Orchestra's expense. In gratitude he dedicated *Palestrina*, which hitherto had been without a dedication, to the Vienna Philharmonic Orchestra. He died on 22 May 1949, seventeen days after his eightieth birthday, and was buried in the Zentralfriedhof near the graves of so many other great composers. At a memorial concert in the Mozarteum Josef Krips conducted the Funeral March from *Die Rose* and the slow movement of his late *Little Symphony*.[96]

Yet amid all the final hardship he continued to compose; and what he wrote forms as remarkable a series of works as does the contemporaneous 'Indian Summer' enjoyed by Strauss. In fact, I would venture to suggest that no one since Beethoven, with the possible exception of Brahms, has reached the sublime and serene simplicity of these late works. As a group they share a brevity that is in no way a euphemism for lack of content – most of them last only about twenty minutes (the three-movement Duo only thirteen), but their concentration is as remarkable as their exclusion of inessentials. There is a preponderance of triple time (often $\frac{6}{8}$

---

[96] Müller-Blattau, *op. cit.*, pp. 126 *et seq.*

Pfitzner conducting in Vienna, December 1944
(courtesy of Annelore Habs and the Hans Pfitzner-Gesellschaft)

with dance-like syncopations, especially in the finales), and
the tortured chromatics of some of his earlier works have
disappeared.

The sequence begins with the G major Cello Concerto of
1935. The rhapsodic opening theme, all but unaccompanied,
leads to a typically simple second subject, a cadenza over a
timpani roll, a song-like *Adagio*, an interlude without the
soloist (shades of the Violin Concerto) and a finale based on
the opening theme. The ending is particularly touching. The
Duo for violin and cello of two years later exists in two
versions, with orchestral and with piano accompaniment; in a
preface to the score Pfitzner writes that the soloists should
treat the work as chamber music, not even memorising their
parts. It is one of my favourite works, displaying the utmost
sophistication in the beguiling way in which theme follows
theme (always slightly different and often at an unexpected
angle). The finale is pure joy. If any of Pfitzner's works could
become popular successes, this should be the first of them.

The *Little Symphony* is in four movements, none of them

exceptionally brief, but it requires a tiny orchestra of strings plus mostly single woodwind and one trumpet, and a harp. It has many of the same qualities as the Duo, plus a witty scherzo; and the recapitulation to the finale features one of the grandest tonal surprises in music. (Rushing scales on the dominant of A flat are diverted only at the very last moment to the home tonic of G – again the semitone relation.) The recapitulation of the first movement, short-circuiting to the second subject, is one of the especially heart-warming moments in Pfitzner. Of all the late works this is the one most obviously by the composer of *Palestrina*. The passage in consecutive fifths early in the first movement is followed by a transition in the melodic and harmonic style of Act Two of the opera, and a passage of development is based on a rhythm tied across the middle of the bar – these are all middle-period Pfitzner characteristics; the slow movement, with its grave theme for violas and subsequent clarinet and flute solos, is from exactly the same world as the Act Three prelude.

Soon afterwards came the C major Symphony, Op. 46, 'for large orchestra', which, being in three joined movements, is actually shorter than the *Little Symphony*. Its opening horn-call theme recurs at the end of the galloping finale; in between there is a slow movement which is basically a single huge melody built from the opening cor anglais solo. (Its atmosphere reminds me of the Introduction to Act Three of *Palestrina*.) There are two sets of piano pieces: *Fünf Klavierstücke*, Op. 47, with evocative titles (written in 1941), and *Sechs Studien*, Op. 51 (1943). Both sets effectively translate late-Pfitzner characteristics to the keyboard. It is surprising that these are the only works, apart from the Concerto, that Pfitzner wrote for the instrument he played himself.

The C minor String Quartet, Op. 50, is an almost impossible work to date by ear alone; its idiom would have been recognised by Schumann, and there is practically a quotation from Mozart (the end of the A major Quartet, к464) in the finale. But again the apparent simplicity conceals very subtle working; and it cannot conceal its deep beauty. The ravishing second subject acts as second subject of the finale, too; the second movement resembles one of those dance-like intermezzos in the late Beethoven quartets, and when it is developed in triplets it achieves a sublimity which would not be out of place in Op. 130.

Not many composers write one cello concerto, let alone three. When Pfitzner decided to write a work for Ludwig Hoelscher he borrowed a theme from his early and unpublished A minor Concerto of 1888 – 'my old age greeting my youth', as he says at the head of the score. The result is a relaxed and wholly lovable work which combines poetry, energy and humour. Pfitzner's slow movements do not often aim for the inner intensity of Bruckner or Elgar, but here the long-drawn solo melody achieves that quality. The soloist shares his cadenza with a clarinettist.

The Sextet, for the unlikely but splendid combination of clarinet, piano, violin, viola, cello and double-bass, a combination which recalls the concertante chamber works of Hummel and Kreutzer, shows Pfitzner greeting not his own youth but Schubert. The relaxation and ease of this music is captivating, and it is to this as much as the instrumentation (and the fact that there are five movements) which puts me in mind of the 'Trout' Quintet or the Octet. Yet, again, the music is no one's but Pfitzner's; and when the violin theme of the *Rondoletto* third movement bounces off at a bewitchingly unexpected set of angles, or when the finale's characteristically step-wise theme turns into a major-key reminiscence of the first movement's G minor to end the work, the listener recognises once more the fingerprints of the composer in a new, joyful form.

Pfitzner's last completed work was the *Fantasy* for orchestra. It is a symphony with two slowish movements joined to a scherzo-like finale in which the trumpet and horn rhythms expand and contract with fascinating irregularity within the prevailing $\frac{3}{4}$. (Much the same happens, but to totally different effect, in the furious drive of the scherzo of the C sharp minor Quartet/Symphony.) The opening of the work builds up from a jumping double-bass figure into a slow $\frac{6}{8}$. Not one of these works would fail to grace the repertoire; what is more, their melodic simplicity should make them readily accessible to an audience. It is proof of the injustice of popular taste that this marvellous corpus of works is so little known.

It is impossible to avoid contrasting the mood of these

compositions with the conditions under which they were written. Of course, it is often unhelpful to draw parallels between the immediate circumstances of a composition and its emotional content; but Pfitzner had written his life into his music before now (following the death of his first wife). The premise may be false; but I cannot help feeling wonder at the character of a man who could produce such music at such a time. There is more here than naïve escapism. The works of this period consistently evoke an inner peace and joy, and surely this was what the old man had found. It might have been Schopenhauer's 'pure, will-less contemplation'; it might have been God. But we may only speculate on these matters, for sadly Pfitzner's views on religion were never made clear.

The picture of Hans Pfitzner with which we are left is of a small and slightly-built man of much strength of character, moody, opinionated, almost entirely self-centred, and with absolute commitment to his own beliefs. In a letter to Willy Levin he wrote: 'I would be losing myself if I were to allow myself to stray in the slightest and to take one step from my path; seen from the outside, people must accept me in my composing as given, they must take me "as I am" '.[97] That was written in February 1909, when *Palestrina* was taking root in his mind; it could be a statement of his whole attitude to life.

He was a highly intelligent and deeply intellectual thinker, of wide reading and culture, as any cursory examination of his writings shows. Strongly as he favoured his native language, he was well acquainted with English writers; the frequent quotations and references in his essays show how genuine was his regard not only for Shakespeare and Byron but also for Shelley and Marlowe. In the world of performance he was a considerable figure. Records show him to have been a profound interpreter of Beethoven; the solo part of his own Piano Concerto bears witness to his keyboard technique; and on one memorable occasion he was conducting *Die Meistersinger* when the Beckmesser became indisposed, and so, leaving the

---

[97] Quoted in Abendroth, *op. cit.*, p. 160 *et seq.*; translated by Daniel Franklin.

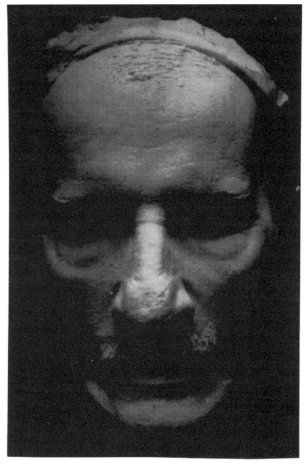

Pfitzner's death mask, 1949
(courtesy of Annelore Habs and the Hans Pfitzner-Gesellschaft)

conducting to the leader of the orchestra, he took over the part himself.[98]

His love for the world of music and the operatic stage in particular took the form of an idealism which he tried to express in his writings. But it is notoriously difficult to find idealism among those who work in the theatre, and it is easy to

[98] *Ibid.*, p. 190.

understand how his resulting frustrations could make him unpopular.[99] He took a high stand on personal, musical and philosophical matters. His essays in reply to those whose artistic beliefs he opposed could all too often descend to the petty, the personal, and the cheaply nationalistic, an unworthy contrast to his music. His attacks on Busoni ('Futuristengefahr', a counterblast to Busoni's *Sketch for a New Aesthetic of Music*) and Paul Bekker ('Die neue Ästhetik der musikalischen Impotenz') make unpleasant reading today;[100] 'Futuristengefahr' was described by Fritz Busch in 1934 as 'a book written from beginning to end in the spirit of the Third Reich'.[101] Pfitzner could be humorous, wistful or bitingly ironic as the mood took him. Busch gives a nice sketch of the front Pfitzner presented to the world:

> Hans Pfitzner showed himself to be the man who had been described to us; dissatisfied with everything, offended directly anyone opened his mouth, and, although advanced in years [this was 1922], after the first rehearsal regularly in love with whatever actress might be taking the part of the young Ighino, Palestrina's son. According to his custom, he drove the theatre personnel to despair by coming too early to unprepared rehearsals. In spite of these peculiarities we did not lose our enjoyment of the beautiful work.[102]

In his attitude to the outside world there were many unresolved contradictions within him. His attitudes to religion and to the world of politics were ambivalent, the central paradoxes of his life. Never confessedly a believer, he perpetually wrestled with the problem of faith. His political

[99] Cf. Edward J. Dent, 'Hans Pfitzner', *Music and Letters*, Vol. 4, No. 2, 1923, p. 128.

[100] 'Futuristengefahr' ('Futurist Danger'; 1917), *Gesammelte Schriften*, Vol. I, pp. 185 *et seq.*; 'Die neue Ästhetik der musikalischen Impotenz' (1920), *ibid.*, Vol. II, pp. 99, *et seq.* The contents of these essays are discussed below, pp. 87–88 and 91–94.

[101] Herbert Gerigk, article in *Die Musik*, December 1934, p. 189, quoted in Antony Beaumont, *Busoni the Composer*, Faber, London, 1985, p. 98.

[102] *Pages from a Musician's Life*, English translation by Margaret Strachey, Hogarth, London, 1953, p. 127.

outlook, always conservative, became increasingly coloured by his personal frustrations and prejudices, until at last he tried to hide from the world of politics altogether. Alma Mahler told a revealing anecdote: one May Day in Vienna, Pfitzner and Gustav Mahler

> ran into one of the socialist processions of workers, marching along to band music [. . .]. Pfitzner was furious at the sight of so many proletarian faces, and escaped down a side-street, whereas Mahler accompanied the workers for some distance [. . .].[103]

It is as if all his life Pfitzner wanted to escape from the 'World of Reality' and take refuge in his own imaginative vision. During World War I he found his refuge in the writing of *Palestrina*; and surrounded by the more personal terror of Nazi Germany he finally managed to enter his own world of truth for good.

---

[103] Kurt Blaukopf, *Mahler*, Thames and Hudson, London, 1973, p. 129.

V

THE DRAMATIC THEMES
OF THE OPERA

Most of the world's great operas tell a story and leave their audience to identify with the principal characters and their fates. Those that attempt to do more, such as Mozart's *Die Zauberflöte*, make a sufficiently obvious contrast that their philosophical intentions are easily perceived, if not always so easily understood. It was Wagner who first took subjects of profound philosophical significance as the norm of opera, and it was his special contribution to the history of art that he presented these subjects, which were of a kind not previously considered suitable for operatic treatment, in the most immediately expressive artistic language the world had known. The thought of his time was heavily influenced by Schopenhauer, and his is the predominant philosophy in Wagner's work, able even to subjugate the epic universality of the Nibelung myth or the simple intensity of the Tristan legend. Pfitzner's work was born under this unprecedently powerful influence.

In *Palestrina* he deals with questions that are not quite so universal as the pursuit of power or the meaning of love, but he hit on a subject that discusses more problems of importance than any one of Wagner's operas (apart from those of *The Ring*). It is this range and scope which make *Palestrina* a work of absorbing interest, together with the quality of the music and the nature of the narrative. To some extent the argument is carried simply by the actions and dialogue of the principals, but as with most worthwhile works of narrative art the situation must be interpreted in a more general sense. To

Pfitzner the conflict between Palestrina and the Council of Trent was a microcosm of the relationship between one man and the world as a whole, and broadly speaking the opera is about the creative artist and his place in the world. As well as studying the relationship between these two parties, Pfitzner has much to tell us about his own views on each of them in isolation.

The Individual versus the World

The quotation from Schopenhauer which stands at the head of the score encapsulates the opera's central philosophical concept. At the same time it tells us what it was in the subject which harmonised so profoundly with Pfitzner's own personality, the conflict between the artist intent only on his own creations and the rest of the world intent on his frustration:

> To the purely intellectual life of the individual, there corresponds just such a life of the whole of mankind whose *real* life is likewise to be found in the *will*. [. . .] This purely intellectual life of mankind consists in its advance in knowledge by means of the sciences and in the perfection of the arts, both of which progress slowly through the ages and centuries and to which each generation furnishes its contribution as it hurries past. Like an ethereal addition, this intellectual life hovers, as a sweet-scented air that is developed from the ferment over the stir and movement of the world, that real life of the nations which is dominated by the *will*. Along with the history of the world, that of philosophy, the sciences and the arts pursues its innocent and bloodless path.[1]

This quotation, which in its clarity and poetic imagery is typical of Schopenhauer's style, emphasises one aspect of his

[1] Arthur Schopenhauer, *Parerga und Paralipomena*, Vol. II, chapter III, paragraph 52 (English translation by E. F. J. Payne, Oxford University Press, Oxford and London, 1974, Vol. 2, p. 75). So far as I know, among previous writers on Pfitzner only Berhard Adamy (*Hans Pfitzner, Literatur, Philosophie und Zeitgeschehen in seinem Weltbild und Werk*, Schneider, Tutzing, 1980, p. 32) and John Williamson (*op. cit*) correctly identify this fundamental quotation. Hans Rectanus, in *Leitmotivik und Form in den musikdramatischen Werken Hans Pfitzners*, wrongly suggests that it comes from *Die Welt als Wille und Vorstellung*.

theory that the world as we know it is a synthesis of two
elements: Will, and Idea or Representation (*Vorstellung*).
Schopenhauer says that in one aspect everything in the world
is an 'object' of perception as perceived by oneself, the 'subject', through the senses. (These sense-data constitute a set of
Ideas, and it is possible to construct a philosophy, that of
Idealism, in which the whole of existence consists of nothing
but these Ideas. Thus one does not 'see' a tree as an object
necessarily existing separately from oneself; the brain
receives, through the medium of the eyes, a series of sensa-
tions which it interprets as a tree.)

But this does not constitute the whole of our experience. If
we look at our own arm, for example, and decide to raise it, it
is true that we perceive an object apparently moving. But
from our own 'inside' knowledge we know why it is moving; it
is doing so under the stimulus of our own will, and can
therefore be seen as one element of our Will itself. By analogy,
all living creatures perceived by us are objectifications of their
own Wills, and the same is true of plants or even inanimate
objects, the only difference being that they do not think.[2]
Schopenhauer puts the difference as that of 'degrees of
objectification of the Will'.

Schopenhauer went on to discuss the nature of the Will,
concluding that on its own it was a blind purposeless striving.
The Will existed merely to overcome obstacles placed in its
path, and the overcoming of an obstacle brought no satis-
faction, for there were immediately fresh obstacles to be
overcome. From this Schopenhauer deduces the ultimate
despair and pessimism of the human condition, for which
there is only one escape: a retreat to a 'will-less' world of pure
contemplation, of pure Idea, in which all consciousness of self
is overcome. In practice, this is to mean the world of Art,
where the product of genius is the expression of pure Idea.
Schopenhauer discusses this at length in *Die Welt als Wille und*

[2] Bryan Magee (in *The Philosophy of Schopenhauer*, Oxford University
Press, 1983, chapter 7) says that Schopenhauer's use of the word 'Will' is
most unfortunate as it implies the existence of consciousness and purpose,
which have no part in Schopenhauer's use of the word as a technical term.
Similarly, Schopenhauer's 'Vorstellung' is not the same as the Platonic
'idea'.

Vorstellung, paying particular attention to music which he sees as a complete microcosm of the Idea of objectified Wills.[3]

The context of the quotation chosen by Pfitzner becomes clearer by considering an earlier extract from the same paragraph:

> [The brain] leads a self-sufficient and independent life [from the body as a whole]. In the same way, the man with great mental gifts leads a second purely intellectual life apart from the individual life which is common to all. Such an intellectual life consists in the constant increase, rectification and extension not of mere learning and erudition, but of systematic knowledge and insight in the real sense. It remains untouched by the fate of his own person, in so far as it is not disturbed by this in its pursuits. Such a life, therefore, exalts the man and sets him above fate and its fluctuations.[4]

Schopenhauer goes on to adduce as an example the life of Goethe, who pursued his investigations into the theory of colour in the midst of the war in Champagne. We should not allow any disturbance in our personal life caused by events in the world around us to disturb our intellectual life. Against this background it is easy to appreciate the significance of the quotation used by Pfitzner. Quite apart from its personal reflection of his own position in working on the opera in the middle of the First World War, it contrasts the creative artist with the egocentricity of the masses as a whole (which is what Pfitzner calls 'the World'); this contrast is the principal theme of the opera. In itself it is also a perfect realisation of Pfitzner's views on tragedy in general, as set out in his essay 'Der zweite Akt Palestrinas – ein Vermächtnis und eine Abwehr' ('a legacy and a warning'):

> There is [. . .] basically only a single tragic problem, with variations: the hopeless struggle of human imagination with the everlasting character of the world, the fruitless search of man to transplant the eternal in this temporal world. [. . .] The twilight of a great character (the hero), the love between

---

[3] In logic there is no reason that any metaphysic should be either pessimistic or optimistic, and Bryan Magee casts doubt on the coherence of this notion of renunciation of the Will in *ibid.,* pp. 242 *et seq.*

[4] Schopenhauer, *ibid.*

sorrowful lovers, the so-called rebellion against the monstrous injustice of the world there are not so many variations [...]. But yet there is something in the world which defied the laws of finality, of transitoriness, the strokes of death and its sentinels, to appear inaccessible to them: that is the *work of art*.[5]

This is the essence of Schopenhauer, and it is the essence of the philosophy of Pfitzner's *Palestrina*.[6]

We have already seen how Pfitzner took the essence of the work right from its conception as a 'triptych', the outer Acts for 'the true world of Palestrina and, in between, the picture of the hectic tumult of the outer world which is hostile to the still, creative work of the genius and could only be represented by the Council'.[7] The contrast is a strong one. Palestrina does not appear at all in Act Two, and indeed is only briefly mentioned, art and artists being insignificant things in the eyes of the World. Only Borromeo appears in all three acts, as a link between the opposing forces. Only through the amateur of art, and, perhaps, through friendship, can the link be made. The World is present in Act Three, in the distance as the off-stage chorus and on stage as the Pope, while at the end Ighino, who is not a creative artist, deserts his father for the World. The various relationships between Palestrina and the different elements of the World are handled with a subtlety that words make merely ponderous by a carefully premeditated key-scheme.[8] If the outer acts show us the world of music, Act Two is anti-musical, and a performance was given at Mainz in 1954 with the second Act spoken instead of sung, emphasising the 'musiclessness' of

[5] Reprinted in *Mitteilungen der Hans-Pfitzner-Gesellschaft*, Vol. 19, Munich, 1967.

[6] Schopenhauer's use of the word 'will' in his technical sense has no necessary connection with determination (it is not even a phenomenon of consciousness), let alone the Nietzschean sense of the same word. Egocentricity may be wilful and anti-art, but it is not necessarily the same thing as Schopenhauer's concept of 'will'.

[7] *Reden, Schriften, Briefen*, p. 27.

[8] *Cf.* pp. 119–23, below.

this world.[9] The World is, indeed, 'the prison of the creative voice',[10] a symbol made literal when Palestrina is thrown into prison on the orders of Borromeo.[11]

Symptom of the ills of the World is haste, the haste which will rush the Council to its conclusion and thus bring about the catastrophe at the end of Act Two; that haste which presses Palestrina to complete his work, which compromises the work of art. Strife and haste are interchangeable at the Council, and the one theme, central to the whole of Act Two (Ex. 56a; p. 175), describes both. Ironically, in Pfitzner's words, the very same evil was responsible for adverse reactions to the second Act itself: 'Something remarkable from the depths of the German spirit came to threaten the success [of the work]: Haste sat down, stupid, unknowing, malicious Haste. It pointed itself principally for the moment at the second Act'.[12] From early in the life of the opera, critics denigrated Act Two, and thereby the design of the whole opera, for its failure to conform to familiar standards of dramaturgy. Agreement or otherwise with this received view must be deferred for the present. But it is at any rate certain that no one who approaches the opera expecting to understand its form in conventional terms will understand its dramatic message. The form is the content.

The Artist as Creator

Many composers have written operas which attempt to examine the relationship of the creative artist to the world. One example which immediately comes to mind for its surface similarities to the plot of *Palestrina* is Berlioz's *Benvenuto*

[9] Rectanus, *op. cit.*, p. 109n. The performance was discussed in *Mitteilungen des Hans-Pfitzner-Gesellschaft*, Vol. 1, Munich, 1954, pp. 8 *et seq.* *Cf.* Pfitzner's comments quoted on p. 277, below.

[10] Abendroth, *op. cit.*, p. 319.

[11] The concept of the 'World' as a mass of faceless humanity, spiritually inert, is a long-established one; St. John uses it in the Fourth Gospel – for instance, Chapter 15, verse 18.

[12] 'Der zweite Akt Palestrinas', *loc. cit.*

Cellini (1838). Here the central figure is commissioned by the
Pope to produce a great statue of Perseus; but his private
relationships and hot temper prevent him from fulfilling this
task until it is nearly too late. The influence of an Italian
Renaissance subject is common to both works, as is also the
presence of the Pope entering towards the end as a saving
figure. In both, a character expresses the wish to leave Rome
for Florence; in both, the creative artist has a pupil (and both
are *travesti* roles); in both there is a vision of dawn breaking
over Rome. But these are entirely superficial similarities, and
in point of fact the two operas belong to very different worlds.
Berlioz's hero triumphs despite his life of immorality and
crime; a murderer, he has his prayers answered. His concluding inspiration which saves his statue in the very process of
being forged is one of Dionysiac personal energy and will, in
keeping with many of the qualities of Berlioz's own score. Art
can excuse anything, and away with religion – that seems to be
the message. It is hard to imagine a philosophy further from
the 'will-less contemplation' of *Palestrina*; and that *Cellini* is
operatically a strange mixture of tragic and comic forms
underlines the difference even more clearly.

The suggestion that the artist is above conventional morality is taken a stage further by Hindemith in his *Cardillac*, the
story of a goldsmith so powerfully in love with his own
creations that to retrieve them he murders his clients. But
Hindemith also wrote, in *Mathis der Maler*, an opera about a
creative artist which is much closer in outlook to *Palestrina*. It,
too, portrays the relationship of the artist to the world through
the symbolic figure of a sixteenth-century genius, and Karl
Schumann has called *Mathis* '*Palestrina*'s extravert brother'.[13]
Hindemith shows the German painter Matthias Grünewald
abandoning his art to better the social conditions of the time
(which is that of the Peasants' War, around 1525), but he
finally realises that he has achieved nothing by so doing.
Cardinal Albrecht of Mainz, in the allegorical guise of St Paul,
tells Mathis that he must be true to the sphere in which God's
gifts have placed him, and that all he creates should be offered

---

[13] Quoted in Hans Rectanus, 'Pfitzner als Dramatiker', in Hans Becker
(ed.), *Beiträge der Geschichte der Oper*, Bosse, Regensburg, 1969.

to the Lord. This is very close to the literal meaning of the Palestrina story, with Mathis having shown more of a social conscience. But Hindemith presents his conclusion as an unarguable truth at the end of the opera, without attempting to justify it. In the absence of religious belief this means a blind trust in one's own abilities, for reasons that we cannot understand, whereas Pfitzner presents his conclusions as the consequence of a fully developed philosophy. We may accept the religious view, and remember that Pfitzner was an agnostic; but it is his opera which tells us more about the condition of man.

Busoni's opera *Doktor Faust*, begun in 1914 and left unfinished at his death ten years later, shares a philosophical and allegorical seriousness with *Palestrina*, and these two operas and *Mathis* seem to form a trio. Again there are surface similarities between Busoni's work and Pfitzner's. The Easter Vespers music of the Prelude to *Doktor Faust* – not just the opening bell evocations but the choruses of 'Pax' as well – naturally invite comparison with the bell interludes and dawn music of *Palestrina*. The $\frac{6}{8}$ *Allegretto* in Busoni's Prelude also has some of Pfitzner's exalted tranquillity, and the Mass scenes in Busoni sound almost like a parody of Pfitzner's scene in which the angels dictate the Mass to Palestrina, so similar is the ethos and so totally opposed the ethics of what is happening on stage (Faust signs his pact with Mephistopheles to the sound of an off-stage choir singing excerpts from the Mass). The conflict between Protestants and Catholics in Busoni's second scene not only looks forward to the similar events in *Mathis* but can also be compared with the conflict between Spaniards and Italians in Act Two of *Palestrina*.[14] But these details are less superficial than they may at first seem. Busoni's philosophy in this opera is also derived from

[14] All these scenes may have a common ancestor in Berlioz's *La Damnation de Faust*. Hindemith is alone in *not* quoting the Protestant chorale 'Ein' feste Burg'; other composers of Pfitzner's time who used it as a leitmotif with Lutheran overtones were Strauss, in *Friedenstag* (1936), where it is scored for pedal timpani, and Havergal Brian, in his Fourth Symphony, *Das Siegeslied* (1933). The latter is a setting in German of the bloodthirsty Psalm 68 ('Let God arise, let his enemies be scattered'), and some hear in it a commentary on the Nazi regime. The chorale is also the most important musical idea in Meyerbeer's *Les Huguenots*.

Schopenhauer, though by taking Schopenhauer's doctrine of 'the eternal will' manages to construct an optimistic conclusion. Life may be a disappointment, its fulfilment of youthful ambition doomed to failure, but those that follow afterwards may reach higher. What matters is the life of the next generation. In consequence creative love is of literally vital importance, not only emotionally but also philosophically. The link with Pfitzner's dictation scene[15] is clear. And most striking of all is that in a spoken Epilogue Busoni concludes his work with a couplet that can hardly be anything other than an echo, conscious or unconscious, of the end of his rival's opera:

Das gibt den Sinn dem fortgesetzten Steigen –
zum vollen Kreise schliesst sich dann der Reigen.[16]

In 1972 Sir Peter Maxwell Davies' opera *Taverner* had its first performance at Covent Garden. Over fifty years after Pfitzner, Maxwell Davies takes another sixteenth-century composer as the subject of an opera set against a background of the religious strife of the Reformation, a historical background also researched with much care. Both operas absorb quotations from the music of their subjects into the style of their composers (although naturally Maxwell Davies has to do more violence to the letter of the original than does *Palestrina*). Both show the composer befriended by a cardinal who is opposed to a ruler (the King or the Emperor Ferdinand); both present the composer's wife or mistress as the source of his inspiration, his Muse. The trial scenes which open both acts of *Taverner*, dogmatic clerics in the background, are related to the council scene of *Palestrina*, and in both we see the contempt in which the composer is held by the Church. The Cardinal's 'He is but a poor musician' could almost be an echo of Novagerio's 'A mere musician – a chorister'.

---

[15] *Cf.* p. 83, below.

[16] 'This is the meaning of the continuing progression – that the dance thus closes a complete circle.'
    The standard singing translation by Edward J. Dent (Breitkopf und Härtel) misses this point completely in a free paraphrase.

Both operas present a parable of the modern composer: Pfitzner himself, or, as Maxwell Davies has admitted, Shostakovich.[17] But this leads to the fundamental difference between the two works. The theme of *Palestrina* is the creative artist and his relationship with the world; that of *Taverner* is the conflict between personal responsibility and political necessity, as it is of Brecht's *Life of Galileo*. In *Taverner* the composer's music is merely a symbol of his own calling, and it could equally well be any other art, science, or trade. The atmosphere, too, is different: in contrast to the 'will-less' Palestrina, Taverner is an angry man ('we always bade him ware of his wrath'), noisy, 'will-full', joining the side of the world. Only at the end is his personality extinguished, to leave, like Palestrina, no relic other than that of his own music as the curtain falls. Yet Maxwell Davies's opera is fundamentally negative, proposing a dilemma to which no solution is offered; positive values (the Catholic tradition, contemporary music) are destroyed by parody, and the lasting memory is of the terrifying vision of Antichrist, for all the world like the parodies of Velasquez by Francis Bacon.

What does Pfitzner tell us about the social standing of the composer? Palestrina, like Mathis and Taverner, was nothing more than an employee of the Church and treated with consequent contempt by the higher ranks. Novagerio's disparaging reference to him has already been quoted, and his comparative, though not extreme, poverty is inferred from the stage directions describing his room: 'Simple to the point of poverty'. But if a man is poor, he may nevertheless reflect lustre on his employer by his fame, however unworthy this may seem to the employee. The contrast between the importance of fame to the outside world and its meaninglessness to the famous man himself is a recurring and poignant idea in the opera. In Act One, Scene Two, Silla says to Ighino:

He is a famous man! What more then does he want?

to which Ighino replies:

That true fame that quietly with time
Wrapped itself round him like a robe of state,

[17] Paul Griffiths on *Taverner*, programme of the Royal Opera House premiere production in the 1983 revival.

Should he still offer thanks for that?
Should a saint be grateful for his halo?
And what is it his fame has brought him
But his colleagues' envy and their open treachery?
His only earthly joy – family, marriage –
Cost him his Papal patronage.
He's scarce fought off the threat of poverty.
Now tell me please what good this phantom's done him,
This fame, which others falsely steal for themselves,
Men who can't hold a candle to my father?

As so often in this superb libretto, Pfitzner invents a literary figure, the 'robe of state', which concisely and memorably expresses his meaning. There is false fame; and there is true fame which is merely the stigma of being what he is, the 'saint's halo'.[18] Yet, despite these words, at the end of Act Three, Ighino shows that he still cares for the noise of fame. In fact, rather uncharacteristically, he suddenly becomes materialistic:

You're the most celebrated of them all,
In far-off times your names will still be spoken,
And not just that, your works will be performed.
The Pope will also pay you handsomely.

And he rushes off into the street to listen to and join the empty plaudits of the World (empty, because, like most listeners to music, they have merely taken someone else's word for it – in this case, the Pope). Fame is the furthest notion from Palestrina's head as the curtain falls.

The importance that Silla attaches to Fame is also significant. Silla sees the applause of the World as one of the chief rewards, if not one of the aims, of the creative artist. Pfitzner saw the hostility of the World to the creative artist, as fostered by the accidents of his own career, as a symptom of the ideal artist's isolation; fame and the plaudits of mankind mean nothing to him. The Palestrina of Act Three is deaf to the voices from outside. Pfitzner's attraction to the Palestrina

[18] I am reminded in this context of the painting by Bernardo Strozzi (1581–1644) in the National Gallery, London, of *Fame*, represented by a goddess whose two musical instruments represent the two aspects of fame: a short trumpet, brazen and brilliant but surely rough in tone, and a wooden theorbo, mellow and satisfying.

legend was no doubt fuelled by the apparent indifference to the World of the historical Palestrina.[19] Certainly the ideas of Pfitzner's intended collaborators, that the successful *performance* of the Mass was to be the centrepiece of the drama, was far from Pfitzner's own concept, centred on the inspiration of the moment of conception.[20]

The end of the opera shows us that Palestrina has found his goal of a peace which denies the self. As a creative artist he has a specific relationship to the world in which he lives and works, but as the subject of an opera it is Palestrina as a man like other men, with the capacity to act as a representative of ourselves, who engages our sympathy and pity. Ultimately more important than the fact that as a composer he is looked on as a mere tool by men of power is that we all live in our own relationship to the rest of the world. Those in power inevitably appear uncaring and uninterested by reason of the numbers over whom they have authority; our own tasks in life may seem unimportant to the world, and we may at times feel that we are mere tools ourselves. In his response to the violence of the world Palestrina is as relevant today as he was during the First World War; because he is true to himself and to the tradition which he maintains. Roger Scruton has pointed out[21] that the only reason that Palestrina is able to carry out his subsidiary political task of bringing a human conflict to a peaceful conclusion is that his primary object is to achieve an individual, inner peace. Few of us are creative artists; but we all understand the conflict of an individual with an apparently uncaring society, and from that point of view the exact nature of Palestrina's vocation is fundamentally irrelevant. And we may all learn from the belief that outer peace may be achieved only if we as individuals achieve inner peace first.

Many other works of art discuss the problems of the creative artist, and nineteenth- and twentieth-century opera furnishes numerous examples. In some cases the fact that a principal

[19] *Cf.* p. 216 below, and also Williamson, *op. cit.*, p. 129.

[20] *Cf.* pp. 31–32 above, and also Williamson, *op. cit.*, p. 131.

[21] In a perceptive article in *The Times*, 1 November 1983.

character is an artist seems almost incidental, a matter of added colour, as, for example, in *La Bohème* (1896) or *Louise* (1900). Of more immediate interest in the context of *Palestrina* are those operas which deal with historical personages; and one can make a further distinction between those which take the events of the artist's life as the centrepiece of the drama, and those which examine the artist's own problems. In the first category come Rimsky-Korsakov's *Mozart and Salieri*, Lehàr's *Paganini*, or Giordano's *Andrea Chenier*. In the second category the subject might be a troubadour or minnesinger (Tannhäuser) or the amateur poet-composer such as Hans Sachs (Lortzing's *Hans Sachs* of 1840, as well as *Die Meistersinger*). Sometimes an anonymous or fictional composer would be the main character, as in Strauss' *Ariadne auf Naxos* or *Capriccio*; in *Intermezzo* the composer is a self-portrait of Strauss himself. Max, the central figure in Krenek's *Johnny spielt auf*, is also a disguised self-portrait of the composer. Such works have the advantage of avoiding the problems of a 'cultural transposition' by using the style of one period to express that of another. Even Franz Schreker's *Der ferne Klang*, for all its evocation of low life and its influence on the Second Viennese School, takes its title from the search by a composer, Fritz, for the true inspiration, the mysterious 'far-off sound' itself. Busoni's *Doktor Faust* must be mentioned in the same context, because it deals with the need of mankind to create.[22] Comprising an important group on their own is a series of works devoted to artists of the Renaissance: Adolf Arensen's *Claudio Monteverdi* and Daniel Lesur's *Andrea del Sarto*, as well as two works already discussed, *Benvenuto Cellini* and *Taverner*. Palestrina's life gave rise to several works, such as the oratorio by Carl Loewe (1845). In 1886 the premiere took place in Regensburg of the opera *Palestrina* by Ernst Melchior Sachs (1843–1917), a pupil of Rheinberger. This included the violent seizure of the manuscript,

---

[22] It is worth mentioning that Busoni made sketches for an opera on the subject of Leonardo da Vinci. In it Leonardo finds himself unable to carry out his commission to paint the Last Supper until he sees the scene in a vision before him. The parallel to the scene in *Palestrina* in which the angels dictate the Mass to the Composer is obvious. *Cf.* Antony Beaumont, *op. cit.*, pp. 314 *et seq.*

but not by the clergy – rather by an intriguer from the papal Kapellmeister who wanted to pass it off as his own work, along the lines of Beckmesser's appropriation of the Prize Song.[23] Pfitzner's work is the pinnacle of this category. At the same time, the years around 1900 saw frequent recourse by German writers for the straight theatre to subjects drawn from the Italian Renaissance particularly, it should be noted, those with a religious flavour. In this context Gerd Ueckermann[24] has referred me to, among others, works on the Borgias by Emil Ludwig, Gräfin Uxkull, Berthold Weiss and Wilhelm Weigand, and on Savonarola by Franz Bockmann, Olga Gabe, Ernst Hammer, Ludwig Kellner, Raimond von Leon, Thomas Mann (*Fiorenza*, 1904), Wilhelm Uhde, Richard Voss and Helene von Willemoes-Suhm, all written within a year or two of 1900.

What is remarkable about Pfitzner's work, therefore, is not his choice of subject but the direction in which he orientates it so as to express a range of profound ideas.

A good starting-point for the discussion of these ideas is to be found in the words given to Palestrina in Act One. He tells Borromeo that he cannot produce to order:

> He can command,
> But not my Genius – only me.

Palestrina is saying that his creativity is in some sense separate from the rest of his personality and he has no control over it. When the spirit moves, he has no choice; as the ghosts tell him, 'he must'. This is a very Romantic view. We would not be surprised to find these words in the mouth of, say, Elgar or Mahler, but it is inconceivable that the real Palestrina could have thought thus – it is an example of what I have called 'cultural transposition'. It is, of course, Pfitzner's own view of himself; it echoes the Romantic notion of the artist as mere medium, as mouthpiece, through which God (or Nature, depending on temperament) finds expression. (This is also

---

[23] Much of this paragraph is drawn from Stephan Kohler, 'Der Komponist als Opernheld', Bayersische Staatsoper programme, Munich, 1979; but *cf.* also Abendroth, *op. cit.*, p. 317.

[24] *Renaissancismus und Fin-de-Siècle*, de Gruyter, Berlin, 1985, *passim.*

the theme of Peter Schaffer's recent play (and film) *Amadeus*.) If the question ever arose in Palestrina's own mind, he would probably have given the answer of the Dead Composers at the beginning of Scene Six:

> For Him – it is His will.

In other words, all music is written 'to the greater glory of God', and it is not surprising that when Palestrina actually makes the comment above, Borromeo's answer is:

> Then God no longer speaks within your soul?

(Earlier Borromeo had described the 'mighty Church' as 'the rock on which your art [. . .] is built'.)

This religious view of art is forced on Pfitzner by the circumstances of the plot, providing some sort of link with Act Two. An expressly atheist Palestrina would be an obvious impossibility, but this is the sort of problem posed by 'cultural transposition'. As it is, Borromeo is suspicious enough of Palestrina's motives:

> There is a stench of sulphur about you!

– i.e., the Devil; and, by implication, a stench of self-centredness and lack of spirituality. But it is the monologue which follows that tells us what Palestrina's real feelings are supposed to be – that is, what Pfitzner's views really are.

> Lucrezia, while you were still alive
> I was secure. Yes, then the source was still alive,
> And while it lived, my life still had its worth.

Love is the source of inspiration – the love of God, or human love, or the love of mankind. Palestrina's immediate response to the voices of the angels in Scene Six confirms it:

> Is there a fount of love [*Liebesquell*]?

'Ein Liebesquell' – the love of God to the sixteenth-century composer; the love for humanity of the man of the twentieth. 'God is love': this is how Palestrina has come to feel of his inspiration, although he has only come to this revelation late in life. Commenting on his solitude, Palestrina said:

> One doesn't feel it during the intoxication
> Of joyful youth, or the giddy round of custom

Which drives one ceaselessly through life.

Only when the inspiration has gone does the composer appreciate it. Deprived of love, he sinks to a state of futility and despair.

Even Borromeo, however, admits that God is not the only source of art:

He who believes God's grace forbids
Mankind's delight in beauty
Is but a man of little faith;
To teach that one's only care in life
Should be to nurse the soul,
This surely is mistaken.

There is no doubt that one of the main influences of Palestrina's inspiration has been his love for Lucrezia. She is like a Beatrice-figure, as in Dante's *Paradise*, a symbolism which gives further point to the paraphrase of the opening of the *Inferno* which Pfitzner inserts into the soliloquy.[25] This tends to be one of the most discussed aspects of the opera, its lack of 'conventional love-interest'. (Lucrezia is the only woman mentioned in the work, and she is dead.) Clearly Pfitzner decided that such an element would be irrelevant to the plot, and the resulting asceticism is one of the opera's most striking characteristics. But there is room for a further thought. It is a commonplace of psychological criticism to identify the process of artistic creation with sexual orgasm, viewing both as, in their different ways, intensely vital and, literally, creative.[26] Abendroth, writing of the music of the opera as a whole, speaks of 'the unspeakable heat which it breathes, having the effect of a smouldering eroticism'.[27] And if this seems an extreme view of the whole work, consider the ecstatic nature of the dictation scene, and also its placing at the end of the First Act, a standard position for a love duet. The metaphor of describing one's artistic creations as one's 'children' is

---

[25] *Cf.* p. 157, below.

[26] The idea was familiar at least as early as Plato, who devoted a lengthy discussion to it; *cf. Symposium*, 207–209, *passim*.

[27] *Op. cit.*, p. 316. Abendroth, writing for the Third Reich, found it necessary to defend the 'manliness' of an opera without love-interest.

familiar – for example, in Mozart's famous letter dedicating his set of six quartets to Haydn. Wagner puts such metaphors into Sachs' mouth in *Die Meistersinger*, and Thomas Mann sounds a similar note in the relationship of Leverkühn and Schwerdtfeger in *Doktor Faustus*. Busoni's *Faust* is centrally concerned with this theme. It is the meaning of the Pygmalion myth, and we may view it as a substitute for that 'love-interest' in *Palestrina*, or as a disguise for love itself.

Yet, even more important than his love for Lucrezia, the idea that lifts Palestrina from his deep pessimism is the message of the Dead Composers when they appear to him in the vision of Act One, Scene Five, that he has been called to a mission in life and that it must be fulfilled. Pfitzner's world-view, as expressed in *Palestrina*, is that man has his pre-ordained task in the history of the world, to accomplish; this is the meaning of the 'letzte Stein' metaphor, echoed by the Dead Composers' own words in the face of the threatened destruction of their music:

> With our works goes our salvation.

It is a pessimistic, fatalist view, the reverse of Goethe's 'Man must strive, and striving, he must err'.

Of course the angels are not 'real' angels, just as the Dead Composers are not 'real' ghosts. They are the personification of the pictures in Palestrina's mind – Borromeo paints for Palestrina the vision in which 'the masters of the Past raise up their hands', and Palestrina is imagining, or dreaming, the scene in his own mind. They are his inner voices, the unseen spring of his creations. Their presentation before our eyes is an enactment of the legend of the inspiration of the Mass. It is a visual metaphor; as Mosco Carner says, it is the same imagery as that of mediaeval paintings which show the artist surrounded by angels.[28]

So despite all this religious imagery, the very kernel of the argument, we are not being told that the only answer lies with God. To the question 'To whom is the artist responsible?' Pfitzner answers that he is responsible only to his work –

[28] 'Pfitzner vs. Berg, or Inspiration vs. Analysis', *Musical Times*, cxviii, 1977, pp. 379 *et seq.* (reprinted in Mosco Carner, *Major and Minor*, Duckworth, London, 1980, pp. 253–57).

which means that part of him which he can call his Genius. In the context of the opera these ideas should be associated with that state of mind which Schopenhauer calls 'pure, will-less contemplation'. The artist may see this as a state of communion with God, or as part of himself. The message of *Palestrina* is not interpretable only by believers.

It is most unfortunate that we know little about Pfitzner's own religious beliefs. Schrott, writing from personal acquaintance,[29] says:

> Out of religion to make art, as with Bach and Bruckner, or out of art to make religion, as with Wagner – those are the two extreme possibilities. Each creator stands for himself. Pfitzner inclines to that which sees in art his religion. He was no believing Protestant.

Yet, as we have seen, he sought bewildered comfort in Christianity after the death of his first wife in 1926; and there is no doubt that his works show, right through his life, the most active interest in the problem of faith. All the operas except *Die Rose* have religious implications, most obviously in *Das Christelflein*, and the unflattering picture of the Council in *Palestrina* may be that of an anti-Catholic (as suggested by Heyworth[30]) rather than of an atheist. Then there is *Das dunkle Reich* ('my "Requiem" '[31]) and the specifically religious parts of *Von deutscher Seele*. In the absence of further evidence I am inclined to the opinion (though it is *only* an opinion) that Pfitzner oscillated. He wanted to be able to believe; there were times at which he came close to belief and others at which his intellect rebelled. Fortunately, we do not have to come down one way or the other to achieve an understanding of the opera, and in particular of the state of mind conveyed by its close. If one is a believer, Schopenhauer's 'pure, will-less contemplation' will be seen as nothing other than a surrendering of will to God.

Whether or not one sees being true to oneself as being true to God, it is the refusal to compromise which is central to

---

[29] *Op cit.*, p. 146.

[30] *Otto Klemperer: His Life and Times*, Vol. 1, p. 91.

[31] *Cf.* p. 58, above.

Pfitzner's character. All that counts is true creativity, whatever its sources. In the words of Goethe's poem *Vermächtnis* (*Testament*), 'Only the fruitful thing is true', and for all his faults even Silla has 'God-given talents', while the non-creative Ighino is 'without meaning'.[32] The creative artist must put his own Genius above everything else.

The conflict between the Individual and the World is the principal axis of the thought expressed in the opera. We have now to consider a second axis, at right angles to the first, as it were, an axis which is at first sight the basis of a less obvious conflict but one which is even more fruitful in its consideration. This conflict is between Intellect and Emotion. Indeed, this is the theme which is illustrated in the opening scenes of the opera: Ighino *versus* Silla, the music of Palestrina against that of the Florentine Camerata.

The conversation between Silla and Ighino can be interpreted, once more, in purely personal terms: Ighino is warm-hearted and dreamy, Silla lively, energetic and self-interested. Borromeo's dislike of, and Palestrina's doubts about, his music are on the surface a mere instance of the generation gap, or of dislike of what is unfamiliar. There is also a suggestion that Silla doesn't like hard work:

> Sweating over the hard things
> High learning has devised.

It is often possible to write music in an avant-garde idiom with much less effort and knowledge than in a language the criteria of which are familiar, as anyone who has tried both will know. It is easier to disguise poor quality!

But Pfitzner introduced the Camerata in opposition to the music of Palestrina, as a symbol of the conflict in which he felt himself involved: Pfitzner *versus* the Second Viennese School. Of course, the connections between Palestrina as seen by Pfitzner and Pfitzner himself, and similarly between the Camerata and the Second Viennese School, are obvious. Each of the latter pair is the artistic avant-garde of the day, by contrast with which each of the former is conservative. *Palestrina* is a monument to musical conservatism, a tribute to the great

---

[32] Suggestion from Chris de Souza in rehearsals for the first English production of *Palestrina*, Collegiate Theatre, London, June 1981.

tradition of music and an affirmation of the artistic beliefs of Pfitzner's predecessors. Palestrina himself has long been held as the ideal exemplar and culmination of the age of Renaissance vocal polyphony.

Even here the situation is not entirely clear-cut, for it leads to a partial contradiction with the previous conclusion that the artist must be true to his own genius, which implies that neither audience nor patrons nor critics need be considered. Taken to an extreme this attitude can lead to works written 'on paper', without respect for performers' requirements, and sometimes all but unperformable as a result. This is a mainly twentieth-century phenomenon, a consequence of the ability of the composer in a changed social environment to write without concern for his public; and this attitude of mind – 'elitist', 'ivory tower', or whatever – is generally identified with the avant-garde. We shall see later that this apparent contradiction is countered by an awareness of the external world of politics.

Let us return for the moment to Pfitzner's conservatism. Close to the first performance of *Palestrina*, in 1917, he published his essay called 'Futuristengefahr' ('Futurist Danger'), an attack on Busoni's manifesto of musical progressiveness, *Sketch of a New Aesthetic of Music*. Busoni claimed, among other things, that music had remained earthbound because of being tied to standard forms. He called for the creative artist to make his own new laws – in form, technique, and even in notes, recommending the use of micro-tones, although he never adopted the latter device himself. Pfitzner saw this as an attack on the most important things in music; form (the body of music) and quality of material were more important to him than free development. In his essay Pfitzner wrote:[33]

> All Busoni's hopes for western music are for the future, seizing up the past and the present as a stuttering beginning, a preparation. What is the alternative? What if we were at a climax or had passed such a climax? If our last hundred or hundred and fifty years marked the blossoming of western music, the shining zenith, which will not recur and is followed

[33] *Gesammelte Schriften*, Vol. I, p. 221.

by a fall, a decadence, as followed the blossoming of Greek tragedy? My feelings incline to this view. [. . .] Previous epochs asked of everything new: is it clear and attractive to me? The present asks: will I not look ridiculously old-fashioned? That is the difference.

The implications of this last remark will be taken up later, but as an expression of Pfitzner's musical conservatism and pessimism this could hardly be bettered.

It is our good fortune that among the critics at the early performances of *Palestrina* was one who, as a major creative artist of the widest culture, not only understood the work profoundly but was also able to give full expression to his reactions: Thomas Mann. He discusses the music and offers some interpretations in his essay 'On Virtue' ('Von der Tugend') in the collection *Reflections of a Non-Political Man (Betrachtungen eines Unpolitischen)*.[34] His knowledge of music was considerable, and the power of music is a theme in many of his novels. But the profound impression that *Palestrina* made on him is particularly apparent in his *Doktor Faustus* (1947), his own testament to the workings of genius, and a book in itself could be devoted to Pfitzner's influence on Mann's novel. Mann describes Pfitzner's position as 'a conservatism that is free, knowing, tender, spiritual, in a word: ironical, not a robust conservatism that believes in authority like that of the Cardinal'.[35] Pfitzner is well aware of the implications of his views, and he is not opposed to musical progress as such.

His view is instead that progress must come from within, as a natural growth from established traditions, rather than a deliberate rejection of what has gone before in order to start afresh, and for the most part he has the history of the arts on his side. This is why, according to Pfitzner, those who are impatient for change will only rarely accomplish anything lasting.

[34] Fischer Verlag, Berlin, 1919.

[35] *Ibid.*, pp. 419 *et seq.*; English translation by Walter D. Morris, Ungar, New York, p. 306. Mann's friendship with Pfitzner lasted until 1933, when Pfitzner was a signatory to a protest over remarks made by Mann about Wagner (*cf.* Thomas Mann, *Pro and Contra Wagner*, translated by Allan Blunden, Faber, London, 1985, pp. 149–67).

The music of the 'great tradition' is given splendid voice in the opera. Apart from the nine dead composers who appear in Palestrina's 'vision', there is Palestrina himself; though it is very doubtful whether the real Palestrina would have felt himself to be conservative, let alone the end of a great tradition. Later generations have admittedly taken his music to be an unsurpassable ideal of its type, but that is not to say that he had no successors (the 'old style' of Monteverdi is an obvious example). Historically, therefore, Pfitzner's 'letzte Stein' idea is dubious. Further weight on the side of the conservative musical element is to be found in the music: the memorable theme which sets the words 'Aus grosser Meister Zeit'[36] appears at pivotal moments in all three acts, underpinning the musical and idealistic structure. There are many other themes associated with the music of the past, but against these is set merely the rather unimportant music of the Florentine Camerata, represented by Silla's awkward song.[37] We have to remind ourselves that the Camerata were the precursors of Monteverdi and hence of modern opera and of the baroque.

It is natural to compare and contrast *Palestrina* with another, more celebrated, German music-drama concerned with the problems of the artist, Wagner's *Die Meistersinger*. It is natural to compare, as Mann did in conversation with Pfitzner, 'Ighino with David, Palestrina with Stoltzing and Sachs, the Mass with the Prize Song'[38] (to which I would add, Silla's song with Beckmesser's, the Pope's singers with the Masters and Pogner, at the end, with the Pope; as will be seen,[39] Pfitzner also makes a veiled reference to Kothner in Ercole Severolus' music). And this was Pfitzner's reply:

> The difference is expressed most clearly in the concluding scenic pictures. At the end of the *Meistersinger* there is a stage full of light, rejoicing of the people, engagement, brilliance and glory; in my work there is, to be sure, Palestrina, who is also celebrated, but in the darkness of his room under the picture of the deceased one, dreaming at his organ. The

---

[36] *Cf*. Ex. 32 on p. 151, below.

[37] *Cf*. Ex. 9 on, p. 135, below.

[38] *Reflections of a Non-Political Man*, p. 311.

[39] *Cf*. p. 192, below.

Meistersinger is the apotheosis of the new, a praise of the future and of life; in *Palestrina* everything tends toward the past, it is dominated by *sympathy with Death*.[40]

It would be hard to find clearer confirmation of Pfitzner's pessimism. This 'sympathy with Death' is an easy concept to find made explicit in the opera. Think of Ighino's description of his father:

> One lives and weeps because one has been born –
> Father, I believe, feels this within him.

This is the very essence of Schopenhauer's pessimistic 'frustration of the Will'. Palestrina's monologue reeks with the idea; and in the meeting with the Dead Composers, he says:

> Why then does cruel death not let me go
> To be like you – with you – in your own land?

This is very nearly a quotation from *Tristan und Isolde*, and perhaps the death wish puts one in mind of Amfortas, too. In the same scene:

> But now my only wish is to depart; [. . .]
> I stare at life's abyss with open eyes,
> And would escape this age – escape
> The burden of seeing mankind weakened by the times.

Before leaving *Die Meistersinger* it is worth comparing and contrasting Wagner's and Pfitzner's views on artistic progressiveness. Sachs makes it clear that for him (i.e., for Wagner) music must be comprehensible to a wider public, and Wagner was keen to make his music accessible by enabling even the impecunious to come to Bayreuth. This is far from Pfitzner's 'ivory tower' in which the creator alone matters, and it is also more in tune with the past than the present in terms of the sociology of the composer. Wagner's initial intention was that Stoltzing should be the central character, winning over the rule-bound Masters in a triumph

---

[40] *Ibid.*, p. 311. The phrase 'sympathy with death ' used by Pfitzner startled Thomas Mann who, as he said, had used it as a 'thematic constituent' of 'a little novel' (*ibid.*) The reference is to *Der Zauberberg* (*cf.* Penguin edn. trans. Lowe-Porter, Harmondsworth, 1960, p. 652) – significantly enough, at the end of a chapter dealing with music and with opera in particular.

of creativity over pedantic critics; but as Hans Sachs came more and more during the composition of the opera to dominate Wagner's thought, this initial message became toned down. Sachs instructs Stoltzing how to continue his Prize Song according to the rules, and it is in this form – admittedly varied with some freedom – that it wins over both Masters and people. At the end the message is that tradition must be respected, and true growth can come from within the existing conventions – which is exactly Pfitzner's message. Neither work, ultimately, gives us an answer to the conflict of conservative and progressive in purely black-and-white terms; both tell us that in writing original music today we must not forget the past. 'Honour your German Masters', says Sachs, in his closing monologue which was, perhaps significantly, an afterthought on Wagner's part.[41]

Finally, as a sidelight on the views expressed above on the lack of 'love interest', it is interesting to note that twice Sachs compares composition with marriage and parenthood – while instructing Stoltzing on how to continue his dream song according to the Rules and when launching the quintet. Wagner identifies the two creative processes more explicitly than Pfitzner.

In these and other ways these two profound masterpieces have much light to shed on each other.

The argument with Busoni was not Pfitzner's only explicit attack on the avant-garde. His next target was the musicologist Paul Bekker, whose influential book on Beethoven[42] seemed to put intellect before emotion and analysis above inspiration, as well as being essentially unmusical in approach (the book contains no music examples). Pfitzner saw all this as characteristic of artistic progressiveness and displaced priorities. He said the book was symbolic of decadence or

[41] *Cf.* Ernest Newman, *Wagner Nights*, Putnam, London, 1949, p. 414. Schopenhauer, who viewed great art as something appreciable only by a minority, may have influenced Wagner in this change of attitude; Wagner was reading Schopenhauer at the time. *Cf.* Bryan Magee, *The Philosophy of Schopenhauer*, p. 348.

[42] *Beethoven*, Schuster und Loeffler, Berlin and Leipzig, 1911.

putrefaction (*Verwesung*) in German music; the role of
inspiration (*Einfall*) should be all-pervasive, as 'an organic
musical whole which cannot be dissected or analysed'.[43] He
does not mean that first thoughts are inviolable and must not
be 'polished up'; his fundamental argument was with the
Schoenbergian school of composition as a whole, which he
saw as embodying the triumph of the intellect at the expense
of the genuine musical content, identified as 'inspiration'.
Mosco Carner looked at the arguments which ensued. He
was surely right when he wrote that

> A listener must first respond instinctively and feel, as Pfitzner
> suggests, the beauty of a given piece. If this is his reaction, then
> analysis will heighten his aesthetic enjoyment when he hears it
> again. If there is no positive response, then all analysis will be
> futile for him.[44]

Pfitzner illustrated his views by looking at Schumann's
Träumerei. Berg replied to Pfitzner by analysing it and made a
number of interesting points but, as Carner says, he 'fails to
explain why it is such a memorable piece [. . .]. To try to
discover by analysis the beauty of an inspiration, is like
searching for the beauty of a rose by tearing off its petals'.
Alma Mahler agreed - 'Music is inexplicable'[45] - and most
music-lovers will have favourite examples of the uselessness
of analysis which tries to pretend that technique can explain
everything.
    Earlier, in 'Zur Grundfrage der Operndichtung', Pfitzner
writes of *die geniale Konzeption*, the 'wonderful conception', as
'the alpha and omega of all art', which is 'inspiration, not just
technique'; what is required is 'a point between free-will and
determinism, a blend of reflection and inspiration'. As to how
this inspiration is to be achieved, 'Where personality is, there
inspiration comes'.[46] Pfitzner valued inspiration above all
things; and this is why the crucial scene of *Palestrina* could not

[43] *Gesammelte Schriften*, Vol. II, pp. 139–62.

[44] *Loc. cit.*

[45] *Ibid.*

[46] *Gesammelte Schriften*, Vol. II, pp. 10 *et seq.*

be the vindicatory performance of the *Missa Papae Marcelli*, as his intended collaborators planned, but its composition – or, to be more precise, its conception, the moment when the idea descends. What we hear in Act One Scene Six is not the detailed composition of the Mass, but the moment of *Einfall* – which nevertheless for Pfitzner meant the largest proportion of a work if it were notably masterly.[47]

In this context, Pfitzner's own compositional methods are important. The sketches for *Palestrina* are preserved in the Bayerische Staatsbibliothek in Munich and have been discussed by John Williamson;[48] he demonstrates that large segments and many organisational details appear to have come to Pfitzner fully-formed in outline, even if some polishing was later needed.

None of this discredits analysis, which has its proper place in criticism. One cannot go on listening to a piece for nothing but the 'gut reaction' it inspires, nor can any piece justifiably produce nothing but such a reaction for its whole length. With time, the reaction of the senses mellows and, fortified by analysis, leads to a deeper understanding of the work. One cannot listen to an extended piece of music with all one's concentration on the emotional content for very long; aspects of technique come to the rescue when the senses tire, and vice versa. Each aspect complements the other.

The critic can serve the artist by helping his audience to understand the artist's aims and achievements, without destroying the beauty. He can draw attention to facets of the work under discussion that his readers may not have noticed; he can convey his enthusiasm for a particular work or artist to the public, and he may convert some to the view that a work or an artist is worthy of investigation. But he cannot bring about any particular listener's positive response to a work; only the work itself can do that.

Nor do Pfitzner's views necessarily discredit the works of Schoenberg, Berg or Webern. (It should be remembered that Pfitzner was writing well in advance of the wholesale rigorous

---

[47] I am indebted to John Williamson (*op. cit.*, pp. 23–47) for this important insight.

[48] *Ibid.*, pp. 148–51.

adoption of twelve-note technique, which did not take place until the mid-1920s.) The problem was that the new sound of the music of these composers went hand-in-hand with pro-longed discussion about technical methods, and despite Schoenberg's reiterated claim that the technique had always to be subservient to the feeling, it was perhaps not surprising that the priorities were misplaced by the public. As it is, the majority will know of the theory of atonality before the music itself is sufficiently familiar for its beauty to become apparent. The misleading impression therefore arises that technique is all and that the results are purely mathematical.

Thus the opera draws a parallel between Palestrina and the Camerata, on the one hand, and Pfitzner and the Second Viennese School on the other. Palestrina may have tri-umphed, in the eyes of posterity, in the sixteenth century. But for all Pfitzner's special pleading, in and through this opera, there is no doubt that the musical mainstream, at least until recently, seemed to go the way of his opponents in the twentieth. Each individual listener can make up his own mind as to whether this was an appropriate course.

The 'Letzte Stein' metaphor shows Palestrina as aware of his position as the last of a line, the conclusion and completion of a tradition. The dead composers tell him:

> The chosen ones long for the one
> Who will complete their circle; you have been selected!

Pfitzner sees himself as being in this position, and he felt that the opera he was writing was not only in the Wagnerian tradition but in all probability the last work in that tradition, completing that particular 'ring'. (Doubtless Pfitzner was also aware of the Wagnerian overtones of that word.) The idea that has been underlying the last few pages, closely allied to the conservative-progressive and inspiration-technique oppo-sitions, is now reaching the surface, the idea that I believe is the most fruitful and fundamental of the whole opera, binding together its many differing strands: the idea of *self-consciousness*. For the creative artist the expression should be interpreted as awareness of one's position in life and history, as a whole and in the particular situations one encounters. In the scene of the Dead Composers Palestrina expresses the problem:

> You lived strong lives in times that too were strong,
> And all unconscious of what was to come,
> Just like a seed within the womb of earth.
> But consciousness, the light that's deathly glaring,
> That rises, trembling like a new-born day,
> Is enemy to art, to fantasy.

Consciousness is enemy to art! The composer who says to himself 'what style must I adopt?', or 'will this seem sufficiently original?', or 'I can't use that progression – I shall look ridiculously old-fashioned', the composer aware of what is expected of him or of his apparent place in the history of his art – he is compromising that art. So it is that the avant-garde, desperately trying to be new and different, succeed only in being false, through awareness of their position.[49] It is hard to deny that the twentieth-century breakdown of communication between composer and general public is connected with the unavoidable self-consciousness of an artist in a world of ready communication, where his work can be discussed immediately all over the world, when more and more critics, teachers and writers (exploiting the possibilities of easy famili-

---

[49] Here again there is no doubt that Mann has taken over this idea in *Doktor Faustus*. Here is Kretschmar (*Doktor Faustus*, English translation Secker and Warburg, London, 1949, chapter 8, p. 61) talking to Adrian Leverkühn, the 'Faustus' of the title:

> For a cultural epoch there seems to me to be a spot too much talk about culture in ours, don't you think? I'd like to know whether epochs that possessed culture ever knew the word at all, or used it. Naiveté, unconsciousness, taken-for-grantedness, seems to be the first criterion of the constitution to which we give this name.

And here is the Devil offering Leverkühn 24 years of creative genius (*ibid.*, chapter 25, p. 230):

> We make naught new – that is other people's matter. We only release, only set free. We let the lameness and self-consciousness, the chaste scruples and doubts, go to the Devil.

Mann sets this central and crucial scene, the longest chapter in the book, in an Italian town that he had visited in 1895 – the town of Palestrina.

arity with any music through recordings) make us aware of
the masterpieces of the past, their history and their relationship to the social system of their time. The pressure on the
composer today *not* to conform, to be original at all costs
regardless of whether the results are attractive to be general
public – a state of affairs made possible by the lack of necessity
for the composer to be answerable to that public in order to
live, through the 'disinterestedness' of the bodies which commission new music – these are, says Pfitzner, writing in 1915,
the forces which can lead only to a dead-end for music. Chris
de Souza draws the parallels within the opera.[50]

> For Palestrina, polyphony [. . .] was giving way to the egocen-
> tricity of monody with its man-centred, self-conscious
> emotional expressivity; for Pfitzner, a thousand years of arche-
> typal wisdom was being thrown overboard for a new
> intellectual technique.

And if that statement over-simplifies the matter by refusing to
acknowledge the fact that the seeds of Schoenberg's technique had already been sown in the late works of Wagner (and
developed by his successors), one may still decide for oneself
whether or not the direction taken by the mainstream of
western music after 1905 was the only and inevitable consequence of what had gone before.

Pfitzner himself wrote of the need to make 'a harmony with
consciousness [. . .]. "Tout comprendre, c'est tout condam-
ner"; a work which is all consciousness, such as the Liszt
symphonic poems, is like a plane – plain'.[51] The essentials of
music are not to be found in pure intellect; the creative forces
are deeper than the consciousness allows, and the consciousness can only organise the fruits of 'inspiration' along
appropriate channels. On the other hand, this 'switching-off
of consciousness is not opium-smoking, or loss of critical
faculties'.[52] The mystery of musical beauty requires reason for

[50] Programme notes, Abbey Opera production, Collegiate Theatre,
London, 1981.

[51] 'Zur Grundfrage der Operndichtung', *Gesammelte Schriften*, II, p. 15.

[52] *Ibid.*, p. 6. Absence of self-consciousness is not mechanical thoughtless-
ness. The following passage from Ruskin (*The Stones of Venice*, London,

its articulation, but it cannot be explained in terms of reason alone. Analysis and inspiration are, for Pfitzner, to be identified with self-consciousness and its absence. John Williamson has pointed out how significant is a chapter heading from Pfitzner's *Über musikalische inspiration*: 'Das Reich des Unbewussten: der Schoss der Inspiration'.[53] Undoubtedly the real Palestrina's self-consciousness had not reached the sort of degree we have been discussing. The type of dialogue that appears in the Borromeo-Palestrina scene of the opera, concerning new music, is very much of our time; self-consciousness began as a Romantic phenomenon, the individual turning in on himself, the artist dramatising his own emotions. This is the reverse of the view of the composer as a medium through which the music passes, as Stravinsky claimed of *The Rite of Spring*, which we have seen is Pfitzner's ideal picture of how the creative artist should work. On this hypothesis, any interference with the message as it passes through must be for the worse; and we are back once more with Schopenhauer, whose ideal life of 'will-less contemplation' means that the individual Will should be kept from interfering with the Truth.

The conflict between the intellectual and the emotional approach to composition, the position of the artist in society, the sources of artistic inspiration, the concept of musical

---

1853, Vol. II, chapter VI, p. 11), incidentally a man of opposite political sympathies to Pfitzner's, provides an interesting commentary:

> You can teach a man to draw a straight line, and to cut one; to strike a curved line; and to carve it; and to copy and carve any number of given lines or forms, with admirable speed and perfect precision; and you find his work perfect of its kind; but if you ask him to think about any of those forms, to consider if he cannot find any better in his own head, he stops; his execution becomes hesitating; he thinks, and ten to one he thinks wrong; ten to one he makes a mistake in the first touch he gives to his work as a thinking being. But you have made a man of him for all that. He was only a machine before, an animated tool.

Without thought, without awareness of humanity, art is impossible, but this is not what Pfitzner means by 'self-consciousness'.

[53] 'The Realm of Unconsciousness: the Womb of Inspiration.' *Cf.* Williamson, *op. cit.*, p. 26.

conservatism – these are the problems which the opera has raised so far, and none of them has any meaning unless set against the background of an artist conscious of what he is trying to do. Mann encapsulated it in two words with which he characterised Romanticism: 'backwards pointing'[54] – not just looking back nostalgically in time, but turning a mirror inwards on oneself. These are the two central thought-processes in *Palestrina*.

This 'reflecting' quality is taken to the extreme of breaking through the convention in the last act. The chorus of papal singers describes their performance of the Mass with the line:

And all the words could be clearly heard

– set in such a way that the words can not be heard at all. And it is difficult, when we come to lines such as

We showed it off to the best advantage
Truly, the performance makes a difference, too!

not to apply the words to *Palestrina* itself.

It could hardly be possible, then, to imagine a libretto or a score more completely conscious of its own significance and position in time than those of *Palestrina*. By definition, therefore, Pfitzner's aim of writing the masterpiece that summed up both the problems of the composer and the tradition it is to end is an impossibility. The whole concept of writing a work that expresses the danger of self-consciousness without being itself self-conscious is self-contradictory. Of course, nothing is quite so clear-cut as this suggests; as I said above, art cannot exist without awareness of the human state, and, just as with the question of artistic progressiveness, a balance must be struck. Excessive impersonality is as sterile as excessive self-consciousness. But the question of whether the music of the twentieth century is excessively self-conscious is not one that is susceptible to quick or dogmatic answers.

---

[54] *Reflections of a Non-Political Man*, p. 302.

The World of 'Reality'

The problems raised and discussed by Act Two of *Palestrina* are fewer than the First and Third Acts, which concern the individual artist – inevitably, for Pfitzner is an artist and not a politician. There is scope for political interpretations of some of the ideas that have already been considered, but I shall concentrate first on those explicit in the text.

The proceedings of the Council of Trent as Pfitzner portrays it raise many questions that a thoughtful listener might like to go away and think about. The Lutheran schism – could it have been prevented or, once begun, healed? Who should have the final word, the Pope or the Holy Roman Emperor? What role should music play in church? Should the vernacular be used in church (or opera house)? To go away and think about, to discuss, yes – but not to see characters discussing them on stage. Semi-academic discussion does not work on stage – as, for example, in Strauss' *Capriccio*, where the arguments fly past at such speed that in the opera house they must seem either trivial or illogical. More effective is the personification of words and music in the characters of Poet and Composer, although the final justification for *Capriccio* lies in the human and beautiful figure of the Countess (whose music is among Strauss' loveliest). In another medium, the plays of Shaw are at their least successful as stage works when their author is putting two sides of a fascinating argument into the mouths of a pair of antagonists; and for the same reason the dialogues of Plato could not be performed on stage. I feel that I want to consider these problems coolly, in my own time and at my own speed; in the theatre, instead, one should be carried along with the fates of the characters.

Pfitzner did not fall into this trap; however interested in the questions raised by the Council he may be, he is content to leave them unanswered rather than discuss them academically on stage. This is the cause of what a critic described as 'reluctance to face conflict'[55] – an odd misunderstanding. In any case, these are not objects of central importance to Pfitzner's conception. Instead, he makes a succession of

[55] Edward Greenfield, *Gramophone*, Vol. 51, February 1974, pp. 1596 *et seq.*

general points. The Council is a microcosm of history in a broad sense – the coming-together of nations, their disputes sometimes solved by diplomacy but eventually toppling over into holocaust. This is a condemnation of the 'real world' of horrifying pessimism. The political view can be found in Mann, a critic less willing to escape from the world than Pfitzner (*Faustus* is as much a condemnation of contemporary Germany as a study of the individual). Mann describes Act Two as 'Nothing other then a colourful and affectionately studied satire on politics, specifically on its immediately dramatic form, the parliament'.[56]

Amid the conflict some further elements emerge. The shooting-down of the rioters in cold blood, where previously the Fathers had merely quarrelled, is the strongest possible condemnation of the inequality of classes – one law for the servants, another for their masters. For all the high qualities demonstrated by some of their leaders, the Italian contingent precipitate the crisis by their impatience in trying to end the Council's business as soon as possible (hence the pun in the servants' words: 'Sie eilen sich [. . .] zum End' – they are hastening to the end of the Council, or to their own end).[57] Pfitzner was critical of 'stupid, unknowing, malicious haste'[58] and by a twist of irony was criticised by the impatient for his construction of this act. But the Spaniards and Lorraine are also responsible for the crisis, too concerned with their personal pride – another aspect of self-consciousness – to back down.

There is no doubting the cynicism and sense of negation which is conveyed by this second act, the reverse of the coin from the individual's world of creation. Palestrina's Mass is of no concern to the Council except as a mere tool of politics. The fine things of the world are eroded and damaged by this cynicism; hence the description of the Council scene by the

[56] *Reflections*, p. 310.

[57] Incidentally, this is possibly also an allusion to Loge's words at the end of *Das Rheingold*, as the Gods are about to enter Valhalla: 'Ihrem Ende eilen sie zu').

[58] 'Der zweite Akt Palestrinas', *loc. cit.*

young critic Walter Seidl as 'musiklos'.[59] Put in these terms
we have the essence of Goethe's Mephistopheles, the spirit of
cynicism 'which endlessly denies'. It is the underlying irony of
this act that this Mephistophelian spirit should be symbolised
by the clergy, and its bitterness may point to some personal
experience of the composer. As Ighino says in Act Three,

> I couldn't understand a world
> Where a thing like that could happen.

But we should not be surprised at the ferocity with which
Pfitzner depicts the world when we remember that he himself
escaped from the terrible 'reality' of the First World War to a
peaceful world of the intellect in which to write *Palestrina*.

There is nonetheless room in discussion of the opera for the
political implications. Mann makes a fundamental assumption in 'Von der Tugend' which helps us to find the link
between music and politics, as well as that between Schopenhauer's two sorts of history; that the life of an individual
artist is most prominently shaped by the events of his time.
This assumption is commonplace in the history of the arts,
although it does not give the whole picture of any individual
artist, nor is it necessary for the view of history to be pushed as
far in the direction of politics as Mann chooses. The political
view nevertheless finds support in several places in Pfitzner's
libretto: for example, in the scene of the Dead Composers the
spirits tell Palestrina that his work will be 'the meaning of this
age'. More obviously, in the very first scene of the opera when
the embryo revolutionary Silla is eagerly anticipating the
prospect of going to Florence, he generalises from one history
to another:

> But I am drawn by all that's fine and new,
> And just as I see life and glory radiant before me,
> So all mankind will gradually rise
> To freedom and unexpected heights!

In the next scene the two boys discuss their ambitions in life.
Here is Silla's view:

> Isn't it better to stand on one's own
> Than to see oneself a small part of the whole?

[59] Quoted in Rectanus, *Leitmotivik und Form*, p. 109.

And later:

> Real strength lies in this: to rule, to be
> The centre of the circle!

But Ighino's is the less self-assertive view:

> Loving communion of good people
> Is the most beautiful thing of all.

And:

> Even the strong man stands to gain
> When many join in selflessness to form
> A whole that makes the work
> And sacrifice worth while.

This is Palestrina's own position:

> Hasn't my father taught us that?
> And nothing lifts the spirit so –
> Nothing on earth offers such sanctuary
> As to be part of a universal whole,
> Not living merely in the 'now'.

In passing, it is worth noticing how these different views further illuminate the central 'ring' metaphor. For Palestrina the ideal is to be part of a group in which everyone is essential; Silla wants to be on his own in the 'centre of the circle'. Both are musicians, but they see things from opposed points of view.

These are, of course, mild philosophical speculations rather than anything of real profundity, but they serve to emphasise how far out of the world Palestrina lives; the boys are more aware of these questions than he. But I think it is unjustified to jump straight to an identification between musical and political conservatism; such an identification would be a serious oversimplification.

Palestrina's pessimism has already been discussed, and it applies not just to music but to the whole of life:

> [I would] escape the burden
> Of seeing mankind weakened by the times.

Mann views pessimism as a defence against reality, echoing Lord Beveridge's 'Scratch a pessimist and you find a defender

of privilege'.[60] Mann's political inclinations were progressive,
and he identifies reactionary views not precisely with musical
conservatism but with this pessimism, saying that *Palestrina*
'completely lacks progressive optimism, and hence political
virtue'.[61] For Mann 'sympathy with Death' and, indeed, all
that was conservative and reactionary, comes to stand for a
political quality which is the opposite of virtuous.

How far is it reasonable to interpret a work of superficially
non-political art in terms of politics – in terms of the discussion of the ends of a society? The answer to this depends as
much on individual taste as on the nature of the work, though
there are many today who, in the view taken by Aristotle that
'everything is subordinate to politics',[62] would have us involve
ourselves politically whenever possible. The artist would thus
be brought out of his ivory tower, as was Mathis in Hindemith's
opera – a step which requires a degree of self-consciousness on the part of the artist. This is the opposite of the
message at the heart of Pfitzner's 'triptych' construction, that
the artist must stay apart from the world, and acceptance of
significant political content in *Palestrina* must therefore lead
to further internal contradiction.

But opposed to the Aristotelian view there is another argument. Assuming that politics means the ordering of the state,
to say that music must be subordinate to politics is to treat the
ordering of the state as an end in itself rather than the means
by which the constituent elements in life, including music,
may be allowed to fulfil themselves. In practice, those who
argue for the omnipotence of politics are generally concealing
their advocacy of some limited ideological principle under the
heading of 'politics' and hoping in this way to direct everything they dislike or think inessential in ways which further
their own limited aims. Under the banner of political slogans
they thus conceal both their real motives and their contempt
for other members of society who do not share those motives.
In their opposite ways this has been demonstrated by the

[60] 'Sayings of the Week', *The Observer*, 17 January 1943.

[61] *Reflections*, p. 423.

[62] Aristotle, *Nicomachean Ethics*, 1.

attitudes towards music of the Hitler regime[63] and the
Stalinist purges of the 1930s and afterwards in the Soviet
Union. Dramatic and narrative art may sometimes display or
conceal political content; but there is no justification for
political arguments to influence creative artists in the abstract
field of music. Ultimately everything depends on the individual's conception of what constitutes politics. Mann is close to an extreme,
taking almost any general expression of the situation of
humanity to be essentially political; I believe, too, that his
view of the virtues of progressiveness should be tempered by
the ideal of natural growth from within established traditions.
The gulf between Pfitzner's and Mann's views on progress
tends to exaggerate the significance of the political content in
the works of both. But whatever one's feelings, there is no
doubt that *Palestrina* leaves one more aware of the world's
problems and suggests a possible attitude towards them.

Noel Coward's witticism that the musical *Camelot* was '*Parsifal* without the jokes' has gone through many permutations,
but anyone who applies it to *Palestrina* has never listened to
the work. There are many facets of humour to be found in it,
from Silla's high spirits to Pfitzner's own joke about the
audibility of the words.[64] But the majority of the humour is to
be found in the portrayal of the 'originals' in Act Two.
Novagerio's obsequiousness, the pomposity of the Master of
Ceremonies, a subdued reproach of Madruscht's over-
seriousness, Luna's calculated mockery and the misplaced
buffoonery of Budoja – all these are most effectively drawn in
by Pfitzner's verbal and musical characterisation. Taken as a
piece, this humour is a sort of loving irony: the sympathy with
which the characters are drawn is unmistakable, but so is the
quiet observation of their faults. This humour led Mann to
one of his most-quoted pronouncements, typically slanted
towards politics:[65]

[63] *Cf.* p. 47–56, above.

[64] *Cf.* p. 98, above.

[65] *Reflections*, p. 301.

Pessimism and humour – I have never perceived their correlation more strongly and never more sympathetically than in the face of the second *Palestrina* act. The optimist, the reformer, in a word, the politician, is never a humorist; he is lofty-rhetorical.

The pessimism is undeniable, though I think that only a German of Mann's disposition would so generalise the applicability of this very individual form of humour. But what is the source of humour? Observation, knowledge of the effect of faults, misplaced sense of dignity; these are the techniques of Pfitzner, and what are they but the self-consciousness of humanity? The ability, on the one hand, to see the ridiculous side, and, on the other, to expose the incongruous is impossible without self-awareness, and these are the sources from which all humour springs. Laughter is a safety-valve to spare us the adverse effects of our self-consciousness, and in its absence the consequences are not comic but tragic. Nations go to war because they cannot, in Wilfred Owen's words, 'sacrifice the Ram of Pride' – they cannot allow themselves to ignore a diminution in their own standing, in their own eyes or in those of others. Men argue, fight and destroy one another to protect their pride in themselves. And this, too, Pfitzner tells his audience. For when the Fathers quarrel, their aims are to protect the pride of Spain or Italy; when Luna and Lorraine come near to blows, it is on account of the trivial question of precedence. Who should come first? Only self-consciousness cares. The servants fight where their patrons had argued, defending the name of their country ('The two words [. . .] *Italy, Spain,* had the effect of a battle-cry'[66]); at the end, they are killed on the orders of Madruscht, the man without humour.

Fame, too, is a manifestation of awareness of what others think of oneself, and in Act One Silla, the representative of self-conscious art, is identified with an awareness of fame; at the end of the opera Palestrina is not thinking of his own standing in the eyes of the world. Pfitzner's identification of

[66] Sforza Pallavicini, *Geschichte des tridentinischer Konzil,* German translation Augsburg, 1835, chapter XX, paragraph VIII, I.

self-consciousness with the operation of Schopenhauer's
'will' is complete.[67]

This, then, is ultimately the single river in which are united
all the multifarious tributaries of ideas contained in Pfitzner's
Palestrina – the contrast between 'will-less' individual creator
and 'will-full' world of reality; the problem of the artist
seeking inspiration and not over-intellectualising; the world
itself, laughing or fighting as it strives to further the multiplicity of individual wills which comprise it. Perhaps the
embodiment of the principle can be found in a single isolated
figure in the opera, the Patriarch Abdisu, the man of primitive
naivety from the home of Christianity itself. He is an operatic
equivalent of Dostoevsky's Prince Myshkin. In an ideal
world, he is the ideally good and venerable man. In the lost-
innocence, self-conscious world of the Council, like some
religious Albert Herring, he is a butt of humour.

How far do the events of Pfitzner's libretto mirror Schopenhauer's philosophy? We have seen the large number of
manifestations of the pessimistic view of the human predica-
ment – Silla's words in Act One, Scene Two (the 'Sorrows of
the World'), and the whole of Palestrina's monologue in
Scene Five are full of that suffering which to Schopenhauer is
the necessary consequence of the rule of Will. And, needless
to say, the whole of Act Two is a specific dramatisation of that
same idea. Even in the outer acts, Silla, Borromeo and Ighino

[67] Here we can see that this aspect of Pfitzner's philosophy goes back to
Rousseau, whose concept of 'amour-propre' is identical to that of self-
consciousness in this later sense. Rousseau, investigating the differences
between primitive man and man in a created society (*The Origin of Inequality*, English translation J. M. Dent, London, 1973, p. 66n), produces his
well-known contrast between *amour-soi* and *amour-propre*:

> Love of self (*amour-soi*) is a natural feeling which leads every animal
> to look to its own preservation, and which, guided by man in reason
> and modified by compassion, creates humanity and virtue. *Amour-
> propre* is a purely relative and factitious feeling, which arises in a state
> of society, leads each individual to make more of himself than of any
> other, causes all the mutual damage men inflict on one another, and
> is the real source of the 'sense of honour'.

It is perhaps helpful to stress once more that our usual use of the word 'will',
akin to 'amour-propre', is not the same thing as Schopenhauer's technical
use of the word.

(at the end) are 'will-ful'. (Silla's attitude makes the association between 'will-ful' and 'wilful' clear.) Only Palestrina is able to preserve his distance from the World and subdue his Will; at the end of the opera he has indeed reached the state of 'losing himself in contemplation'. His state of mind as the curtain falls can be seen as a perfect achievement of Schopenhauer's ideal:

> If, raised by the power of the mind, a man relinquishes the common way of looking at things, [. . .] the final goal of which is always a relation to his own will; if he thus ceases to consider the where, the when, the why, the whither, of things, and looks simply and solely at the *what*; if, further, he does not allow abstract thought, the concepts of the reasons, to take possession of his consciousness; but instead of all this, gives the whole power of his mind to perception, sinks himself entirely in this, and lets his whole consciousness be filled with the quiet contemplation of the natural object actually present – if thus the subject has passed out of all relation to the will, then that which is so known is no longer the particular thing as such, but it is the *Idea*, the eternal form, the immediate objectivity of the will at this grade; and, therefore, he who is sunk in this perception is no longer individual, for in such perception the individual has lost himself; but he is *pure*, will-less, painless, timeless *subject of knowledge*.[68]

But there is more to it than this. The whole subject is inextricably intermingled with a religious outlook (the contrast between Palestrina's and Pfitzner's religious beliefs serving to bring about considerable confusion about the exact religious attitude of the work), and of course the religious outlook is, for Schopenhauer, an unnecessary hypothesis. One positive quality that Pfitzner puts forward – the only one, indeed, which is explicitly present in Palestrina's mind at the end – is the sense of fulfilment and completion which is a God-given idea (literally – at any rate in the context of the opera) and which is meaningless without reference to God. And this, after all, has been the specifically announced meaning that Palestrina's life has been given. It is a constructive alternative to Schopenhauer's nihilism, but then so is any

---

[68] Schopenhauer, *The World as Will and Idea*, English translation Kegan Paul, London, 1883/6, §34.

alternative which is based on religion. It need hardly be said that the principal claim for the existence of religious belief is to supply meaning to life which, if looked at in purely humanistic terms, is very difficult to see as other than meaningless.

So *Palestrina* stands in the tradition of nineteenth-century German art in its taking over from Schopenhauer its general atmosphere of pessimism, as well as one or two specific ideas chief among which is that conflict between the creative artist and the 'world' as embodied in the quotation in the score. But perhaps more important is the overall ethic that Mann described as 'Cross, Death and Grave'.[69] And yet for all its 'sympathy with death', at the very end there is real – human *and* religious – optimism. It is a strangely warm-hearted and gladdening conclusion, because Pfitzner has had the courage and the inspiration to end with a positive answer to some of the dark questions posed by the modern philosophies of man.

[69] *Reflections*, p. 297.

VI

THE MUSIC OF THE OPERA

Given the date, place and circumstances of its origin, it is almost inevitable that *Palestrina* was written using the leitmotif system. But, just as there is a world of difference between the sonata styles of, say, Haydn and Schumann, so is Pfitzner's leitmotivic technique significantly different from that of Wagner and of other composers who used the system, such as Strauss, Korngold and Elgar.

As with Wagner, Pfitzner's leitmotifs are just as likely to stand for abstract ideas as for concrete objects or individual characters. Bernard Shaw poured magnificent scorn on composers whose technique was limited to 'one fixed theme attached to [each character] like a name-plate to an umbrella, blaring unaltered from the orchestra whenever he steps on stage'; rather, 'the more complex characters, instead of having a simple musical label attached to them, have their characteristic ideas and aspirations identified with special representative themes'. Shaw went on to point out how Wotan, for example, is represented sometimes by the Valhalla motif and sometimes by the Spear motif, to take only a simple case.[1] Similarly, Palestrina himself has at least four individual themes, and even a comparatively minor character such as Cardinal Madruscht has two (*cf.* Exx. 62 and 63, pp. 179 and 180). This abundance of material gives Pfitzner wide choice in his expression of a character's thoughts and in the estab-

---

[1] 'The Perfect Wagnerite', *Major Critical Essays*, Constable, London, 1932, p. 256; reprinted in *Shaw's Music*, The Bodley Head, London, 1981, Vol. 3, pp. 520 and 519.

lishment of subtle cross-relationships, even while it makes considerable demands on the memory of the audience. The various subtle shades of meaning that can be inferred from the appearance or even the non-appearance of the many different motifs is a constant source of fascination.

In my description of the work I have avoided giving every single motif a short title, a practice which can lead to dangerous over-simplifications, especially when, as here, different motifs reflect subtly different aspects of the same idea. And even when a motif seems to have a straightforward meaning, it can later turn out to have deeper ones, too: for instance, Ex. 12 (p. 137) presents not merely Rome but the city in all its grand yet backward-looking splendour; and in Act Two it represents the Pope as a political and possibly reactionary force. Equally, simplistic labelling can obscure the differences of usage and status of the themes. Thus Ex. 24 (p. 145) recurs merely as a reminiscence at the end of Act One, with musical and emotional recapitulatory effect; Ex. 8 (p. 134) simply represents the boy Silla and his lively nature; while Ex. 1 (p. 129) occurs with profound and complex meaning in a wide variety of contexts. To dignify Ex. 24 with a title like 'psalm motif' seems ridiculous; and the association of Ex. 1 with the word 'creativity' is really only a shorthand for its central musical and philosophical functions. Indeed, it is characteristic of Pfitzner the 'abstract' musician to base sections of the music on themes with no very specific 'meaning'. Such ideas as Ex. 18 (p. 140) or Ex. 33 (p. 151) recur in different contexts, and it is possible to infer interpretations for them; but such interpretations seem to me less important than their purely musical role.

The other important aspect of leitmotivic technique to which Shaw's words draw attention is the extent to which the motifs are varied. Comparatively little attention seems to have been paid to this aspect of Wagner's method; to take only one example, consider the many different directions in which the second phrase of the Siegfried motif is made to turn. Pfitzner, too, gives much thought to the differing shapes of his motifs, even from his earliest dramatic works. It is rare in *Palestrina* for one to leap out of the texture; often, we tend suddenly to become aware that a primary or a secondary line has become a quotation of music already heard. Even quotations of external material, such as a phrase from the *St. Matthew Passion* (p. 198), are usually so subtly introduced as to be easily overlooked. Examples of the sort of development which an idea may undergo vary widely. The intervals of Ex. 1 are several times quoted in rhythmic diminution, the briefest passing mention. The harmonic nature of Ex. 4 (p. 130) enables it to appear naturally at almost any point; the cadential nature of Ex. 6 (p. 131) can be interrupted. The huge and magnificent Council theme, Ex. 7 (p. 132) can be extended sequentially almost indefinitely, while its strong line enables it to be identified easily in diminution, and the rising octaves which open it can act as its harbinger. Ighino's theme, Ex. 15 (p. 138), is altered in harmony and in orchestration as his moods change. The one really prominent symmetrical tune in the opera, the Emperor's Ex. 29 (p. 149), is hammered into a number of ingenious shapes (though its identity is always so obvious when it appears that these variations do not always avoid predictability). In what follows I have mentioned the different forms of the motifs as they occur, but the exact nature of the changes is always of interest and importance – and complicated to put into words.

In his later instrumental works Pfitzner takes this idea to an extreme; no theme ever recurs identically. The way in which the variations are accomplished in, say, the Duo for violin and cello, Op. 43, is fascinating.

The techniques by which Pfitzner develops his themes are wide-ranging. As much as Wagner he is capable of building large sections from small motifs in the manner of a Beethoven symphony; the way in which so much of Act Two, and in particular the Prelude, is built up from the three-note cell of Ex. 56*a* (p. 175) is invariably impressive. Alternatively, and this is where Pfitzner's abilities as a writer of lieder become apparent, he can draw out a theme continually to build a long paragraph out of an apparently endless (melodic) line, an ability which, in a very different way, he shares with Strauss. The whole of Act One, Scene Two, and especially such passages as that between figures 20 and 22 in the score (Silla's inability to believe that there is anything the matter with Palestrina), furnishes a good example of this. Some of

Pfitzner's themes appear not be so malleable as those of
Wagner; he shows that they are instead more ductile.[2] This is
an aspect of Pfitzner's mastery of counterpoint evident in all
his major works; indeed, his ability to think symphonically
and polyphonically at the same time is extraordinarily impressive, and, of course, such a style is ideally suited to an opera
on the subject of Palestrina.

In consequence of this broad palette of techniques the
movement of the music can vary in pace over a huge range. It
is not easy to think of any music in the sonata tradition that
moves at a more furious pace than the Prelude to the Second
Act; equally, if Pfitzner does not demonstrate Wagner's
almost miraculous ability to effect the most gradual of trans-
itions, he is able to produce an impression of almost complete
immobility while always being able to move forward again
without a jerk. Much of the scene with the Dead Masters in
Act One displays this stillness, as do parts of the first scene of
Act Three. (A *locus classicus* in Pfitzner's instrumental music is
to be found in the first movement of the Piano Concerto.)
Such an ability allows Pfitzner to introduce so closed and
static an object as a chorale (Ex. 32, p. 151), for he knows that
he can avoid an embarrassed pause at the end.

A key to understanding Pfitzner's style is that his devel-
opmental procedures often include the substantial altering of
the intervals of a phrase while keeping its rhythm unchanged,
a procedure later used more thoroughly by Havergal Brian.
Examples of this device abound in Pfitzner's instrumental
works. For instance, in the C sharp minor String Quartet the
main theme has the rhythm

which takes on a seemingly limitless number of shapes during
the first movement. The development section builds up a

_____

[2] Malleable: 'capable of being hammered into shape'; ductile: 'capable of
being drawn into long thin wires'.

climax of tremendous power using this rhythm together with more traditional methods, such as rhythmic diminution, sequence and accelerating harmonic rhythm; Beethoven would not have disowned such a passage. The slow movement of the Piano Concerto also furnishes a good example of this, varying the theme the rhythm of which is

In *Das Herz* the recovery of the young Prince at the end of Act One is greeted by a celebratory theme in $\frac{6}{8}$ rhythm; his subsequent death in Act Two is announced by a much more ominous theme in a rhythm clearly designed to refer to the earlier context. In *Palestrina* Pfitzner does not really apply this method to the principal motifs, but rather prefers to build scenes from themes of more musical than dramatic significance such as Exx. 18 or 33 (pp. 140 and 151). But of at least equal importance is the use made of this method to establish relationships between the themes. Exx. 21 (p. 142), 33 (p. 151), 37 (p. 154), 45 (p. 163), 51 (p. 166), 66 (p. 182), 70 (p. 186), 78 (p. 193) and 86 (p. 206) all share a rhythm of a long note held across the middle of the bar followed by three quavers, which may or may not be conscious but which is at any rate a unifying element. Themes with a note held across the middle of the bar before releasing their energy are deeply characteristic of Pfitzner – the themes of the Piano Concerto and the Violin Concerto, the C sharp minor Quartet and the first movement of the Violin Sonata all share this feature, although with the exception of the Sonata the three equal quavers which follow are specific to *Palestrina*. Again, in the opera the rhythmic connection between Exx. 2 (p. 130) and 12 (p. 137) is obvious, as is that between Exx. 18 (p. 140) and 20 (p. 141).

But there are more direct ways in which Pfitzner establishes the fundamental identities underlying his material. The simple fifth with which the opera opens sets off reactions in all sorts of directions. It evokes the sixteenth century and, more specifically, provides a direct link with Palestrina's Mass, as we shall see when we come to look at the Dictation Scene, while at the same time it is wonderfully characteristic of Pfitzner himself. The fifth appears very obviously in the Old Masters theme, Ex. 25 (p. 146), and in the motif of 'highest joy', Ex. 52 (p. 167); and 'filled in', it becomes the motif of the Mass, Ex. 51 (p. 166). (It would, I think, be over-ingenious to try to discover meanings in every jump of a fifth in the examples.) Many themes feature rising or falling scales, aiming perhaps consciously for the smoothness of Palestrina's own style; Exx. 7 (p. 132), 12 (p. 137), 15 (p. 138), 36 (p. 154) and 43 (p. 161) are examples. There will be other relationships that each listener will no doubt observe for himself; one must not treat the music as if it were based on Schoenbergian tone-rows, but there may, for instance, be a reason for the undeniable similarity between the shapes of Silla's Ex. 8 (p. 134) and the Mass theme, Ex. 51 (p. 166).

Two other aspects of Pfitzner's thematic working deserve notice. One is the reappearance of a theme on a different degree of the scale, a device no doubt learnt from Beethoven (the 'In gloria Dei Patris' fugue from the *Missa Solemnis*, for example) and one which gives such reappearances the impression of viewing an object from a new and oblique angle. Again, this is most noticeable in the chamber and orchestral works (the Duo again provides a particularly fascinating set of examples) but its occasional use in *Palestrina*, such as with the loneliness theme, Ex. 39 (p. 157), is worthy of remark. The other aspect is the tendency, used with such frequency in the late works that it becomes practically a mannerism, of anticipating the theme of a new movement or section by varied fragments before it arrives. Pfitzner may have taken the idea from Schumann (for instance, at the end of the slow movement of Schumann's Piano Quartet); in *Palestrina* we see this fingerprint with the Trent theme at the end of Borromeo's Act One solo, with Borromeo's theme immediately before his entry in Act Three, and elsewhere. Korngold is one of several other composers to have adopted this device (in *Die tote Stadt*, for instance), but I know of no one who uses it so often and so individually as Pfitzner. The logical corollary of this procedure – that of finishing a work with a shortened but unmistakable reference to an earlier theme, a favourite gambit of Max Bruch – is also omnipresent in the instrumental music, though it is hardly a 'procedure' worthy of note in the same way in a leitmotivic opera.

For nearly two hundred years the composers whom Pfitzner saw as being in the 'great tradition' had used tonality as their method of creating large-scale form, and it is certainly the most important structural feature in *Palestrina*. Like all tonal composers, Pfitzner articulates his form, on every scale from the largest to the smallest, by means of key structure; tonality was what was in his mind during composition, and the opera cannot be fully understood otherwise. In answer to the often-voiced objection that such things cannot be heard without perfect pitch, it is the duty of the analyst to make up for the absence of perfect pitch or a score by helping the ear to follow what is happening – and one can hear relative tonal progressions without perfect pitch.

Pfitzner's tonal architecture is fairly easy to follow – not as easy, perhaps, as that of Bruckner, whose phrases often move from one four-bar period to the next by simple sequence, but easier than, say, Elgar, whose themes themselves are often modulatory and whose minor harmonies often obscure the major tonality. Busoni presents even more problems in this respect: long sections of *Doktor Faust* change tonality with almost bewildering frequency, to the extent that it becomes hard to distinguish local chromatic colour from change in fundamental tonality, a problem that does not arise even with Reger, whose habitual use of distant keys as mere colour is notorious in some quarters. Busoni's very fluid tonality is a symptom of his progressive tendencies, together with his Berg-like use of closed forms, and it is in these fundamentally opposed attitudes to tonality rather than in quibbling over the relationship to Schopenhauer that the major difference between *Doktor Faust* and *Palestrina* lies.

By the time of *Palestrina* Pfitzner was in sufficient command of his language to direct the tonal movement with complete control. It is not usually hard to decide what key the music is in, and Pfitzner is afraid neither of long diatonic passages such as the D minor of the Introduction to Act One

nor of passages in which the tonality remains obscure for
some time (whereas in the earlier operas I sometimes feel that
corresponding passages lack the inevitability of a composer
entirely certain of what he is doing). In the scene of the Dead
Masters the tonal progressions are deliberately undynamic
and diffuse; all sense of the drive of sonata style is absent, but
the keys change frequently enough to enhance the weird
impression. This is only one of several devices through which
Pfitzner evokes the unreality of the scene, and by temporarily
relinquishing sonata movement he also links the music more
strongly to that of those Masters themselves.

Pfitzner's modulations also display his technical mastery.
Often they are effected by the classical method of a short
period of tonal ambiguity, and the clarity of Pfitzner's thought
is shown by the way in which it is usually easy to hear the
relationship of the two keys after the modulation has taken
place. Where the ambiguity has no modulatory effect, so that
it is instead a simple interpolation of chromatic harmonies,
the chords themselves are often as distant as those of Richard
Strauss' famous harmonic sidesteps. But whereas with
Strauss the result is usually acerbic and witty, Pfitzner's
sidesteps sound melancholy and wistfully expressive.

The use of tonality as a structural principle in opera goes
back at least to Mozart. It is rare for any single opera movement in Mozart, apart from the extended finales, to move very
far afield from the key in which it starts, but that key will have
its own place in the progress of the act as a whole. And each of
his four great operas is centred around one key, beginning and
ending there: *Don Giovanni* in D, major and minor, *Die
Zauberflöte* in E flat, and so on.

Wagner, consciously seeking to build on Beethoven's
language, expands his ideas in a natural way. The essence of
Wagner's operatic language, set out in *Oper und Drama*[3] and
borne out by the works, is that the sentiment of each line and
each change in the dramatic situation is associated with an
appropriate modulation – or, if a line shows no contrast of

---

[3] English translation Evans, Reeves, London, 1913 (especially Part III,
Chapter III, in this context).

ideas, with no modulation at all.[4] As a principle for the setting of texts, this is perfectly adequate but hardly very original. When in *Messiah* Handel modulates from F sharp minor to D major at the words 'gross darkness [shall cover] the people; but the Lord shall arise upon thee', he is doing the same thing. Pfitzner's use of the principle has to be studied in the context of specific examples, so at this stage I shall confine myself to mentioning his fondness for modulating to a key a semitone away. This is a sort of extension of Neapolitan harmonies, and it is seen on a grand scale in, for instance, the spectacular shift in the *tutti* in the first movement of the Piano Concerto from E flat to E. (Interestingly, the same modulation also occurs in the penultimate verse of the song 'Der Gärtner', Op. 9, No. 1, and, in reverse, in the second subject of the finale of the Duo for violin and cello.) The ease with which the move takes place in, say, the 'Nachtgruss' chorale in *Von deutscher Seele* has the air of a magician doing the impossible. Even as early as *Der arme Heinrich*, Agnes' first entry, with her theme in A minor, is presaged by the same theme in G sharp minor, and it is not long before the tonality becomes B flat major; by the time of *Palestrina* the device is being used with more subtlety. Dominant-tonic relationships are not totally eschewed, but this semitone move is definitely a Pfitzner fingerprint.[5]

It is all very well wandering from key to key as the moment suggests, with no eye on the final objective, but without a clear idea of the path to be followed the composer soon becomes hopelessly lost. To switch metaphors, there must be firm structural support for spans as vast as the acts of German Romantic opera. Wagner developed one such method of tonal coherence.

Indications of an integrated tonal structure appear in *Tann-häuser*, in which the Pilgrims' music is generally in E major, though when it returns at the end of the opera it is in the chief

---

[4] *Cf.* also, for a clear summary, Bryan Magee, *Aspects of Wagner*, Ross, London, 1968, chapter 1.

[5] Harold Truscott pointed out (in *Music-Journal*, No. 2, London, 1948, p. 38) how Pfitzner continually makes subtle use of the *avoidance* of dominant preparation.

key of the final act, which is E flat. In the Second Act, the
choral rejoicings are consistently in B major, returning there
from whatever other keys have been reached in the meantime.
Some motifs or themes have a particular tonality, to which the
music returns regularly when those themes are quoted.
Clearly Wagner is not making much of this concept at this
stage in his career; otherwise, he would surely have moved to
a distant key for the Venusberg music instead of persisting
with the Pilgrims' key of E as in the Overture.

Lohengrin represents a significant step forward in the use of
this idea. It begins and ends with the music of the Grail in
A major, a tonality which recurs for all reappearances of the
Grail music and for Lohengrin himself. Other keys throughout the work are related to this. Act Two opens in gloom in
the relative minor, F sharp, the same key as Ortrud's oath
later in the act. Typical of Wagner's mature use of key is the
depressed tonality of A flat for Elsa's entrance in Act One,
contrasting with the heightening of B flat for her song of
thanksgiving in Act Two and the Bridal March.

It is possible that Wagner found the scheme of 'one idea,
one key' rather restrictive, and it can give the impression of
anchoring the tonality in too static a manner. Certainly *The
Ring* is freer in its key structure. Wagner did not feel obliged to
finish an opera in the same key as he began it: *Das Rheingold*,
and hence *The Ring* as a whole, begins in E flat with one of the
most famous examples of sustained tonality in all music, but
both *Das Rheingold* and *Götterdämmerung* end in D flat.
Tristan begins in a very chromatic A minor and ends in B
major, surely a conscious progression of tonality representing
a vastly expanded version of the concept of dramatic modulation. But *Die Meistersinger* and *Parsifal* begin and end in the
same key, C major in one instance and A flat in the other; in
both works the identity of thematic material at beginning and
end is reinforced by the identity of tonality.

Neither is the principle of coincidence of motif and key
consistently used in *The Ring*, although the inconsistencies are
full of interest. For example, the Valhalla motif is in D flat
throughout *Rheingold* and *Siegfried*, but in *Die Walküre*, referring to Wotan's machinations on behalf of the Wälsung twins,
it is in E major, the key with which that opera so unforgettably

ends. More predictably, most of the music associated with tragedy – the themes of Siegmund and Sieglinde, the Siegfried motif itself, and the funeral march – are in C minor, a key inevitably thought of as tragic since Beethoven's day. An interesting and often-mentioned touch is the depressing of the chords of E minor/C major of Brünnhilde's awakening to E flat minor/C flat major at the beginning of *Götterdämmerung*.

It is all too easy to impose external formal schemes on such works as these; in his analyses of the Wagner operas,[6] Alfred Lorentz took such schemes to an extreme, and I don't think he should be swallowed whole. On the other hand, such regular associations as these can hardly be coincidence, and it is a variant of this idea that Pfitzner adopts in *Palestrina*.[7]

Palestrina is constructed about a nucleus of four principal keys, which in themselves and in their relation to one another focus the elements of the drama. The work begins and ends in D minor and this key – appropriate in view of its modal tendencies – is associated with the world of Palestrina himself and the 'creativity' of his music. Exx. 1 (p. 129), 2 (p. 130), 4 (p. 130), 5 (p. 131) and 6 (p. 131) are all in D minor and Ex. 6 is the cadence that ends the work. Governing this D minor is its dominant, A major, associated with the angels who dictate the Mass to Palestrina, with his dead wife Lucrezia, and with love as a whole – the sources of his inspiration – as well as being an appropriately bright key in its own right. One of the most significant tonal features of the entire work occurs in Act Two during Morone's 'inspired' address to the Council, where the music modulates to A major at the words 'Engel des Friedens seid [Be angels of peace]'.

In contrast to these keys of 'creativity and inspiration', the second act centres on E flat major, the furthest possible remove from A, as appropriate for the 'reality of worldly

<hr />

[6] For example, *Das Geheimnis der Form bei Richard Wagner*, four vols., Max Hesses Verlag, Berlin, 1924–33.

[7] Strauss' use of tonality is looser yet. He is more likely to use the principle of progressive tonality – for example, in ending the Marschallin's monologue in Act One of *Der Rosenkavalier* in E flat, a semitone below the key which dominated the love music at the start – than of identity of motif and key.

activities'. The act begins and ends in this key. Half-way
between A and E flat is the neutral key of C, which is
associated with the Pope, the Holy Roman Emperor, the
Spaniards (C minor), the off-stage crowd in Act Three, and
with Palestrina's pupil Silla. These are participants in the
drama who do not belong to Palestrina's world, but neither
are they a serious enemy of it (at least by the time the Pope
appears in Act Three). The real enemy is the Council of
Trent, representing the World, as had always been Pfitzner's
intention.[8] It is perhaps ironical that his plan involves the
Pope and the Emperor sharing a key, for in the outside world
they are opposing powers. But it enables Pfitzner to emphasise that the Pope's visit has no lasting effect on Palestrina; he
and the others pass him by. Once again the chosen key works
very well for its themes – the almost childish qualities of Silla's
song and the simple breadth of the themes of both Pope and
Emperor.

This means that the keys of A, C and especially E flat are of
prime importance in Act Two, and here Pfitzner completes a
'diminished seventh' of keys by punctuating the debate in the
Council by a 'voting' theme, Ex. 80 (p. 196), in G flat. This is
a very satisfying conception, and, so far as I know, unprece-
dented, although it seems to be derived from the 'Wolf's
Glen' scene of *Der Freischütz*, and Sibelius uses C, E flat and
G flat as basic keys in his Fifth Symphony. Pfitzner uses one
other key as a principal structural feature: B flat minor dominates the last Act and shows the bewildered, convalescent
Palestrina in a state of total unself-consciousness.

It is possible to go further and examine the structure of an
opera according to purely musical criteria, as if it were a
symphonic poem or symphony. Wagner does not always pay
much attention to this aspect of his operas; as Robert Gutman
says, 'He never hesitated to sacrifice clarity of tonality to an
immediate dramatic need'.[9] Perhaps *Die Meistersinger* is
closest to Pfitzner's usage. First, large expanses of music are

[8] *Cf.* the lecture quoted above, p. 32: 'This could only be the Council, the
starting-point for decrees hostile to art'.

[9] *Richard Wagner: The Man, His Mind, and His Music*, Secker and Warburg,
London, 1968, p. 373.

related to a single key: the Masters, the Chorale and the Prize Song C major, Sachs's cobbling song B flat, 'Wach' auf' G major, while subtle use is made of the limited notes of Beckmesser's lute and the Nightwatchman's horn. But more than this, most of the individual scenes end in the key with which they began and with references – often subtle – to the same music; for instance, Act One, Scene One (Walther and Eva), in C, Scene Two (Walther and David) in D, and Scene Three (the Trial Song) in F. Further, use is made of the strophic form of the set numbers to punctuate scenes with similar passages all in one key.

From this point of view, all Pfitzner's operas are constructed with much care. *Der arme Heinrich* must, in its outer acts at least, be as strongly structured as any first opera. The thematic and tonal symmetries of Act One are complex and very pleasing; its extended and overlapping uses of ternary ABA form are well set out by Hans Rectanus.[10] The last Act blends structure effectively with drama by punctuating the development of the plot by successive phrases of a 'Christe Eleison' and a 'Dies Irae' sung by a choir of monks. The effect, though less original, is very impressive, and perhaps the nearest we come in Pfitzner to an explicit closed form.

Structural elements appear early in Act One of *Palestrina*: beginning in C major, there is a clear establishment of the dominant, marked by an orchestral interlude, before returning to C with the same music as before. Such a procedure, obviously borrowed from sonata form, is not used again, and one wonders whether its use could be construed as support for the old tradition. Instead, Pfitzner used the 'motif and key' principle to punctuate or enclose a scene or section with a theme recurring in the same key. There is the 'framing' effect of the double theme, Exx. 6 and 7, placed at extremities of Borromeo's monologue in Act One, Scene Three, and in a slightly different sense there is the ternary effect, in the Dead Masters scene, of enclosing Ex. 41 by sections based on Exx. 25 and 40 (pp. 146 and 157). But the best example is during the Debate in Act Two, where the G flat of Ex. 80 (p. 196) occurs four times, separating the debate's different

---

[10] *Leitmotivik und Form, op. cit.*, pp. 58 *et seq.*

topics by the taking of votes.[11] At the same time Severolus'
interruptions, in his Lydian/Dorian mode, have the same
effect in 'syncopation', as it were. This double structure
anchors the music very firmly, and I cannot avoid picturing
the result as a row of identical columns supporting a massive
building. In Act Three, with C major 'Evviva's reaching
Palestrina from outside, the effect is reversed – it is the spaces
between the columns which are the same each time. Pfitzner
uses this device, akin to rondo form, not only in *Heinrich*, his
first opera, but in *Das Herz*, his last (Act One, Scene One),[12]
while in *Die Rose* the Vorspiel and Act One are full of the ABA
plan.[13] But Pfitzner does not go as far in his use of 'closed'
forms as Berg (both *Wozzeck* and *Lulu*), Schreker or, more
relevantly, Busoni, who uses rondo form explicitly in *Doktor
Faust* (Letztes Bild).

The strong parallels between the structures of the first two
acts are particularly interesting. In both, the first scene begins
in C and there is then a clear establishment of another key
(G minor or E flat) before returning to C at the end of the
second scene (and with the same music as at first). Both acts
then move to B, minor or major, at the end of the third scene.
At the ends of both acts there is a huge orchestral climax,
dying away only to be repeated to bring the curtain down, and
only reaching the final tonality in the very last bars. The
shorter third act does not attempt to continue the pattern; it
would be out-of-place and probably too predictable. The
essence of the work is, after all, the contrast between the 'two
worlds', and the different results of the two worlds on the
same tonal basis are clearly indicated by this parallel as it
stands, the one returning to C major, the other with E flat
annihilating its rivals. The second act can be thought of as a
distorted reflection of the first, or as a development of it, in
which case the recapitulatory elements of Act Three complete
the analogy to a sonata form.

I can think of only one other opera that makes its second
part a conscious paraphrase of its first, and one that Pfitzner is

[11] *Ibid.*, pp. 58 *et seq.*

[12] *Ibid.*, p. 170.

[13] *Ibid.*, pp. 83 *et seq.*

unlikely to have known. The idea of drawing parallels between Pfitzner and Berlioz is almost grotesque. But Acts One and Three of *Les Troyens*, the opening acts of their respective 'parts', show many parallels, not only in the large-scale organisation of the individual numbers (lively opening chorus, mezzo-soprano solo, ballet, short entrance *scena* for the tenor, ensemble), but even in the detailed shape of the musical ideas.

In view of the underlying tonal scheme of *Palestrina*, it is intriguing to find that not only does the main 'Council' theme, Ex. 7 (p. 132), share the centrally important 'letzte Stein' cadence with Ex. 6 (p. 131); its principal tonality is not the 'Council' key of E flat, which symbolises discord, but the same D minor as Ex. 6. When, further, the rhythmic similarity between the other Council theme, Ex. 59, and Ex. 5 (pp. 176 and 131), which is so strongly related to Ex. 6, is taken into account (the similarity with Ex. 59 is particularly apparent in the lowest part of Ex. 5), there can be no question of coincidence or accident. Pfitzner would seem to be suggesting that despite the unflattering picture he is to present of the Council's deliberations, he has to acknowledge that fundamentally and in many important respects it was a sincere, impressive and indeed creative human achievement. After all, Morone is presented as a genuinely inspired man.

Examination of tonality leads naturally to harmony. Pfitzner's harmonic vocabulary is comparatively subdued; his most aggressive effects are usually obtained not by extravagant chromatic dissonances but by unusual juxtapositions of simple chords. In *Parsifal* Kundry enters to a jamming-together of most of the notes of the scale to form a full dominant thirteenth; in *Palestrina* Madruscht enters at the end of Act Two, with murderous intent, to a C major triad, first inversion, emerging via a diminished seventh from E flat minor. Admittedly seven bars later there is a crunch on D, E and F natural; but that is a rare exception, and it has a motivic basis. Of such harmonic excesses as those of Richard Strauss in his earlier works there is, unsurprisingly, no trace.

Inversions of secondary sevenths are among Pfitzner's favourite harmonies, whether as unprepared dissonances or as pure (and uncloying) consonances (the latter a frequent

colour in the late works). He is also partial to a sort of multiple
suspension, or single suspension within a seventh, of which
the chord which opens and colours much of *Der arme Heinrich*
is typical. The opening is actually quoted in *Palestrina*
(*cf.* Ex. 27, p. 147), and similar harmonies, usually freer of
tonal associations, are often heard in the Dead Masters
scene.

Bernhard Adamy[14] points out that the libretto is Pfitzner's
one big achievement in non-polemical writing (six sonnets[15]
and a few other fragments being unimportant). It is obviously
significant that Pfitzner's most successful opera is the only
one written to his own libretto. The form of the libretto
provokes some interesting speculations. The metre is generally iambic pentameter, though the lengths of the lines
change frequently; two striking instances are the final quatrain of the whole opera which consists of three tetrameters
and a dimeter, and the splendid moment when the Pope
enters in Act Three and sings six lines of unrhymed dactyllic
hexameters. It is conceivable that the sudden association with
the number three at this point is symbolic of the Holy Trinity
in the same way that it is in the Sanctus of Bach's B minor
Mass. Pfitzner's preference for verse rather than prose
became explicit when he rewrote some of Hans Mahner-
Mons' libretto for *Das Herz* in blank verse;[16] clearly he
preferred a more marked rhythm to complement the music.
The question of rhyme is much more involved. No one
rhyme-scheme prevails, though there are many instances of
couplets and quatrains, both ABAB and ABBA. Adamy attempts
to find large scale poetic structures in the libretto,[17] but I am
rather sceptical and prefer to see in the incidence of rhyme a
mirror of the dramatic situation.

It is noticeable that strong rhyme-schemes appear when
there is some sense of a set-piece in operation – not only the

---

[14] 'Das *Palestrina*-Textbuch als Dichtung', *Symposium Hans Pfitzner*,
Schneider, Tutzing, 1984, p. 23.

[15] Reprinted in the Appendix to *Gesammelte Schriften, op. cit.*, Vol. II.

[16] *Cf.* Abendroth, *op. cit.*, pp. 332 *et seq.*, and Adamy, *op. cit.*, p. 43.

[17] *Ibid.*

obvious instances of Silla's song, the Spaniards' mockery or the Emperor's lines about the Old Masters, but also, for example, in the preliminary exchanges at the beginnings of all three acts: between Silla and Ighino, between Severolus and Novagerio, between the singers of the papal chapel.[18] Each of these instances consists of irregular variations on quatrains and couplets, with an occasional quintet. Borromeo's monologue follows a non-repeating scheme in which rhyming couplets keep giving way to quatrains and quintets before settling down into six ABAB quatrains. But it seems to me particularly interesting and significant that in several places an important passage begins in blank verse and gradually develops rhyme as it proceeds, as if order is being imposed on chaos. Palestrina's Act One monologue does this, continuing with more and more rhyme through the dictation scene to his final solo which ends with two couplets. In the long scene in Act Two between Borromeo and Novagerio, rhyme is established as the mode of address only when the two prelates have sat down over 'fruit and red wine',[19] after which a very irregular rhyme scheme runs for about a hundred lines. Morone's address begins, after its introductory prayer, without rhymes and turns slowly into quintets, and his final speech, restoring peace after the quarrel, runs into the concluding AABCBCDD with a transition using the dissonance of 'künden' and 'finden'. Ighino's lines in the final act run in the reverse direction, from entirely regular quatrains to blank verse as he is seen to be more and more out of touch with his father.

In performance, the effect of rhyme depends on the regularity of the vocal phrase-lengths. At times the symmetry is

---

[18] Reading the libretto at these points, I am reminded of the sort of detached give-and-take in Shakespeare where one or other of the characters is not emotionally involved in the conversation – *cf.*, for instance, the Romeo-Mercutio conversation in *Romeo and Juliet*, Act One, Scene Four. Although the libretto does not resort to alternate single lines from different characters until the last act, Pfitzner's writing seems to me to derive from the stichomythia used on occasion by Shakespeare (e.g., *A Midsummer Night's Dream*, Act One, Scene One, lines 136–40) and ultimately from the ancient Greek tragedians.

[19] *Cf.* p. 182, below.

obvious (such as at 'aus grosser Meister Zeit'), and at others it
is certainly present, Ighino's

> Die Mühen werden meine Freuden,
> Wenn das Gefühl mich ganz entzückt,
> Dass junges Leben alter Zeiten
> Und wie durch Zauber nahe rückt[20]

in Act One, and his

> Nun bist du mir wieder gegeben,
> Und die Messe durchklinget die Welt.
> Erwache nun auch zum Leben
> Für dein Kind, das umschlungen dich hält![21]

in Act Three being two examples. Both come before interruptions and indeed many of the solos end with strong
rhymed couplets or quatrains; an idea also perhaps borrowed
from Shakespeare's use of a rhyming couplet at the end of
each scene, though I feel that it may also reflect the pronounced end-of-paragraph effect of the cadences at the ends
of solos in Wagner's music-dramas. Elsewhere, the very fluid
lengths of the phrases through which the music grows organ-
ically in the orchestra tend to smother the effect of rhyme, and
in any case the result is far more fluent than it was in the first
two operas, *Der arme Heinrich* and *Die Rose*, with those turgid
rhymed couplets of Grun's. Wagner had to make the same
progress to maturity; the symmetrical phrases of *Lohengrin* are
often incredibly square, and one can practically hear Wagner
learning how to avoid this weakness as he progressed through
the first two parts of *The Ring*. Pfitzner's vocal line usually

---

[20] 'When that ecstasy informs me,
   My efforts are repaid with joy,
   The youthful life of times long past
   Seems magically to be born again.'

I have used Veronica Slater's translation of the libretto (*cf.* note 22 on p. 32,
above) throughout, except for a small number of my own minor alterations;
these are indicated by the initials (OT).

[21] 'And now you've been returned to me,
   And the Mass rings out through the world,
   Awake now once again to life,
   For your child, whose arms embrace you.'

follows the rhythms of speech rather than verse in this respect, and it moves at a pace substantially closer to that of real speech than was the case in his first two operas. The vocal line itself is often musically subsidiary, but it is always a genuine part of the texture (and it is often not supported by the orchestra); its interplay with the instrumental lines creates a complex rhythmic counterpoint, and the results in terms of phrase structure are often exceptionally subtle. One fascinating example is the passage leading into the G minor orchestral interlude in Act One, Scene Two (*cf.* p. 140). If there are times when it is not always clear why the verse does or does not rhyme at any particular point, the reason may not be any lack of poetic technique on Pfitzner's part so much as an echo of the musical structure already taking shape in his imagination as he wrote the libretto.

The orchestration of *Palestrina* is a special source of pleasure. The forces required are huge:
   four flutes, two doubling piccolo,
   alto flute,
   three oboes, one doubling cor anglais,
   three clarinets, two doubling E flat clarinet,
   bass clarinet,
   three bassoons,
   double bassoon,
   six horns,
   four trumpets (in F),
   four trombones,
   bass tuba,
   timpani,
   percussion (bass drum, cymbals, tam-tam, triangle, hand-
      bells (Schellen), suspended cymbal),
   two harps,
   celeste,
   organ,
   viola d'amore, and
   strings,
   plus, in the last act, an off-stage band consisting of two
      piccolos, two clarinets in C, two mandolins, guitars,
      bells, tam-tams (numbers unspecified).

But, far more than in any work by Mahler or Strauss, the
object of prescribing this vast array is not to make a loud
noise, but to make available a sequence of very subtle tone-
colours. The multiplicity of flutes, for example, is used in the
very opening bars, four independent lines doubling four solo
violins; later, in the scene with the Dead Masters, there are
the extraordinary sounds of four low flutes and alto flute
playing *piano* chords above nothing but double basses divided
into four parts (full score, figure 127 on page 178, and
elsewhere). The E flat clarinets are not used for Berliozian
witches' broomsticks, but for the extraordinary other-worldly
music which accompanies the Patriarch Abdisu (Ex. 76,
p. 191). The viola d'amore plays a total of eight bars in the
whole work, three in Act One and five in Act Two; in both
places it is hard to hear. Its presence is no doubt more for
psychological than aural effect; its two appearances coincide
with Borromeo and then the Pope mentioning 'the angels'.
Something approaching the full orchestral force is called for
in only five places: the two bell-climaxes at the end of Act
One, Scenes Six and Seven; two chords in the prelude to Act
Two; and the two passages of uproar, among the Council and
among the servants, at the end of Act Two. For the most part
the score is quiet, and warm and rich in colouring. The very
frequent and varied use Pfitzner makes of solo strings is of
particular interest. The principal violin and, even more so, the
principal viola have a marvellous evening, while such effects
as harmonics on three solo cellos and two solo violins or, as
previously mentioned, multiple divisions of the lower strings,
abound in the later scenes of Act One. The whole score is the
achievement of a man who both knew and loved the orchestra; time after time the sonorities drawn from the orchestra pit
delight the ear.

Act One

The Introduction to the first Act establishes at once two
important concepts. It is divided into separate sections which
mirror the Schopenhauerian duality of the work, concerned
on the one hand with Palestrina and on the other with the

Council of Trent. The two are combined to form a third section leading to the First Act proper, thus echoing the overall triptych shape of the three-act work. In addition, the opening itself establishes the predominantly mystical atmosphere of the First Act and also the contrapuntal nature of both score and subject.

The first sounds heard are the rising open intervals of Ex. 1 in a Dorian D minor, scored for four flutes and four solo violins – a sound which simply glows with an inner light; this music is like no other.

Ex. 1

The strange, rapt intensity of this theme, which represents Palestrina himself as creative artist and, by extension, the whole concept of 'inspiration', is an idea of fundamental importance, informing the whole score. The purity of the counterpoint and the open intervals evoke the world of Palestrina, and the music has a similar objectivity, but the voice is equally unmistakably Pfitzner's own – a blend at once sublime and mysterious. The continuation, figure *b*, will become a separate motif in its own right, representing the musical masterpieces of earlier times. It reaches a chord of G major, but the anticipated plagal cadence is not completed.

Pfitzner continues with a cloudier counter-statement of Ex. 1 in G minor in which *a* is given to four clarinets and four solo violas, *b* to the original four flutes and solo violins. Much of the reflective music in both the outer Acts will be associated with viola tone. This first shift of tonality, to the subdominant, is significant both of the non-assertive nature of the composer's world and for the importance which the key of G minor will assume. Soon the polyphony gives way to Ex. 2 in the violins; its characteristic rhythm is that of the name

'Pierluigi' and it represents Palestrina as a human being. No detail of this expository section is wasted: the oscillating fourths under the ensuing *fermata* (Ex. 3) outline the Phrygian harmony of another of Palestrina's motifs, Ex. 4. Here is the composer as representative of the past tradition.

Ex. 2

Ex. 3

Ex. 4

From the hints of B flat in Ex. 2 we have reached a half-close on the dominant of D minor (although the chord is a bare fifth, the C sharp being omitted); after it, that key is resumed, four flutes maintaining the quiet intensity with Ex. 5, still another of Palestrina's motifs. This one is associated with the fulfilment of his creative mission and, with it, the completion of a chapter of musical history. After a half-close, Ex. 5 is restated with a high oboe countersubject, closing into A minor with magically evocative harmonies. Ex. 2 is repeated,

Ex. 5

restoring D minor, and the subdominant is reached for the beginning of Ex. 6, a beautiful variant of Ex. 5. This is linked to Palestrina's own voiced awareness of his role in his words which conclude the opera:

> [...] den letzten Stein
> An einem deiner tausend Ringe, Du Gott![22]

Ex. 6

This theme, with its cadence via the dominant of A minor back into D minor, will be the music on which the final curtain of Act Three falls, and wherever it appears it has a strong feeling of finality. I shall refer to the end of Ex. 6 as the 'letzte Stein' cadence, though in giving it a name I am risking hubris. Thomas Mann said that it 'cannot easily be given a name'[23] and explained that not only did it refer to the 'last stone' but that it recurs at Ighino's 'Da wird es still in ihm und leer'.[24] Mann writes,

[22] '[...] the final precious stone
On one of Your unnumbered rings,
Thou God!'

[23] *Reflections*, p. 310.

[24] 'He became silent and empty within'.

It is also at the same time the symbol of Palestrina's psychological condition after the death of his wife, the symbol [. . .] of
his special type of productivity, a productivity of pessimism, of
resignation and of longing.[25]

Here it concludes the opening section of the Introduction,
balancing the earlier half-close of Ex. 3; so far the music has
evolved in slow and long-drawn sentences, forming a single,
unified paragraph, its intensity harmonic and contrapuntal
rather than symphonic. After a drum-roll the violins play
Ex. 7, a very long and majestic theme representing the Council of Trent and in this case in particular its ceremonial
aspect.

Ex. 7

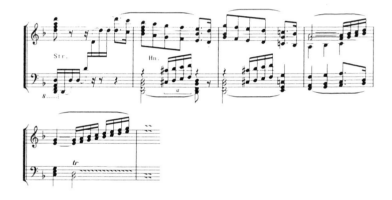

Its initially bare harmonies are strangely augmented by a horn
playing parallel consecutive fifths with the melody, a detail
unique to this first appearance of the theme. It blends into a
restatement on trombones of Ex. 6, with which it shares its
key; the significance of this fact has already been discussed in
terms of the drama,[26] but musically its effect is very clear here
in the Introduction. In spite of a few momentary changes the
tonality has stayed in D minor practically throughout, laying
a solid tonal foundation for the opera even though the Act

[25] *Reflections*, p. 311.

[26] *Cf.* p. 123, above.

which follows begins and ends in C. D minor is the fundamental key of the whole opera and its persistence here is also consonant with the slow-moving and restrained character of the music heard so far. (On the other hand, the rate at which ideas have been presented in the Introduction is remarkable: six in the first 47 bars alone, without any sense of haste. The fact that the second section of the Introduction consists of a single very long idea makes a helpful contrast.) The Introduction is rounded off with a combination of Ex. 7 in cellos and basses with Ex. 1 in violins and woodwind. But the expected D minor cadence is replaced by a chord of G, soon darkening to the minor, as staccato chords on cello and harp presage the C major accompaniment to the song we are about to hear; and after a further G minor reference to Ex. 1, with the staccato chords on fewer and fewer numbers of cellos and violas, the curtain goes up.

Scene One

A room in Palestrina's house, not very spacious, and fairly gloomy, with heavy, dark furniture. Everything is simple to the point of poverty. In the middle of the room there is a large work-table, strewn with unused manuscript paper. On the back wall hangs a large portrait of a beautiful middle-aged woman – Lucrezia, Palestrina's dead wife. To the right of the door a large window – the only one – shows a distant view of Rome. There is a chair by the window. It is late afternoon. During the course of the opening scenes, especially the third and fourth, darkness falls.

When the curtain rises, the seventeen-year-old Silla is discovered sitting in his master's armchair, almost swamped by its size. Lounging back, one leg thrown over the other, he is trying over a new song he has written, accompanying himself on a viol. He breaks off frequently as his thoughts wander.[27]

The opera's division into scenes is the old-fashioned one which defines a change of characters on the stage and not a change of location. Indeed, the location, Palestrina's room, remains unchanged throughout the first and last acts (and that of the Council throughout the second).

---

[27] Pfitzner's stage directions at the head of each scene are reproduced from the full score (translated by Veronica Slater, except, as with the translation of the libretto, (OT) indicates that I have made alterations to her version.)

The opening scene is deliberately low-key emotionally; Pfitzner is presenting the second of his two main conflicts, that between the conservative and the avant-garde in music, through the personality of Silla. He is an enthusiastic and well-meaning youth, but he has not yet discovered that there are other ways of looking at the world than his own. His self-centredness is reflected in his clarinet motif, Ex. 8. Its key is generally C major, as it is here, but it often moves further afield.

Ex. 8

At present he is full of enthusiasm for the new ideas and music of the Florentine Camerata, although he is a composition pupil of Palestrina, the greatest living master of the 'old style'. From Silla's usurpation of his chair, it would appear that he dreams of taking over his master's position, in fame if not in style. His song, and the 'viol' accompaniment, Ex. 9, which is actually played by two violas in the orchestra pit, sounds, and is meant to sound, strange, though the harmonies remain beautifully plangent.[28]

[28] The chords, Ex. 9, and the Silla motif, Ex. 8, are found in the manuscript of a setting for voice and piano of a poem by Goethe, beginning:

> O gib, vom weichen Pfühle,
> Träumend, ein halb Gehör!
> Bei meinem Saitenspiele
> Schlafe! was willst du mehr?

Only a few bars of the song appear to have been written, but in them the origin of the Silla motif is clear. The manuscript of the song is dated 5 May 1909. It would seem that Pfitzner, seeking the appropriate 'new and strange' style for Silla's song with string accompaniment, associated the words 'Bei meinem Saitenspiele' with this scene, and the result has the further benefit of being describable as a 'monody', being a single vocal line with chordal, non-horizontal accompaniment. (For full details of the Pfitzner manuscripts and the Italian background to the Goethe poem, *cf.* Wolfgang Osthoff, 'Pfitzner-Goethe-Italien: die Würzeln des Silla-Liedchens im *Palestrina*', *Analecta Musicologica*, No. 17, Cologne, 1976.)

Ex. 9

The song's strangeness rests in its tonality, nominally C major but with a pull towards A minor and F major, as in the Lydian mode; in its phrasing and unexpected cadences; and in its irregular metre and the odd juxtaposition of its vocabulary ('Schönste, ungnäd'ge' and 'Dame, Nymphe', for example), the sort of mannered techniques that are common to the avant-garde of any period. It effectively forms a contrast to Palestrina's own 'perfect', perhaps reactionary, art.

Silla's interpolated comments, in distant keys, show that he is less interested in his own song than in his urge to go to Florence, where all that he considers exciting is taking place. His interruptions take the form of an ABCB quatrain, perhaps showing that, for all his wish to be progressive, his mind actually works rather conventionally. At the words

Welch herrlich freier Zug
Geht doch durch unsre Zeit![29]

there is a Straussian upsurge of orchestral excitement based on Ex. 8, leading, from a plunge into E major, via F, B flat and the dominant of G, to Ex. 10 in B major on clarinet and strings. It is clear how varied – and even how irrational – is Silla's anticipation. Ex. 10 represents Florence – or at least all the exuberance and gaiety of Florence as Silla imagines it. Those themes in the opera which represent places – Florence, Rome, Trent, Bologna – are not so much pictorial as expressive of the character of each particular city in the context of the story and its symbolism. Silla speaks of 'the singing voice, long shackled by polyphony', and in a typical illustrative

---

[29] 'A glorious breath of freedom
Is pulsing through our times!'

Ex. 10

touch the woodwind play four bars of rather plain C major, Ex. 11, a shock after the very lively writing which has just reached F sharp major with signs of going on to C sharp. The principal line of Ex. 11 is derived from Palestrina's *Missa Aspice Domine*, which was published together with the *Missa Papae Marcelli* in the Second Book of Palestrina's Masses (1567). The counterpoint is not Palestrina's.[30]

Ex. 11

This theme *may* suggest that polyphony is academic and stultifying to inspiration or it *may* be an ironical comment on the music of Silla's song.[31] But Florence, Silla's motif and the conflicting keys of F and B minor regain the centre of attention, in writing which is just as polyphonic – Ex. 10 in canon at the third and with three auxiliary parts – and much less stiff.

Silla goes to the window and looks out at the view over Rome. To him it is merely an 'old hole', the home of an outdated art which might at best 'sprout a few new buds'. But the motif representing the city, Ex. 12, is noble and majestically restrained; it incorporates the 'Pierluigi' rhythm of Ex. 2,

---

[30] *Cf.* Wolfgang Osthoff, 'Eine neue Quelle zu Palestrinazitat und Palestrinasatz in Pfitzners musikalischer Legende', *Renaissance-Studien: Helmut Osthoff zum 80. Geburtstag*, Schneider, Tutzing, 1979, p. 199, and John Williamson, *op. cit.*, pp. 176–79. The *Missa Aspice Domine* does not seem to exist in a modern edition, so bar numbers are unavailable, the 1567 edition consisting, naturally, of separate, unbarred parts.

[31] I am indebted to Harold Truscott for this observation.

showing that Rome is a symbol of the same eternal qualities as
Palestrina himself – an appropriate symbolism for the 'Eternal
City' to assume. The dominant of D minor had been reached,
but the new motif strides in grandly in G flat.

Ex. 12

Modulating to B flat, minor and then major, it gives way
smoothly, after a rising pendant played by strings and harp
(Ex. 13) to a vivid picture of the city's bells giving tongue
(Ex. 14), reaching C major again, the key which began the
scene.

Ex. 13

Ex. 14

But Silla is drawn only to what he thinks of as 'fine and new';
there is an *accelerando* as the dominant of A minor, with Ex.
14, resolves to A major, the quaver rhythms of the bells
speeding up and breaking into semiquavers related to Ex. 10.
The music moves via B flat to the dominant of G minor.

Scene Two

Ighino enters, to the sounds of his motif, Ex. 15, in G minor on a solo viola. (The theme is equally capable of being harmonised in the relative major, and both versions will often be heard.)

Ex.15

It is clear at one that he is less brash and self-assertive, more prone to melancholy, than his older friend. He can be thought of as a 'pale relection' of other characters; here he is the opposite of Silla, who unlike him is a creative artist, however misguided his aims. In Act Three he stands in the same contrasting relation to Palestrina, and it is his lack of creativity which is the flaw in him, ultimately leading him to the side of the world rather than the creative individual. This is what Palestrina means when, in his monologue in Scene Four, he calls Ighino 'wholly without meaning' – 'ganzlich sinnlos'. Silla wants to tell Ighino that he is off to Florence, but he never gets round to doing so – their Master and his sadness is the subject of discussion.

Ighino's initial exchanges with Silla are dominated by a lively counterpoint in the pattern of Ex. 16 (the liveliness of the two youngsters), still on solo viola.

Ex.16

Soon the violins play Ex. 15 in diminution, and the lively Florentine music continues. Here is the first of many examples of Pfitzner's ability to make clear reference to a theme even when its outline is much changed. There is a gradual slip to B minor (= C flat) while Ighino is saying that he doesn't know the answer to Silla's question of whether it is better to stand alone or be a small cog in a big wheel. To Ex. 15 at its original slow pace he says, with touching naivety, that all he does know is that

> Loving communion of good people
> Is the most beautiful thing of all.

These words –

> Die liebliche Gemeinsamkeit
> Von guten Menschen unter sich
> Ist doch das Schönste allezeit

– like the rest of the conversation are written in the simplest of metres and ABAB rhyme, as if the boys are merely making up their answers as part of a game. The lively nature of the orchestral writing throughout this paragraph reinforces this impression, little rhythmic figures in the woodwind contributing an element of play.

Silla laughs at Ighino's simplicity, as the tonality slips further to B flat, and says that for him the only worthwhile role is leader ('Mittelpunkt im Kreise' – the centre of the circle; the symbolism both anticipates and contradicts the 'letzte Stein' image. Silla and Palestrina are both musicians, but they have opposite views). Silla suggests that singing in the choir is a wearisome way of labouring under the rule of others: 'Sweating over the awkward things high learning has devised, aren't we like donkeys harnessed to a yoke?' The 'awkward things of high learning' are illustrated by an ingenious variant of the dry C major of Ex. 11; the imitation is inverted to produce a mirror canon.

Ex. 17

Harps and pizzicato strings express – ironically? – the 'singing of the choir'. The 'donkey's yoke' is more naively illustrated by the jangling of small bells with cellos, basses and double bassoon.

Ighino takes the opposite view, and in his extended reply the music works round through gradually less complicated polyphonic textures from a local E to B minor (where his own Ex. 15 is heard), B flat, and finally G minor. (The phrase-structures in both voice and orchestra, in the approach to this key are interlinked with exceptional subtlety.) Here, in the original key of his motif, we hear Ex. 1, and although a florid solo clarinet part with harp prevents it from sounding as timeless as at the beginning of the Introduction, the key and the voice's temporary silence make this obviously an important emotional and musical staging-post in the structure of the Act. The G minor is 'interrupted' by a chord of C exactly as the D minor of the Introduction was by a chord of G. Ighino has just sung of being 'magically born again': inspiration is a rebirth, and hence this 'recapitulation' in a new key. These, he says, are his father's beliefs too, to work with others as part of a larger whole. The keys change rapidly and the music reaches a big climax on D major.

From this dominant of G minor the horns extract the F sharp as a pivot note to begin a long paragraph that acts dramatically as a development section. Ighino comes round to the reason for his own sorrow – that of his father, and its causes. In B minor a flute introduces a new theme, Ex. 18; sparsely accompanied by a few short chords including a rising-octave figure, it is extended freely for 25 bars as a more-or-less continuously evolving melody with some sequential repetition.

Ex. 18

Suddenly Ighino names 'my father's grief', and there is an outburst of feeling based on the second phrase of Ex. 18, in G minor over a pedal E flat. The outburst ends as suddenly as it began; in D major Silla suggests that Ighino is only imagining things. Ex. 18 returns more perkily on the clarinet but takes a different turning after three bars, under the influence of Silla's semiquavers. The 'tag' (*x*) of Ex. 18 undergoes various shifts in accent as the woodwind discuss it; the cellos take it up and the movement slows as the theme is fragmented.

Silla is puzzled. Why should Palestrina be sad – he is famous, isn't he? A strong cadence apparently establishes A, but two more chords move on from G to D, the same key with which the paragraph was initiated. This chord-progression (Ex. 19) is later heard in other keys, and can be thought of as the 'fame' motif.

Ex. 19

Ighino's answer begins with a distant but clear variant of Ex. 18*y*, a typical Pfitzner transformation. Linear extensions of the 'tag' move slowly onto a pedal F, which rises to F sharp as part of the dominant of E, and here Ex. 19 returns; despite its harmonic sidestep (like Strauss's recurring cadence in *Don Quixote*) it completes the cadence in E,[32] whereas before it took the music on to a new key. This contrasting use of the same sequence to describe the different attributes of Silla and Ighino is very subtle.

E major is maintained only for a moment, as the tonality sinks to D flat for the appearance of the beautiful new Ex. 20 in the violins.

Ex. 20

---

[32] The woodwind are notated as F flat.

Ighino is well launched on his answer to Silla, an answer which is more in the nature of a meditation than an explanation to his friend. He muses on

That true fame that quietly with time
Wrapped itself round him like a robe of state

and Ex. 20 can be thought of as the 'Feierkleid' ('robe of state') motif. It is at once repeated in B flat. A strong dissonance emphasises the envy of Palestrina's colleagues, by which time the first violins are beginning to weave a long thread of melody in which occasional references to the 'tag' confirm its derivation from Ex. 18. Its sequences move unhurriedly, shadowed by the vocal line, through various keys in the area of A flat minor, and die away on a high G flat. Lower strings restore A flat minor with Ex. 20, while at the same time we hear the cadence of Ex. 4; Palestrina cares nothing for false fame. Faint references to the 'tag' are made before suddenly Ighino moves to G minor and the cadence back to D minor of Ex. 6, where we hear Ex. 1. Ighino is talking of Palestrina's past achievement. The 'heaviest blow' which ended, apparently for ever, the composer's creativity, the death of his wife, is marked by a *fortissimo* chord of G minor, the subdominant of D minor. It leads to a chromatic move to the very distant key of D flat minor where the Lucrezia motif, Ex. 21, steals in for the first time.

Ex. 21

The theme is in the first violins, but the voice part complements and stretches the line in a fascinating way typical of the whole work. Now the 'tag' leads to Ex. 6 in G minor, its rhythm stutteringly augmented. All the spirit seems to have gone from the music; there is scarcely any movement other than the voice. Violins pass from a derivative, Ex. 22, of Ex. 21 to a lonely variant of Ex. 20 and an augmentation of Silla's Ex. 16.

Ex. 22

'I have a happy nature, I am fond of life, but now I too find everything so sad.' With these words Ighino reaches the dominant of G minor, and here simultaneously we hear Ex. 1 (in D) on oboes and bassoons, Ex. 20 on cellos, and Ex. 19 on three solo violins; such is the mixture of his feelings. By now we are close to the end of the paragraph, and Pfitzner indicates this by returning to Ex. 18 with its original fragments of chordal accompaniment, suggesting a distant relationship to a ternary form behind the paragraph as a whole. Apparently we are about to move to A minor, but Ighino brings up the dark phrase: 'The sorrows of the World', and at once we are in E flat minor. 'One lives and weeps because one has been born'; nothing could be closer to Schopenhauer than this. A deeply expressive orchestration of Ex. 15 in B flat minor (muted violas) brings Ighino's monologue to an end in spiritual emptiness as the music, whose movement (rather than pulse) has almost imperceptibly become slower and slower, now comes to rest in F minor. (Incidentally, it is worth pointing out how much more satisfying is this 'narration' of essential background information by Ighino than those in, say, *Il Trovatore* or even *Parsifal*. Here it is an integral part of the musical and dramatic structure.)

Silla has been touched by this. But he doesn't really understand, and his idea of cheering Ighino up is to sing him his song, in preparation for which he moves into G major. Ighino is far too upset to be interested (interruption of B minor), but the self-centred Silla is not going to miss his opportunity of showing off his composition. So now we hear the whole thing, in the original Lydian C major (and it sounds no less strange). The first section of the First Act thus comes to an end with a (nearly) complete recapitulation of the fragments which opened it.

The first two scenes of the opera are musically inseparable, forming a single unit within the design of the First Act. The unit begins and ends in the Lydian C major of Silla's song, and while Silla is alone on stage we are never very far from C. The first important move comes after his view of Rome, where the turn to A, accompanied by an *accelerando*, prepares the establishment of G minor for Ighino's entry at the beginning of Scene Two. This is the dominant minor of the framing C as well as the sub-dominant of the Introduction's D minor – at once a classical tonal progression and the unassertive relationship characteristic of the outer acts of the whole opera.

Local key changes do not prevent G minor from returning at the pivotal interlude where Ex. 1 returns. The ideas and keys have been stated and brought to a momentary full stop; now we can move further afield. In the ensuing discussion between the boys there is less feeling of a stable tonal centre until Ighino moves to G minor once more at his identification of the true cause of his father's sorrow. The final C major is not very strongly prepared, for this is by no means the end of the Act; but the complete rendition of Silla's song rounds off the unit neatly and satisfactorily.

Scene Three

> *Cardinal Borromeo has entered the room, followed by Palestrina; they have remained standing just inside the doorway. Borromeo is between forty and fifty, a tall, intelligent-looking man with intense eyes; Palestrina is past fifty, his hair greying, especially at the temples. Silla breaks off suddenly as Ighino, who has noticed the newcomers first, nudges him. Both sink to their knees. Silla, with a mixture of fear, embarrassment and suppressed laughter, lowers his eyes before the Cardinal's frowning disapproval. Ighino gazes anxiously at both men.*

Borromeo's theme, Ex. 23, announces his presence, its B flat and E flat contradicting the key, as surely as the new orchestration contradicts the sound, of Silla's song, and as Silla breaks off Borromeo voices our thoughts:

A strange cacophony to hear
Where a strict master dwells!

Ex. 23

Ex. 23 expresses his ill-humoured side and contains a prominent tritone, though its rhythm is more important than its intervals, which change without altering its identity in typical Pfitzner fashion. The tonal scheme is interrupted by Borromeo's entrance, and for a while no one key is allowed to establish itself. If Ex. 23 has any particular tonal implications, they are of the dominant of D minor, although Palestrina's words to the boys, less aggressive than Borromeo's, move back by way of recollections of Ex. 4 towards the Lydian C major. Another new idea, Ex. 24, appears here, accompanying Palestrina's instructions to the boys to 'go upstairs, and be ready to practice the Psalm at dawn'. It will recur as a reminiscence at the end of the Act. Both boys leave, to an augmentation of Ighino's theme and an inversion of Silla's.

Ex. 24

Palestrina apologises for his pupils. We are soon in the vicinity of A major, but this darkens momentarily to A flat minor; to Borromeo, Silla's music sounds 'sinful' (Ex. 8 distorted in diminution). Palestrina is more broad-minded. His own music may certainly seem to him in tune with the great tradition:

The art that masters through the ages
Have built into a mysterious alliance,
Into an ever-growing edifice [...].

The first line is set to a rising idea, Ex. 25, on the cor anglais
and solo double-bass in octaves; it is the principal theme of
the masters of the past and recurs several times in the first two
acts.

Ex. 25

Here the pedal A associates it with D minor and hence with
Ex. 1, as does the fact that it contains the interval of a fifth as
well as its inversion of a fourth, though in fact its tonality is
often ambiguous; it could almost as well be F major. The
strange orchestration looks forward to the Dead Masters
scene, in which this theme takes a prominent place. The
second line introduces another theme, Ex. 26.

Ex. 26

From hints of F major the music is directed by way of A flat
(= dominant of C sharp) to F sharp major, as Palestrina goes
on to tell us, to semiquaver music developing Exx. 8, 9 and 10
and again sounding rather Straussian, that the Florentines
have gone back to the theories of the Greeks. For all he knows
they, and Silla, may be right. The orchestra develops the
opening of Ex. 10 in close imitation. It is characteristic of the
unself-conscious artist that he has a detached tolerance of
new theories about his art.

There is a diminuendo and the music slows markedly as
Palestrina sings a *legato* version of Silla's song, Ex. 9 ('ob jetzt
die Welt nicht ungeahnte Wege geht'[33]), in B major, turned at
the end of the line towards F, whereupon Ex. 6 begins in

[33] 'Maybe the world is set on pathways never imagined.'

G minor. Its cadence into D minor is interrupted by a
diminished seventh chord and the process starts again in A
minor, moving to E minor. Palestrina is lamenting the possibility that 'what we thought eternal is bound to pass away'.
Ex. 6 continues as an E minor ostinato in the bass and
associates itself with the rising scale which grows out of the
Council theme, Ex. 7, as Borromeo takes up the argument
under *marcato* wind chords. When he refers to 'the great
Church', the music briefly reaches C major, the key associated with the Pope and the Emperor. At the words 'Ihr
scheint mir krank in eurer Seele seit langsam schon',[34] the
rising scale is turned into a reference to the opening 'sorrow'
theme from *Der arme Heinrich* (Ex. 27).

Ex. 27

Original orchestration appears at Borromeo's description of
'die Engel halten Wacht und wollen Lobgesänge haben':[35] a
solo viola d'amore, celeste and cymbal, with harmonies on
three solo cellos. As with Janáček (in *Kát'a Kabanová*), one
wonders whether the viola d'amore is being used more for its
evocative name than for a sound not very far removed from
that of an ordinary viola, especially as, with plenty going on
above and below, it is hard for its characteristic timbre to
make itself felt.

After a page or two of obscure tonality we have now
reached D major – not quite the D minor of Palestrina's
creativity nor the A major of the angels. But we are abruptly
thrown back by way of D flat to C major. A passage in which

[34] 'It seems to me that your soul has long been sick' (OT).

[35] 'The angels keep their watch and wish for hymns of praise.'

The Vienna State Opera production of Palestrina *in 1969:*
Act One, Scene Three: Renate Holm as Ighino,
Trudelise Schmidt as Silla, Gerd Feldhoff as Borromeo,
and Horst Laubenthal as Palestrina
(photograph by Helmut Koller, Vienna)

Palestrina is accompanied by a solo string trio turns into the
rising scales common to Exx. 6 and 7 on the dominant of
A flat, with a fleeting reference to Exx. 8 and 10. Borromeo
goes on to tell Palestrina of the progress of the Council of
Trent: from a tonally oblique angle, rising octaves herald a
full statement of Ex. 7, but before this Ex. 6 takes us in its
usual way from G minor to D minor. The Pope's 'stern
command' brings first references to the motif of haste, Ex. 56
(p. 175), which will dominate the Second Act. Borromeo's
ensuing solo is built around a new idea, Ex. 28;[36] it begins in
the lower strings, continuing in imitation in the violins.

[36] John Williamson (*op. cit.*, p. 153) says that Ex. 28 refers to the Pope's
word, adding that 'the combination of contexts (here and in Act Two)
provides a clear definition of its meaning'. I have to say that I do not find the
definition 'clear'; it might equally well refer to the dogmatic questions
before the Church, as its recurrence in Act Two coincides with the discussion of church music. Nonetheless, the fact of its recurrence is more
important than any intrinsic meaning, and perhaps it should be regarded as
a theme whose significance is primarily musical.

Ex. 28

We also hear the octaves of Ex. 7; all these themes are carefully blended together. A sort of Lydian C/F major is eventually established. Whom could the errors of the new style offend more than Palestrina, Borromeo asks, voice and orchestra sharing the outline of Ex. 7, and the contrast of old and new is pointed by Ex. 4. For the objectors, all past church music must perish (fierce dissonances) and everything return to Gregorian chant. The chant-like music with which these words are illustrated is an ingenious derivative of one of the most striking themes in the whole opera, that of the Emperor Ferdinand (Ex. 29).

Ex. 29

Presumably at this point Pfitzner anticipates how church music was eventually to be saved. The key, as almost always for this theme, is C; a few pages earlier, C minor had been anticipated, but the dominant resolution was sidestepped and now the key is reached from the more unusual (but Pfitzner-ian) direction of B major. The fate of polyphonic music, consigned to the flames, and Borromeo's sorrow at the thought, is described by Ex. 30, a variant of Ex. 29; a typical Pfitzner effect is that this, its first appearance, is hidden in the lower strings, and we only become aware of it gradually. It is followed by a chromatic theme, Ex. 31, a relation of Ex. 26.

Ex. 30

Ex. 31

This passage culminates in a fierce dissonance. The music
now tries several keys, with Ex. 31 now clearly heard as
Borromeo states his views:

> Klein glaubig, wer von Gottes Güte
> Wohl glaubt, dass sie dem Menschen wehrt
> Die Freude an der Schönheit Blüte.[37]

Those who are of his opinion have been fortunate to receive
the support of the Emperor himself. We have the resolution
into pure diatonicism of Ex. 29 in C major, given its full shape
for the first time. The theme is given to woodwind, but the
violins double the climactic phrase only, a procedure typical
of Elgar. Pfitzner now sets a translation of the very words of
the Emperor's letter of 23 August 1563:

> Aus grosser Meister Zeit
> Das wohlerfund'ne Alte,
> Weil es den Geist der Frömmigkeit
> Erwecke und erhalte.[38]

This broad chorale, Ex. 32, significantly begins identically to
b in Ex. 1, as the art of the past is truly creative. In addition,
the last line of Ex. 32 is melodically identical to the first six
notes of Ex. 29, and the strings immediately prove that this is

[37] 'He who believes God's grace forbids
Mankind's delight in beauty
Is but a man of little faith.'

[38] '[. . .] all that is well-made
In masterpieces of the past
Since that awakens and upholds
The spirit of piety.'

no coincidence by continuing with the variant, Ex. 30. The whole chorale is of a type found several times in *Von deutscher Seele*, as well as in the songs (such as 'Der Gärtner', Op. 9, No. 1). Its parenthood in the Lutheran tradition is clear, but its tonal progressions are less predictable, in this case moving from B minor through D minor and with a cadence from E minor to G.

Ex. 32

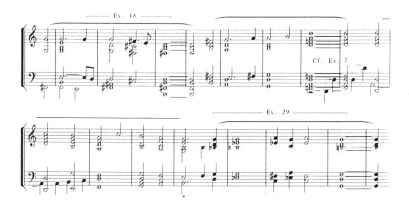

Restarting the movement after so formal a period is always a problem. Pfitzner's solution is to work Ex. 30 contrapuntally, accompanied by its own diminution. Borromeo could now carry his point of view in the Council, despite the numbers opposing him. The strings introduce Ex. 33, an important motif representing his plan and its success in the Council, though it contrives to suggest the devious and not wholly constructive side of all such discussions by its tonal precariousness.

Ex. 33

It runs through the next few pages, straddling a silent bar, with fluid tonality in a seemingly endless melody, a wonderful example of Pfitzner's 'ductile' technique. It develops into figuration based on rising fourths; Ex. 34 gives a glimpse of this process.

Ex. 34

Borromeo's plan is certainly constructive – to have a new polyphonic work written which would reconcile all the arguments, thus saving polyphony and setting the norm for all future compositions. His exposition of this ideal also includes references to the creativity theme, Ex. 1, in C sharp, E and the 'inspiration' key of A (Ex. 1*a* later in diminution), a sudden *forte* irruption of Ex. 33, the Council theme, Ex. 7, and the Emperor's theme, Ex. 29. This is at once followed by a new variant of Ex. 1 in the violins, now back in D minor. The culmination is Exx. 6 and 7, in D minor again, thus rounding off as a single unit the long span of Borromeo's exposition that began with the same music nearly 300 bars earlier. Palestrina is the only man who could write this work; who else could bring both pure style and religious feeling to it? The half-close of Ex. 4 resolves from F to the darkness of B flat minor with the two parts of Ex. 1 combining in the woodwind. Borromeo's charge is to 'rescue music here in Rome'; and the Rome theme is heard in all its breadth (Ex. 12), the city standing for the art as much as the music itself does. Borromeo's plea is rounded off by Ex. 1 and the Pierluigi motif, Ex. 2, in the orchestra, firmly in D minor; it concludes an immense paragraph of noble music.

But Palestrina refuses to accept the task, doubting his ability to write such a work. His first words are accompanied by a violin line which turns into the theme of Borromeo's idea, Ex. 33. The orchestra suggests Borromeo's surprise and impatience with fragments of a compound idea which is only heard coherently later, as in Ex. 37. Borromeo repeats his entreaty, to a new idea, Ex. 35, in A flat; occurring also in Acts Two and Three, it suggests Borromeo's endeavours and

Act One, Scene Three: Gerd Feldhoff as Borromeo
and Horst Laubenthal as Palestrina
(photograph by Helmut Koller, Vienna)

struggles, which are not helped by his current misreading of Palestrina's character and creative genius.

Ex. 35

The progress of keys reflects all this inner tension; for instance, when A major is reached ('Ihr schätzt sie wahrlich niedrig'[39]) its brightness is contradicted by its approach from the key a semitone below. Later, hints that the Council and Emperor would also be 'not amused' remind us of the more important issues (Ex. 29 with a beautiful oboe countertheme, and then combined with Ex. 7). The orchestration here also emphasises the barrier between the two men; Palestrina is

[39] 'Do you then value these so lightly?'

accompanied mainly by strings while Borromeo has plenty of woodwind and brass.

> Ist dies Pierluigi Palestrina,
> Der unermüdliche, schaffensfrohe Mann?[40]

asks Borromeo (Exx. 2, 4). 'Er ist's nicht mehr',[41] replies the composer, and a sad dotted rhythm, Ex. 36, is heard, expressive of his weariness and his closeness to death – spiritually if not physically.

Ex. 36

Borromeo is becoming impatient, his thoughts turning towards his return to Trent. Palestrina's G sharp minor gives way to Ex. 37 in E, but with hints of the Trent theme, Ex. 38, in the bass.

Ex. 37

Ex. 38

---

[40] 'Is this Pierluigi Palestrina,
The joyous, inexhaustible creator?'

[41] 'That he is no longer' (OT).

*Act One, Scene Three: Gerd Feldhoff as Borromeo
and Horst Laubenthal as Palestrina
(photograph by Helmut Koller, Vienna)*

The anticipation of an important new theme by varied fragments of it, already seem with Ex. 29, is a process so characteristic of Pfitzner as to become at times a mannerism; there are countless examples in the instrumental music. Borromeo describes the Masters of the Past praying for Palestrina's aid and the Old Masters theme, Exx. 25 and 26, accompany his words. After a big orchestral climax over a pedal D, Exx. 37 and 38 are stated, Ex. 37*b* having its intervals augmented as Borromeo's anger rises. Ex. 26 returns sadly in A minor on a solo flute as Palestrina repeats his refusal; the second bar is taken over by the brass while versions of Ex. 37 appear in the woodwind. The intervals in the strings continue to widen and the music gradually increases in momentum as the definitive version of Ex. 38 emerges. This motif, together with still wilder versions of Ex. 37 (violent tenths abounding), brings the whole scene to a climax as Borromeo storms out.

Nach Schwefel riecht's in Eurer Näh![42]

Ex. 38, in B minor despite the chords of C, is the motif of Trent. Its galloping rhythms suggest both the fury with which Borromeo is returning there and the intellectual vigour and hot tempers to be found in the Council, although its key stamps it as a predominantly neutral background to events. It takes over the dotted rhythms of Ex. 36 and in the heavy brass beneath screaming strings it forms a huge orchestral climax on a first inversion of G, ending with Ex. 37 in the strings.

Although the C major which began the scene is still present in some of the harmonies, we have clearly moved much further afield tonally and emotionally than we were permitted to do while only Silla and Ighino were on stage – which is appropriate at this more advanced stage of the musical structure, and especially bearing in mind that this scene contains some of the most important intellectual arguments in the work.

Scene Four

> *Palestrina, who listened to the last, unexpected outburst with some dismay, stares thoughtfully after Borromeo for a while; then he turns back to the room sadly, but quite composed.*

Palestrina is left alone, in more than one sense:

> Der letzte Freund, der mir noch wohlgesinnt,
> Nun geht auch er.[43]

His vocal line is anguished and angular, with a falling seventh taken over from the brass and echoed in the strings. The sense of motion has slowed down, the agitation died away; B minor slips down to B flat minor. The tone of the violas is prominent throughout this scene; a solo viola introduces the loneliness theme, Ex. 39, before the bleak and bleakly-set words:

---

[42] 'There is a stench of sulphur about you!' – *cf.* p. 82, above. I recall the glint in the eye of John Brockeler, portraying the fanatical side of Borromeo, at Munich in 1990.

[43] 'The last friend who was well-disposed towards me,
  Now he's gone too' (OT).

Wie fremd und unbekannt sind sich die Menschen!
Das Innerste der Welt ist Einsamkeit.[44]

Ex. 39, here at its first appearance poised over a chord of G
first inversion, demonstrates another Pfitzner characteristic:
appearing later on different degrees of the scale, it displays
different aspects from different angles. Incidentally, the second phrase of Ex. 39 is all but identical to the finale theme, in
its second phrase, of the C sharp minor String Quartet of
1925.

Ex. 39

Next comes another theme, Ex. 40, which suggests the
unreal world of fantasy (Palestrina's 'the intoxication of giddy
youth').

Ex. 40

At first heard in combination with Ex. 39, it is at once freely
inverted by the violins and appears several times during the
remainder of the scene, at one point augmented in the bass.
Palestrina feels himself 'alone, deep in a forest [...] in the
middle of life', an obvious reference to the opening of Dante's
Inferno. It is given form here by a striking moment of orchestration, two low trumpet chords with strings divided into
fourteen parts. We are now in C sharp minor and Ex. 39
begins on this tonic; perhaps it is significant that the key is
now the same as that of the Op. 36 Quartet, which is one of
Pfitzner's most profound and inwardly expressive works.
Suddenly the tonality drops to C, en route to F. The bass line

---

[44] 'How strange and unknown men are to each other!
The inmost thing on earth is solitude.'

in the opera has now settled down to a long, slow motion which underpins the texture both of this scene and the next, increasing the unearthliness of the vision. Palestrina reflects that while Lucrezia was still alive he was secure and he could still feel that his life had value. With a quiet affirmation of A major, and following intimate repeated chords which will return in the last Act, a solo violin plays a beautiful version of Ex. 21. Next Palestrina's thoughts turn to Ighino; but for all his love for his son, Ighino is not a creator and thus is 'ganzlich sinnlos'.[45] The solo viola gives out a tender version of Ex. 15 in B flat minor, leading to a four-part canon on Ex. 25 (chromatically altered) for double-basses. Above this the rising fifth and seventh of Ex. 1*a* are heard on the solo viola. Palestrina has an access of feelings of the futility of life when viewed in this pessimistic, God-less light; his work will eventually be destroyed by Time anyway, so what does it matter if it is all burnt tomorrow? The emptiness is emphasised by the extraordinary writing for four low flutes and alto flute above double-basses still playing four independent lines. Not even the thought of the music of the past (Ex. 1*b* combined beautifully with Ex. 25) can comfort him – what is there in life at all? With the despair the tonality has drifted from B minor onto a nebulous and almost keyless chord which combines A, B flat, D and E flat, going on to suggest the dominant of D minor.

Scene Five

In the meantime, forms have begun to take shape in the ghostly violet light that has filtered through the room: they have approached silently and slowly from the darkened background, and now surround Palestrina. They are dressed in the clothes of several different countries – Spain, the Netherlands, Italy, Germany, France – and seem to belong to several earlier centuries. The earliest – perhaps

---

[45] 'wholly without meaning' (OT).

from the thirteenth century – wears a Monk's habit.[46] *Their ages
vary, too, from youth to venerable age; and so does the quality of
their clothes. They are the masters of previous epochs, Palestrina's
great predecessors.*

*During his last words they have been standing motionless,
smiling strangely at him; now they answer his despairing cry 'What
for?'*

The music does not resolve into D minor. The trombones
outline a rising fifth, E flat – B flat, the opening of Ex. 1 (or
Ex. 25) but suggesting an unexpected and mysterious tonality, more than merely a flat supertonic. Beneath Palestrina's
last agonised high A the nine voices reply 'Für Ihn' – it is for
God alone – to the same rising fifth, and flute and bass clarinet
in octaves play the principal melodic germ of the scene,
Ex. 41.

Ex. 41

At the same time the harmony breathes the same air as Ex. 4
and, in addition, Ex. 2 recurs throughout the scene as a
reiterated personal plea. As in the third scene, the orchestration emphasises the contrast between the characters,
Palestrina with strings alone, palpitating fitfully, and the
spirits with mysterious still brass. Perhaps this was inspired by
a similar device in the *Todesverkündigung* scene of *Die Walküre*. The key changes from C to D minor and back, typical of
the sense of unreality. Palestrina recognises two of the nine
spirits, whose voices range downwards from high tenor to

---

[46] The score makes it clear that this refers to the First Master, and one
wonders whether Pfitzner conceived his nine Masters in chronological
order – a view inconsistent with the score's identification of the contemporaries Isaac and Josquin as Second and Fourth Masters
respectively.

deep bass – the fourth, in fifteenth-century Burgundian costume, is Josquin des Pres, and the second is Heinrich Isaac,·
often known as 'Harry the German' and addressed by Palestrina as such here. The others are unidentified; perhaps
Pfitzner selected these two names especially as spiritual forerunners of Palestrina. Certainly the music does not evoke
specific styles; it is generally archaic rather than specifically
authentic.

The spirits greet Palestrina formally, to a combination of
the harmony of Ex. 4 and the rhythm and melody of Ex. 2,
while a sudden *fortissimo* on Ex. 1*b* – the 'music of the past' –
gives emphasis to their standing. A cadence into A minor is
produced. The strings mention Ex. 40; is this a dream? After
some unstable tonality Palestrina's E flat is answered by the
spirits with a falling fifth starting on D, the reverse of their first
entry. There is a short passage based on Ex. 26, first heard
augmented in the bass and then at twice that speed in the
violins; then the nine spirits continue with a complete nine-
part passage built on the ubiquitous interval of a fifth and on
Exx. 41 and 25. The paragraph ends with a strikingly
sixteenth-century cadence to a close on F as the spirits echo
the basic image: Palestrina is the one to complete the circle of
the chosen ones!

A new motion begins with the F minor of Ex. 42 on cor
anglais and solo cello as Palestrina tries to say that he is not
the man to write anything now.

Ex. 42

Ex. 2 is inverted, now audibly related to Ex. 42; back in
common time, Ex. 36 recurs much augmented as he says he is
an old man. This is in A minor, slipping to G sharp and then
further as the First Master brings a cadence in B minor with

the Pierluigi motif of Ex. 2. Variants of Ex. 42, now in
B major, set the music in motion again, but soon we move to
C minor and then G minor as Ex. 42 is combined with
another theme, Ex. 43. The latter is a variant, without the
dotted rhythm, of Ex. 36.

Ex. 43

At the line 'Wo's in mir blühte, ist jetzt tote Stelle',[47] the
clarinet plays Ex. 22 and Ex. 2 is inverted. This is the end of
his inspiration and his own negation (note the *falling* fifths),
and the overall shape is like a dying reminiscence of Ex. 21.
The key is D minor. Ex. 25 continues to appear in the bass as
the second principal Old Masters theme. Now come the lines
quoted above referring to artistic self-consciousness.[48] They
are set against an orchestral background in which a solo E flat
clarinet plays the whole of Ex. 42 in common time.

The spirits know that Palestrina is wrong, that his anguish
is merely part of the creative process, its labour pains. They
exhort him to complete his task on earth, and the rising fifth to
which they first sing 'Dein Erdenpensum' ('Your task on
earth') is that of Ex. 1*a*, accompanied by Ex. 41 in the
woodwind. Significantly, this is the first time since their first
two notes that all nine Masters sing in unison, and the key is
D minor. Palestrina says that he will not listen, but his reply
brings forth a chromatic distortion of Ex. 2; again he is being
false to himself. He says that he has comforts 'neither in
Heaven nor on Earth', a clarinet with Ex. 15 telling us that
even Ighino can bring him no joy. Soon a new figure, Ex. 44,
is heard. Rectanus, associating it with the 'letzte Stein' image,
points out the 'hammering' – i.e., forging – suggestion of its
repeated semitones.[49]

---

[47] 'What blossomed in me once is barren now.'

[48] *Cf.* p. 95, above.

[49] *Leitmotivik und Form*, p. 115.

Ex. 44

The whole of Ex. 1 recurs at the words

Und so, wie du nun musst, so mussten wir im Leben.[50]

The key is A minor, the dominant minor of the key of creativity, and later turns to A major with the angels. A version of Ex. 4 is followed by a return to the rising intervals of Ex. 25; over an organ pedal C, the spirits talk of God as 'der alte Weltenmeister'[51] and, accompanied by Ex. 44, of the history of humanity as God's forging 'rings and precious stones for the shimmering chains of the ages'. And, with a return to D minor, they state complete the opera's final and first-written lines, thus making explicit for the first time the central image of creativity and the role of the genius, from which idea the whole of the opera springs.

During the spirits' plea, the crux of their message, Ex. 5 has made three appearances and eventually it is allowed to complete itself as Ex. 6, to the key words 'der letzte Stein'. Slowly, with repetitions of 'dein Erdenpensum', the spirits fade, amid *tremolando* harmonies identical to the first chord of Ex. 4 (single desks of violas and of cellos playing arpeggiated figures is enough to prevent the texture from becoming completely static), followed by sequential, hypnotic repetitions of Ex. 41 over the dominant of D minor. Palestrina is left perplexed, unconvinced and once more alone.

It will be noted that several of the principal themes first heard in the Introduction have been heard again, in their original D minor, in the closing stages of this scene. Admittedly they are viewed in slight distortion, as it were, through the other-worldly context of the dead composers' music, but this device does give the effect of a recapitulation of the Introduction at this stage of the First Act. Yet the tonalities of this scene as a whole are often only sketchily

---

[50] 'Just as you are now compelled, so were we in our lives.'

[51] 'The age-old Master of the World.'

defined, open intervals and the ambiguity of Ex. 25 prevailing. These factors and the orchestration combine with the totally unhurried pacing of the scene to take us outside the normal world of time. The impression of inevitable progress characteristic of the pace of sonata movement at the point of recapitulation is wholly unsuited to the drama at this moment. Pfitzner's ability to control and sustain the slowest pace is nowhere better illustrated.

The scene as a whole falls roughly into ternary form, the compound-time, Ex. 42 section separating the expanses of static music based on Exx. 25 and 41.[52]

Scene Six

Palestrina, who remained in the armchair throughout the last scene, now sits upright, but with closed eyes; it is completely dark.

As soon as the spirits have disappeared, he begins:

Allein, in dunkler Tiefe
Voll Angst ich armer Mensch
Rufe laut nach oben.[53]

Thus, accompanied by the motif of his loneliness, Ex. 40, on oboe and cor anglais, Palestrina returns to his reliance on God. Converting a chord of C sharp minor to A major, he is answered by an angel who has appeared unnoticed and who sings Ex. 45, the opening phrase of the Kyrie of the *Missa Papae Marcelli*, in canon at the octave with a trumpet and then by Palestrina.

Ex. 45

With this theme the Mass itself opens, though there tenor I is answered an octave higher instead (by the soprano). This is

---

[52] *Cf.* Rectanus, *Leitmotivik und Form*, p. 146.

[53] 'Alone, in deepest darkness,
Wretched and terrified,
I raise my voice to heaven.'

the most significant appearance so far in the opera of the key of A major, and the effect of reaching this bright key in so simply effective a way cannot fail to make its point. Edward Dent pointed out how the effect is heightened by the entry of a high soprano after so much music involving only male voices.[54]

To Palestrina, repeating the music as he writes it down, this is the direct inspiration he has been seeking, and which he describes as 'ein Liebesquell',[55] Ex. 46.

Ex. 46

The symbolism of this has already been discussed.[56] A clarinet plays some rising fourths, Ex. 47, and, over Palestrina's last words, a clarinet, then an oboe and then a solo violin play a sequence of falling thirds, Ex. 48.

Ex. 47

Ex. 48

This is similar to a later phrase from the Kyrie of the Mass (tenor II, bars 14–15 in the Lockwood edition) and repeated in a version closer to Pfitzner's, as quoted here, in other voices

[54] 'Hans Pfitzner', *loc. cit.*, p. 131.

[55] 'A fount of love.'

[56] *Cf.* p. 82, above.

in succeeding bars. But Pfitzner makes no further use of this phrase, and its appearance may be coincidental. The music moves to the subdominant. Two more angels have appeared; one sings the opening phrase of the Christe (Ex. 49) while the second has an original countersubject.

Ex. 49

As Palestrina repeats Ex. 49, the first angel joins in, and then a whole choir of angels with Ex. 47 augmented as a *cantus firmus*. Prominent in the music is not only the rising fourth, but a rising scale of five notes – a 'filling-in', as it were, of Ex. 1 – and the music shifts to C major.[57]

A particularly lovely orchestral interlude follows, in F major, the harmonic vocabulary that of *Parsifal* at its most diatonic. It begins on high violins with a phrase from Palestrina's Gloria, Ex. 50, and during its Lucrezia's theme, Ex. 21, shows that she too is appearing to Palestrina to aid his inspiration.[58]

Ex. 50

For her music, however, the key switches from A major via C sharp to E flat minor, the furthest possible from A, perhaps

[57] Typical of the contrapuntal elaboration employed here by Pfitzner is the canon by inversion between Palestrina (at the words 'Wie durch die eig'ne Brust') and the First Angel's 'in unum Deum'.

[58] Osthoff, in 'Eine neue Quelle', p. 198, identified the first phrase of the Lucrezia theme with a phrase from the *Missa Papae Marcelli*, Kyrie, tenor II, bars 33–36. *Cf.* also Williamson, *op. cit.*, p. 192.

reminding us that in truth Lucrezia is not an angel even though Palestrina thought of her as one. In purely musical terms this modulation means that we travel further, covering a wider range, in the course of the scene than would have been the case with what is otherwise a fairly restricted range of key. The solo violin plays a distant derivative of Ex. 21, which is later taken up by all the strings. 'In terra pax hominibus,' sings the first angel, and Lucrezia repeats these words in German. 'Frieden' – peace – is the gist of her message, the peace both of God's love and of the creative artist's sense of fulfilment at the conclusion of this task. Throughout the scene the equating of creativity with love is constantly present. When the angels repeat the word 'hominibus' they do so to some parallel modal chords which momentarily recall Vaughan Williams' use of this device. The music modulates to B flat and when Lucrezia finishes we hear Ex. 51, a motif which stands for the whole Mass itself; it is based on two phrases from the Sanctus combined to create a line that Palestrina could not possibly have written[59] but which embodies all the elation of the inspired composer.

Ex. 51

More than that, in combining the rising scale of five notes with the rising fourth Ex. 51 unites in one theme the two

[59] The energetic rhythm and 'hiccup' before the leap of the fourth are much more the province of the school of the Netherlands. Osthoff (*loc. cit.*) gives a series of examples, of which that from Josquin's instrumental *La Bernadina* is the closest; and to them I would add the second Kyrie of Josquin's mass *Pange Lingua* and the very beautiful *Du tout plongiet* by Antoine de Brumel.

principal melodic germs both of Palestrina's Mass and of Pfitzner's opera. It is well fitted to express the creative achievement which is one of the most fundamental of all the symbols in the opera.

It enters in three-part canon in the strings, in B flat, over a dominant pedal which adds a slightly valedictory sense. Further imitations follow at other pitches. Immediately Palestrina sings Ex. 52 to the words 'Zu überschwenglichem Glück' – the motif of 'highest joy' – continuing with Ex. 51, which he takes up to a high B flat.

Ex. 52

Ex. 52 almost never appears except in the company of Ex. 50 (the one exception being five bars from the end of the First Act), linking the joy specifically to the creation of the Mass. As if further confirmation were required, it begins with the rising fifth that began the 'creativity' motif, Ex. 1. It 'balances' Ex. 51 perfectly, like a very free inversion.

The impression on the listener that the entry of this theme marks the coda or epilogue to the scene is very strong; it has a cadential finality. Its key of B flat is also the same as the B flat minor of much of Palestrina's soliloquy, possibly a further reason for the previous interruption of a key (E flat minor) closely related to B flat but very far from the expected A major. Throughout the Dictation Scene the interruptions by Palestrina and Lucrezia are carefully planned to punctuate the Mass music in an effectively symmetrical way.

Now the boys' choir sings a Gloria, based on 'Filium Dei Unigenitum' from the *Missa Papae Marcelli* (Ex. 53).[60] The rising scale with which it continues leads sequentially through various keys to C major. There the three solo angels sing Ex. 51, rising this time to a thrilling top C. Palestrina is giving thanks to the power of eternal love which has brought him at

[60] *Cf.* Osthoff, *loc. cit.*, and Williamson, *op. cit.*, p. 192.

Ex. 53

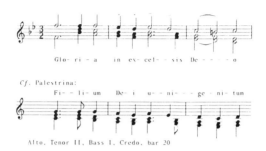

last the peace he has sought. 'Dona nobis pacem', sing the boys; and Palestrina finishes his labours on an unforgettable *piano* high C, accompanied by the motif of joy, Ex. 52. Rectanus has pointed out[61] how the whole structure of this scene is planned against a background of increasing contrapuntal complexity: the Kyrie begins with one angel, the Credo all three plus the boys' choir. 'In terra pax' is an interlude for Lucrezia and one angel, and the Gloria is then *tutti*. Between these sections Palestrina comments on his own emotions, while continuing to write. Throughout, Pfitzner employs all the devices of contrapuntal and imitative writing – augmentation, diminution, stretto, and so on – to portray the filling of the air with the beating of angels' wings.

The impression that the scene has to give is that the whole of the Mass has been dictated to Palestrina and written down by him. As anything like a complete performance of the Mass is obviously out of the question, Pfitzner was faced with a very difficult task in order to convey that impression, and there can be little doubt of the skill or the success of his solution. Of the music of the Mass, he only quotes directly four ideas, the opening phrases of the Kyrie and Christe (Exx. 45 and 49) and the Gloria and Sanctus phrases which give rise to Exx. 51 and 53, plus possibly the brief phrase from the Kyrie already referred to (Ex. 48). Ex. 45 is the principal figure of the whole Mass. As far as modern scholarship has been able to establish, it is not borrowed from another work or another composer; neither can it be called a genuine 'head-motif', for it does not

---

[61] *Leitmotivik und Form*, p. 147.

stand at the beginning of every movement. It opens the first Kyrie, shared antiphonally between the six parts; at the 'Patrem omnipotentem' which opens the Credo (bass II, followed by bass I at the chordal setting of 'factorem coeli'); and in three-part canon at the beginning of the second seven-part Agnus. In addition variants occur at the Gloria (bass II then bass I) – the fourths of Ex. 47; at 'Dominus, Deus Sabaoth' in the Sanctus (bass I, then bass II); at the beginning of the Osanna (bass I – bass II answers with a falling instead of a rising sequence); and at the beginning of Agnus I (all parts).

Otherwise all the music that the angels sing is original, although it is written to sound as if it might come from the Mass. Set against the ripe music of later Romanticism Pfitzner does not need to follow the 'academic rules' that roughly describe the so-called 'Palestrina style': the new lines are often much less smooth than anything Palestrina could have written. In addition the whole tessitura, enforced by writing in the bright key of A major, requires the three solo angels to have fully-developed operatic voices, which militates against the possibility of achieving the sort of sound which would be expected in a modern performance of the Mass. In any case, Pfitzner *had* to invent music for the words 'Gloria in excelsis Deo' and 'Credo in unum Deum', for they were, by the custom of the time, not set by Palestrina, but must be sung to the conventional intonations – a custom which persisted in such later works as Bruckner's E minor Mass of 1866 (which quotes Palestrina in the Sanctus) and Stravinsky's Mass of 1944–48. That Pfitzner has managed to achieve not merely a contrast but also a satisfying cohesion in the uniting of his own style with the music he has taken from or given to Palestrina is in itself a remarkable demonstration of the qualities of that own style. It is a genuine reconciliation between the languages of the sixteenth and early twentieth centuries.

The reconciliation is achieved most obviously by the linear nature of so much of Pfitzner's score, and by the lyricism of his lines, which often sound vocal even when given to the orchestra – another basically Italian feature. By reducing the quantity of chromatic harmony he is able to come close to Palestrina's modes, and indeed several of the opera's motifs are strongly modal (Ex. 1 is Dorian and Ex. 4 Phrygian, for example). And, as has already been mentioned, there is a motivic unity between the two works as well. The all-pervading fifth of the opera is the inversion of the fourth which is so strong a feature of the Mass. In addition the rising scale of a fifth is not only a basic element of Ex. 51 but it also appears frequently in the Mass (and not only in the Sanctus). Rising and falling scales are so much a feature of Palestrina's style that the figure can hardly be thought of as a consciously used element of the work (though such scales build the Credo to a powerful climax). But the use of the five notes in the opera is another of the several very carefully planned techniques by which Pfitzner achieves the necessary unity in this scene.

It is unfortunate that the public of today tends to associate angelic choirboys with the empty sentimentality of Hollywood, a phenomenon which was splendidly parodied by the Marx Brothers (in *The Big Store*, 1941). Care must be taken not to let the scene come close to visual kitsch. But in a fine performance of the opera doubts are left behind and, as Lord Harewood says, 'it succeeds in giving an impression of the artist's exultation at the moment of creation'.[62]

The transition to the last scene of the Act is one of the most extraordinary passages in the whole work. Musically it is based on the bell motif, Ex. 14, although this is combined with references to Exx. 51 and 52. Ostensibly it is a picture in sound of the bells of Rome as the city wakes to the new day, but the passage, beginning in C major over a tonic pedal, reaches a tremendous climax of such violent chromatic intensity, the bass turning to the tritone A–E flat, that something much deeper is implied.[63] It gives the impression that after the huge exertion required in writing the Mass, Palestrina's mind has been stretched to the utmost, and these are the terrifying after-effects. It has been a tremendous mental strain.

The view that Pfitzner's portrait of Palestrina shows a

[62] *Kobbé's Complete Opera Book*, 8th edn., Putnam, London, 1969, p. 974.

[63] A similar, though far less violent, effect is obtained in the accompaniment to Pfitzner's song, 'Michaelskirchplatz', Op. 19, No. 2.

Romantic and not a sixteenth-century composer was discussed earlier.[64] The reaction after the completion of a major
work is attested to by late Romantics such as Mahler and
Elgar,[65] two of the most highly-strung of composers. The
dissonance of the music here reveals that Pfitzner, if not
Palestrina, showed the same reaction. Another, structural,
reason for the dissonance of the bell passage will be revealed
in Act Two.

The bell music reaches its shattering climax, there is a
fermata, and the Rome theme, Ex. 12, bursts out in all its
unhurried majesty in G flat major in the full orchestra. The
crisis is over. As it dies down, its pendant from the first scene,
Ex. 13, and a variant of the bell music, Ex. 54, follow.

Ex. 54

The bell music lasts for nine bars – exactly the same length as
the passage based on the same music which will end the next
scene, and with it the Act.[66]

Scene Seven

*The room is as it was before, but with the rosy light of dawn filtering
through the window [. . .]. Palestrina, overcome by his exertions,
falls back in his chair; his right arm hangs down, the pen slips from
his fingers. Sheets of music lie strewn on the table and the floor; he
sleeps deeply, and remains asleep until the end of the Act.*

*Silla suddenly appears in the doorway. After a glance at the
sleeping Palestrina, he gestures to Ighino to follow him into the
room. The boys have come for morning practice.*

Pfitzner could have ended his Act here, but imaginatively he
follows the tension of the two previous scenes with a little

[64] *Cf.* p. 81–82, above.

[65] *Cf.* for example, Elgar's letters to Jaeger, *Letters to Nimrod*, ed. Percy
Young, Dobson, London, 1965; also Jerrold Northrop Moore (ed.), *Elgar
and his Publishers*, Oxford University Press, Oxford, 1987.

[66] Rectanus, *Leitmotivik und Form*, p. 148.

vignette that lightens the mood (in just the same way as the final reappearance of the Page at the end of *Der Rosenkavalier*). There are structural reasons, too, for the existence of this scene: it perfectly counterbalances the first scene of the Act, and it has its reflection in Act Two.[67] The sequence of the music (Exx. 12, 13, 54) echoes Ighino's entry at the beginning of Scene Two, and it alternates with Ex. 24 from Scene Three; the boys have prepared their psalm. They discover Palestrina asleep (the Silla motif, Ex. 8, of which we heard rather a lot in the opening scenes, is used only sparingly here), and the music runs in a lively $\frac{12}{8}$. 'What happiness – he's been composing', says Ighino, accompanied by the motif of a different sort of joy, Ex. 52, and they read through the sheets of music. This first re-appearance of Ex. 52 is in E flat, looking back to the first two notes of the Dead Masters in Scene Five as well as emphasising the all-round importance of the rising fifth. The action is illustrated by an ingenious contrapuntal combination of Exx. 15, 45 and 11 as Ighino reads the Kyrie, and of Exx. 8, 49 and 11 in two-part imitation (Silla reading the Christe): Ex. 55.

Ex. 55

The presence of Ex. 11 implies that to them it is old-style counterpoint, seeming drily academic, maybe, to Silla. He

[67] *Cf.* pp. 203–5, below.

says that it is in 'the old style, but not so weighty', while to the
less intellectual Ighino it just seems beautiful. Silla reflects
that an old man has written so much in a single night; a solo
violin with Ex. 38 reminds us of the loneliness of that night.
But his last words are

Ich glaube nicht, dass grade dieses Werk
Dem alten Meister grosse Ehre macht.[68]

To which Ex. 8 suggests that this is a judgement typical of his
impetuosity.

The drama of the act finished, the last nine bars are a
tremendous crescendo based on the bell motif, Ex. 14, like a
resumption of the ending of the previous scene. This time,
however, B flat minor returns with an almost physical sense of
effort to pure C major, the motif of happiness is added, and
the bells and tam-tam which have added to the climax main-
tain their pealing through the crescendo on the final chord.
Yet at the end, we realise that the final C major has only been
established for half a dozen bars; nor was it prepared by a vast
passage of irresistible resolution, but by a sidestep from an
unusual direction. There is much more to be said in the
opera, and after so much careful preparation in the rest of the
Act – the tonic-dominant move of the first double scene, the
spreading emotions of Borromeo's argument, the tonally
static yet ambiguous nature of the Dead Composers' music
and the contrasting long stretches of broad tonality in the
Dictation Scene – the place for a full resolution is not here.
The tonal scheme confirms the D minor Introduction as
being distinct from the rest of the Act, the latter starting and
finishing in C.

There is no doubt that the impression left in our minds at
the end of this first Act is that of powerful and dramatic work.
It has been a long act (it runs for about an hour and forty
minutes), and much of it has been slow and meditative, but,
starting and finishing with youthful naïvety, it has encom-
passed solemn events. Apart from the central monologue, it is
in effect a sequence of duets: Silla and Ighino, Borromeo and
Palestrina, Palestrina and the Dead Composers, Palestrina

[68] 'I hardly think that this will be the work
To bring great honour to our ancient master.'

and the angels, Silla and Ighino. Some have suggested that the
work should end here, and indeed the first Act on its own
could make a complete musical and dramatic entity were it
not for the deliberately inconclusive and even disturbing way
with which Pfitzner has ended it. But by moving on to the
contrasting 'reality of worldly activities', the scope and scale
are expanded immensely: from the ivory tower to the whole of
life.

Act Two

We have seen how the Second Act takes us to a different
world from that of the outer acts. In it there is less concentration on the profounder emotions, and Pfitzner takes the
opportunity of this 'externalisation' to produce a wonderfully
coherent musical and dramatic structure. The main keys are
E flat, the conflict key of the Council, and C major, the
Council's more neutral aspect. The A major of the angels has
a small but important role, and the 'diminished seventh' of
keys is completed by G flat which is used at the moments of
formal council voting. Such a tonal scheme in itself constitutes a highly imaginative concept.

   The Prelude to Act Two is a substantial piece, formally and
physically strong enough to stand on its own. Pfitzner differ-
entiates it from the Introduction (*Einleitung*) to the other two
acts by giving it the title of 'Vorspiel'. Its first notes
immediately tell us that we are in a very different world from
that of the First Act, indeed, exactly Schopenhauer's 'reality
of worldly activities'. It begins in a rather chromatic E flat, the
furthest pole from the A major of the angels, with Ex. 56 on
six horns; the first three notes (*a*), equivalent, of course, to the
next three, constitute a motif which runs through the whole
Act in one form or another. It refers to the strife within the
Council, and in particular over the haste with which it is being
'rushed to its conclusions'; Ex. 56*a* will be conveniently
referred to as the haste motif. After this initial idea and its
continuation (*b*) have been set out, the quaver movement
settles down to a tonally vague rhythmic background based
on perfect and diminished fifths over which the trumpets

Ex. 56

interpolate isolated notes, then pairs of notes. The pairs
gradually take on a more definite shape, and after nine bars
they coalesce into Ex. 56*a* inverted and suggesting A flat
minor. If Ex. 56*a* is the motif of haste, its inversion suggests
the reverse, the wish to discuss matters carefully and at
length. The continuation, Ex. 57, in a tentative E flat, is a free
inversion of Ex. 56.

Ex. 57

Developments follow in the violins, with persistent references
to Ex. 56*a*. There is a hint of G flat, and then of B minor, with
figuration in the strings which recalls Ex. 56*b*. Shortly piccolo,
trumpet and horns introduce an idea in triplet rhythm, Ex. 68
(p. 185), later to be associated with the delegates' cries of
'Placet! Placet!', in its usual key of G flat, but the three-note
figure, Ex. 56*a*, returns and builds up a climax, continuing
with the bustling rhythmic background figuration. Again the
trumpet builds up fragments of Ex. 56*a* in inversion, though
this time in the space of only two bars, and the inversion leads
to E flat minor and a big crunch on a chord of C major (first
inversion) with added sixth, out of which Ex. 56*b* grows.
Shortly a jump of a rising major seventh, an interval to be
associated with Discord, becomes prominent, emphasised by
the piccolo and inverted in the bass, and another climax is
reached with Ex. 56*a* both as originally and inverted, over a

bass E flat. With repetitions of Ex. 57 the climax subsides, the
bass drops to D, and in the appropriate 'sonata' key of B flat
Ex. 58 enters in the woodwind.

Ex. 58

This sounds like – and structurally is – a 'second subject', and
although it obviously begins as an augmentation of Ex. 56*a*
inverted, it soon acquires elements of its own – a typical
Pfitzner procedure. In the Act which follows, this theme,
associated with the Archbishop of Prague, will be felt as a
calming influence associated with the wish to take matters in
their proper order.

What we have heard so far would make a very satisfactory
exposition to the first movement of a large-scale symphony
(though it would be unusual for two such big climaxes to have
been reached so soon), but Pfitzner has not forgotten that this
is an operatic prelude. After some hints of Ex. 56*a* augmented, rising octaves introduce Ex. 59 in G minor (here the
theme is quoted in its later version in D minor).

Ex. 59

This is one of the themes associated with the Council itself,
and to fit its grave tread into the headlong pace of the Prelude
it is written in 'three-bar' rhythm (three bars of the Prelude
correspond to one of Ex. 59).[69] Octave leaps continue and
lead to the other main Council theme, Ex. 7, already familiar

---

[69] Harold Truscott pointed out how Pfitzner achieves here 'the combination of a real slow tempo with a real quick tempo' (*Music Survey*, No. 1,
London, 1947, p. 14).

from the first Act. Ex. 7 is stated twice, in G minor and then in its usual key of D minor (as it was at the end of the Introduction to Act One). As it ends, in B flat, Ex. 56*a* creeps upwards from the bass, again in augmentation.

Suddenly the mood lightens as the key changes to C and the motif acquires an anticipatory triplet, Ex. 60, and the curtain goes up.

Ex. 60

Just as in Act One, and introduced by the same modulation, Pfitzner starts with a scene on a low emotional level which sets out important ideas.

Scene One

The great hall of Cardinal Madruscht's palace in Trent. The hall has been prepared for the last full meeting, a so-called General Congregation, before the ceremonial conclusion. On either side of the stage about four tiers of benches and chairs have been arranged in semi-circles for the Cardinals, Cardinal Legates and Nuncios. On the stage, the Cardinal Legate Bernardo Novagerio. The Master of Ceremonies, Bishop Ercole Severolus, is standing near him.

The opening scene acts as a dramatic exposition of some of the most important elements of the Act, following the musical exposition of the Prelude. Under the direction of the Master of Ceremonies, servants are arranging the hall for the final meeting. It is appropriate that their motif, Ex. 60, is derived from that of haste, for the servants will be at the centre of the strife caused by the prelates' arguments at the end of the Act, arguments which have been brought on by haste. Most of this first scene consists musically of developments of Exx. 56 and 60. The Count of Luna, spokesman of the King of Spain and

perhaps a direct descendant of the character in *Il Trovatore*, is
to have a special seat to himself – contrary to protocol but for
reasons of political expediency – and while Serverolus and
Novagerio are exchanging some light-hearted banter about
this arrangement the C minor motif of the Spaniards, Ex. 61,
is heard in the orchestra.

Ex. 61

When Novagerio hopes for no more quarrels about rank,
there is a brief move to the 'strife' key of E flat, where the
Council theme, Ex. 7, makes an appearance in diminution in
the violins. Ex. 60 then takes us on to E minor for another
reference to Ex. 61; the second half answers the first in D
minor. Novagerio tells Severolus that the speeches are to be
kept short today, that he must interrupt if anyone shows signs
of going on too long, and the watchword is 'Schnell zum
Schluss',[70] Ex. 56a, this time in B flat. Ex. 56 makes another
full appearance at the condemnation of those who, like Lainez, speak too long, and now Novagerio calls all the servants
together, back in C major once more. He tells them that they
must behave themselves in future, saying

> Kennt ihr den grünen Turm?
> Und kennt ihr auch die Wiege drin?
> Die Kinder da drin man wiegt
> Schrein sehr laut, und gar nicht vernügt.[71]

[70] 'Quickly to the close' (OT).

[71] D'you know of the green tower?
D'you know of the cradle in it?
The children that are rocked in that
Cry aloud in misery.'

I am informed by Pfitzner's step-daughter, Frau Annelore Habs, that the
'green tower' is the Vatican prison, and that to be rocked in the cradle
meant to be tortured on the rack.

The transition from the vigour of Ex. 56 to the much slower pace with which he speaks is impressively controlled. His words are set to another prominent rising major seventh. The music of the Prelude returns, and the servants are left in no doubt that Cardinal Madruscht (Ex. 62 in C minor, again anticipating the next scene) will not tolerate any recurrence of their brawling.

Ex. 62

They swear to keep the peace, but we have our doubts: their cadence is in E flat. C major has given way to the other main key of the Act.

Scene Two

The Cardinal Christoph Madruscht enters. He is a powerfully built man who, despite his ecclesiastical robes, gives more the impression of a warrior, a nobleman. He looks serious and out of humour; as he descends the stairs, Novagerio goes towards him in a friendly and cheerful manner. They greet each other, shake hands, and then come downstage together.

Madruscht's Ex. 62 makes prominent use of trills; this is the 'German Bear', although, as we shall see, this may be a libel on the original.[72] Novagerio has described him as one not to be trifled with, and in his brusqueness and that of his music we feel that he is capable of being utterly ruthless if the need arose. Novagerio shows him such respect that he seems to fawn on him.

The long musical paragraph which follows is based on Ex. 63, heard first in the strings, and at once drawn out into one of Pfitzner's typical long lines of melody.

---

[72] *Cf.* p. 259, below.

Ex. 63

This is the more prepossessing side of Madruscht; but the key is the conflict key of E flat. On the other hand, Ex. 62 is generally in C minor, the same key as the Spaniards. At Novagerio's mention of the Kaiser there is the inevitable C major reference to Ex. 29. When he refers to Bologna, major mediant harmonies become the local tonic of E major and we hear a smooth chordal theme in the woodwind, representing that city (Ex. 64).

Ex. 64

This theme is a pictorial, rather than structural, feature, for it does not recur; but it balances the Rome and Trent motifs. Bologna is contrasted with 'German, inconvenient Trent', and we hear Ex. 38 in its former distant key of B minor, followed by the haste motif augmented.

This music now achieves a calmer form in the woodwind. Novagerio goes off at a tangent to talk about the weather – he describes the day as 'ein schöner Tag! Ein Gottestag!'[73] (one thinks perhaps of the opening of Act Two of *Der Rosenkavalier*). These words are accompanied by some C major

[73] 'A lovely day! A God-given day!'

woodwind chords that sound rather *Meistersinger*ish though in fact they are a quotation from Pfitzner's own song 'Herbstbild' ('Autumn Scene'), Op. 21, No. 1, of 1907, to words by Hebbel (Ex. 65).

Ex. 65

The picture-painting of this song is obviously appropriate (the month, it will be remembered, being November), but why Pfitzner should choose such a moment for self-quotation is unclear.[74] Perhaps the word 'Herbstesnebel' in the libretto sent his mind towards the song. Madruscht wants to stick to his original topic, and Pfitzner makes a fresh start with Ex. 63 in E flat.

Novagerio succeeds in getting away from him to greet Borromeo, who has just arrived. With a sudden modulation

[74] Other Pfitzner operas include somewhat esoteric self-quotations, after the manner of Strauss and Elgar. *Heinrich* develops the second half of the song, 'Der Gärtner', Op. 9, No. 1, and *Das Christelflein* makes use of the finale theme from the D major String Quartet, Op. 13.

to B major, a clarinet plays a new theme, Ex. 66, accompaniment to the greeting and conversation of the two legates, and subsequently drawn out into a long melodic line.

Ex. 66

Ex. 66 is actually heard in the figuration of the Prelude (eighth bar of Figure 2) and so is associated with the 'haste' of Ex. 56, but the listener is unlikely to be aware of the derivation. Clearly B major is effectively C flat in this context. The orchestra plays the 'discussion' theme, Ex. 33, leading to an orchestral accompaniment whose rhythm is that of Borromeo's Ex. 23. A reference to the Council theme, Ex. 7, in D minor follows, as Borromeo compliments Madruscht on his efforts to do his best for the Council, and Madruscht, to his C minor trills, offers Borromeo refreshment, duly brought by the servants to the sounds of Ex. 60, suddenly in C major. We are back in the key, and with the theme, which began Scene One – just as we were at the corresponding point in the First Act.

Scene Three

> [*Madruscht*] *goes towards a group of Italian ecclesiastics who have just entered the back of the hall. Novagerio and Borromeo remain in the foreground.*

Borromeo and Novagerio sit down to discuss in advance some of the matters which will be considered. At Novagerio's first reference to the Emperor, Ex. 29 is ingeniously split between the vocal line and the violas, though in a different way from the corresponding moment in Act One. Needless to say, we are still in C. Novagerio and Borromeo begin by trying to weigh each other up; their opening pleasantries are accompanied by instructions such as 'cautiously probing' and 'meeting his eyes' in the libretto. These formalities over, they sit down to share their 'fruit and red wine'. Back in B major as

before, we hear Ex. 66 and then a characterful new idea,
Ex. 67. Superficially this theme is associated with refresh-
ments, but here as elsewhere the implication is that sharing of
comestibles can be seen as confirming an alliance; there is also
a veiled association with the Eucharist, helped by the key of
A major, which is connected with spiritual matters. Novagerio has his own way of diplomacy.

Ex. 67

But now Ex. 67 leads back to 'Schnell zum Beschluss' and
Ex. 56 in F sharp minor. (Here the voice part is allowed four
syllables, whereas before it had only three.[75] The reason for
this is not clear to me.) We move to B minor, where Borromeo
remarks with somewhat uncharacteristic ruthlessness, 'May
the blood of the heretics flow like this!' – uncharacteristic, that
is, in the context of his place among the warring elements of
the Council of Trent, but we can remember that Act One has
shown us the stern side of his character. There is a moment of
extraordinary orchestration here, with *col legno* violins and
stabbing flutes above the texture. But Novagerio and Ex. 67,
now in A flat, return us to a more civilised world. The
Emperor's Ex. 30 and later Ex. 29 in the bass, preceded by
references to the Rome theme for the Pope (Ex. 12) and to
Borromeo's plans (Ex. 35), accompany Novagerio's description of the behind-the-scenes negotiations between these
powers, in which Morone is an intermediary. Novagerio tells
of the danger that the Emperor's son may be inclined towards
the heresy of Lutheranism; when he refers to 'der Lutherpest'
the orchestra turns Ex. 29 into the most famous of all
Lutheran chorales, 'Ein' feste Burg'. (Pfitzner's invention in
these scenes is amazing, and nowhere more than in the
variants he achieves of Ex. 29.) But the Spaniards will stand
firm, and we hear a combination of Ex. 61 (the Spaniards)
and Ex. 29 in canon with itself (Ferdinand and Maximilian).

[75] *Cf.* p. 178, above.

Act Two, Scene Three (photograph by Helmut Koller, Vienna)

For once the key is not C but C sharp minor/E major. Pfitzner's liking for graphic illustration appears here in the libretto: Novagerio describes the beliefs of the Emperor's son as 'sour grapes to the old fox – he leaves the sweet ones on the vine', and in illustration he picks up one of the grapes he has been eating and drops it on the ground, to the accompaniment of Ex. 67. Perhaps the Emperor aims for the domination of the Catholic world (the Spanish theme, Ex. 61, on trombones combined with Ex. 29 again in C sharp minor), thus making a mighty union with Rome (Ex. 12), but to pacify the Emperor Novagerio suggests that his wishes as regards the matters before the Council should be granted (Ex. 29, back home in C, but giving way to Ex. 66 in B major). Borromeo says that there are important points here – Ex. 56*a* returns together with its inversion – but Novagerio, accompanied by impatient figuration, says that the Pope must have the last word:

Der Papst, der will – der Kaiser muss.[76]

[76] 'The Pope decides, the Emperor must obey.'

But as the Council is to have the upper hand over the Emperor, Ex. 29 is now in the Council key of E flat, together with fragments of Ex. 56, the first half augmented.

Now comes the topic of central interest to the opera, the question of polyphony and church music. Starting with the theme of Borromeo's plan, Ex. 28, significantly in D minor, Novagerio refers to Borromeo's success in debate and assumes that all is going smoothly as regards the composition of the trial Mass (Exx. 33 and 34). A very brief reference to Ex. 1*a* in diminution in A flat (strings, then woodwind, after the words 'Wie steht es mit der Komposition?'[77]) remind us that the real problem is actually that of inspiration. Novagerio hopes that all will soon be able to give their assenting vote of 'Placet' (Ex. 68, in G flat).

Ex. 68

Of course, Borromeo can report only that no progress has been made; the last he knew was that he had instructed that Palestrina be thrown into prison for his failure to compose the required Mass setting, and he has not yet been bailed out by Ighino's producing of the Mass manuscript (we are not told about this development until Act Three). Ex. 31 returns from Act One. Novagerio had thought that all was settled, 'like an Amen' – a line amusingly illustrated by a plain C major chord in the woodwind – but he can't remember the composer's name. Borromeo, with Ex. 4, reminds him; but Borromeo, remembering the arguments in Act One, is not pleased. Violins anticipate a new theme, Ex. 69, expressive of his ruthlessness, the Church Militant in action. For a moment he is able to keep his temper, Ex. 35 from Act One returning in a fairly placid A flat,[78] but then muted trombones suddenly

---

[77] 'How is the composition going?'

[78] Rectanus (*Leitmotivik und Form*, p. 118) points out that not only the key but also the instrumentation is all but the same as it is in Act One.

Ex. 69

break out with the F minor, over a discordant G, of Ex. 69.
Fame did not tempt Palestrina, and nor did the Pope's
specific wishes; here there is a first suggestion in the vocal line
and solo cello of the Pope's Ex. 70. (This is the Pope in
person; up to now he has been presented in his official
capacity only, by the Rome theme, Ex. 12.)

Ex. 70

This music coincides with another sudden shift in tonality, to
E major, but we soon go on to A minor and Novagerio's
amazement that 'a mere musician, a chorister' could be so
stubborn in the face of such high authority.

The leaping tenths in the vocal line and the violins show
that already Novagerio is thinking of using force. He is in a
hurry; there is still plenty of Ex. 56 to be heard. The quirks of
so insignificant a person must not be allowed to hinder the
progress of the Council of Trent. A new rhythmic variant of
Ex. 56*a* now makes its appearance, Ex. 71, referring to
Palestrina's imprisonment.

Ex. 71

The Pope and the Emperor would both be enraged by such a
delay, says Novagerio, and now more clearly we hear the
benevolent theme, Ex. 70, associated with Pope Pius, the
previous dissonant chromatics stepping up from the region of

F sharp to pure G major, followed by a diminution of Ex. 29 on, rather than in, C. In what follows, however, the inversion of Ex. 56*a*, carried through various regions to E minor, implies that for all Novagerio's impatience the writing of the Mass will be the solution to the problem. Novagerio's contempt for the Artist is clear:

Das kleine Menschenwerklein muss entstehn.[79]

A far cry from the mysteries of Act One! For the World the Mass is tiny almost to the point of insignificance.

Novagerio invokes the power and importance of the whole Council, with Ex. 59 in E minor, firmly anchored over a tonic pedal (and with a solo cello very busily filling in the harmonies). There is a mention of Borromeo's anger (Ex. 69). With major sevenths in the voice part and in an anguished violin solo, Novagerio makes his threat of force explicit:

Für solche Leute ist ein wahrer Segen
Des alten vierten Paulus' Institut![80]

A fragment of Ex. 59 in the clarinets reminds us of the Council's requirements. Sadly Borromeo remembers with remorse how he used to feel for Palestrina:

Er war ein Meister – wie beklag' ich ihn![81]

It appears that we are about to be given a lyrical and reflective interlude in slower tempo. The orchestra gives us Exx. 25 and 24 in violas and solo cello, there is a diminuendo, and a rising sixth takes us beautifully into B major – but all that Novagerio can say is:

Ei Freund, das Unverdauliche
Wird ausgespien.[82]

[79] 'This little man-made work must come to be.'

[80] 'The ancient institute of Paul IV
   Is a blessing for men like this!'

The 'ancient institute' in question is the Roman Inquisition; *cf.* p. 239 below.

[81] 'He was a master – how I mourn for him!'

[82] 'Friend, what is indigestible
   Must be spat out.'

and the B major turns out to be the comparative banality of Ex. 67.

The Cardinal of Lorraine has entered and is talking to Madruscht; their presence gives a suitable pretext for breaking off this uncomfortable conversation. With Ex. 62 in C minor we prepare for the E flat of the new scene.

We have reached the end of a long expository section (though not the end of the dramatic exposition of the act as a whole). Much of what has happened may seem to be mere illustration of local detail; but in fact we have now made exactly the same tonal progress as in Act One (to the end of a scene dealing with Borromeo's anger), from the neutrality of C, beginning Scene One and ending Scene Two, to B at the end of Scene Three.

Scene Four

> *During the last scene, the hall has been gradually filling up with laymen and ecclesiastics of all nations and ranks; they are now grouped mainly by nationalities [. . .]. From here onward the stage begins to fill up even more.*

Lorraine's grave E flat viola theme, Ex. 72, which is accompanied only by a tonic pedal, begins the scene and runs very beautifully through the following conversation; Lorraine and Madruscht are among the most serious-minded of the delegates, although the key shows that Lorraine is in reality a destructive influence.

Ex. 72

The viola line moves towards C flat, recalling the corresponding move in the Prelude. Madruscht pessimistically describes the gathering as 'mehr eilig als heilig',[83] with Ex. 56 reinforcing his words. He does not want to rush matters. He expands these criticisms to the sound of his trills, Ex. 62, and criticises

---

[83] 'More hasty than holy.'

Lorraine, to Ex. 72, for moving to the Italians' side. At Lorraine's counter-criticism of the Emperor we hear the predictable C major of Ex. 29, but Lorraine goes on to tell us, more significantly, the Morone has just at this moment returned from his mission. Novagerio is keen to get the Congregation under way; we move easily to D minor for Ex. 7 in diminution, while Ex. 56*a* creeps in in the bass. Madruscht, still cold and pessimistic with his Ex. 62, is cynical about the prospects of achieving anything:

> Da eine Christliche Einigung nicht zu erzielen,
> Lasst uns, da wir denn doch nun müssen,
> Getrost das Ding zu Grabe tragen.[84]

And he goes to take his place. Ex. 72 appears on the dominant before going back to the tonic E flat for a full statement, rounding off another ABA section. The long passage since the beginning of the scene centred on E flat marks this as a critical stage in the Act; whereas before everything had been a consequence of the C major at the beginning of Scene One, from here onwards the Council's arguments take over in earnest.

Archbishop Brus of Prague has been on the edge of the group. His conservatism and his German background makes him Pfitzner's own mouthpiece as, to Ex. 58, nobly orchestrated in G flat with solo viola and cello in octaves, he comments sadly:

> Wie verwickelt und kalt hier alles geschicht.[85]

Madruscht grimly brings this conversation to an end after some tonal meanderings with a very final C minor cadence:

> Des Kaisers Wille – ist jetzt unsre Pflicht![86]

[84] 'Since we cannot reach a Christian agreement,
Let us, since we must,
Bring it to a decent end.'

[85] 'How deviously and coldly it's all done now.' John Williamson, who points out Brus' uniquely German position (*op. cit.*, p. 163), further notes that, perhaps for that reason, Brus is allowed to present 'ecclesiastical matters of great spiritual weight', and that his theme is much stressed whenever it appears.

[86] 'The Emperor's will - is now our duty!'

But now the mood lightens. The contingent of Spaniards has
assembled and in a long, self-contained paragraph derived
from Ex. 61 they poke fun at the horde of Italians. The music
is basically diatonic though with grotesque shifts from
C minor in and out of D flat and related areas. The phrase
structure is regularised, but complete symmetry is avoided
with some clever touches. The Count of Luna enters to mock
the Italians' baggage; his high spirits, scorn and self-
importance are well worthy of his family name. The same
bells that illustrated the donkey's yoke in Act One, Scene
Two, return at the words:

> [. . .] auf dem Eselein
> Kommt der Heilige Geist
> Aus Rom im kleinen Tornister gereist![87]

Another episode follows immediately: the Bishop of Budoja
enters flamboyantly and greets his Italian colleagues with
such lack of restraint as to justify the Spaniards' mockery.
Budoja's music is fresh, chatty and rather trivial, as befits the
buffoon of the Council who does not know when to be serious
(Ex. 73; note the presence of Ex. 56 on the solo clarinet).

Ex. 73

His key is D major. Again, when Budoja mentions expenses
for attendance, assuming that they will be available, Ex. 56*a*
in the bass warns that this will lead to trouble. Among
Budoja's satellites is the timid Theophilus of Imola, who has
his own chattery motif (Ex. 74).

---

[87] '[. . .] see the Holy Ghost
Riding all the way from Rome
In the satchel of a donkey!'

Ex. 74

By contrast, the pace at once slows beautifully and, to Ex. 58, now far away in E flat, the Archbishop of Prague is pointed out. 'Prague – is that in Germany?' asks a young doctor (a travesti part) – a nice instance of the lightness of touch with which Pfitzner continually invests these scenes. Budoja goes on to mention the heretics, the 'Lutherischen Schweine', and again 'Ein' feste Burg' is heard, this time in the strings (Ex. 75).

Ex. 75

Morone briefly reminds us of more serious matters, but now we move to B minor for the third episode: Abdisu, Patriarch of Assyria, has arrived. His outlandish high tenor voice and strange orchestral accompaniment with E flat clarinet and solo violin, in clashing tonic/dominant harmonies (Ex. 76), and an extraordinary pentatonic trumpet counter-theme, show how exotic and other-worldly he appears to the assembly.

Ex. 76

But in fact he, of all those assembled, is the only representative of the Home of Christianity itself. Compared with him, it is the others who are the strangers.[88] Budoja, taking his arm, finds him a place; Exx. 73 and 76 combine.

So far, although half the Act is over, all has been expository. The characters and ideas, together with their music, have been set out on a sort of palette before us; we have heard the main keys, and the increasing importance of E flat has prepared us for trouble. In the Congregation of the Council which follows, all are brought into conflict, as in a development section.

Preliminary overtures based on Ex. 59 silence Budoja and it is time for the Congregation to begin. Severolus, as Master of Ceremonies, stands and formally bids everyone to take his place. He is the Kothner of the Council and the $\frac{5}{4}$ rhythm of Ex. 77 may well be a conscious reference to Kothner's two bars of $\frac{5}{4}$ in *Die Meistersinger.*[89]

Ex. 77

The modal inflections and even rhythm of Ex. 77 are backward-looking elements which place Severolus firmly on the side of the Establishment. The theme effectively punctuates the debate which follows like a recurring refrain, though the notes are never exactly the same (another Pfitznerian trait). Severolus announces the ranks to the falling scale of Ex. 7, which, as Rectanus points out,[90] enables the notes to sink in pitch as the ranks diminish: first, starting on E, the Archbishops and Prelates; next, a tone lower, Ambassadors and Envoys; finally, a tone lower still, Theologians and Professors.

A tremendously impressive orchestral interlude in D minor describes the ceremony of place-taking, spelt out in detail by

[88] This observation is Chris de Souza's.

[89] *Die Meistersinger*, Act One, p. 314, in the Eulenberg miniature score; the observation is by Rectanus (*Leitmotivik und Form*, p. 129).

[90] *Ibid.*, p. 129.

Pfitzner's stage directions. First we hear Ex. 59, moving from
D minor to F for Severolus (Ex. 77). Fragments of Ex. 59
introduce the acolytes (Ex. 60 chromatically altered – these
are no longer mere servants), and then there is a full statement
of Exx. 7, emerging obliquely, and 59 in G minor, moving
back to D minor. This is one of the grandest passages in
German opera. Severolus, over a tonic pedal and with a most
solemn and beautiful violin countersubject, announces that
Morone, First Papal Cardinal Legate, will address the
assembly.

Scene Five
The General Congregation has begun. Three chords bring us
from D minor to the distant key of A flat, where Ex. 78,
appearing in cellos and basses, forms the musical basis for the
centrepiece of the Act, Morone's splendid address.

Ex. 78

A beautiful and important melodic phrase (Ex. 79) appears at
the words 'angels of peace', with another switch to a key a
semitone away, A major, the 'key of the angels'.

Ex. 79

Morone asks for the blessing of God on the Emperor, and
there is a magnificent full statement of Ex. 29. This, in its
usual C major, is so grand and striking a motif and so much
heard in this Act (the bold outlines of the theme making it an

event whenever it occurs) that the Emperor's presence is felt
as strongly as if he were there in person. Ex. 29 moves with
grand effect to a half-close on G; and G major is taken up as
the local tonic, without being further established.
There follows immediately a drawn-out version of Ex. 79,
as Morone appeals to his colleagues, after which G major
becomes minor. The Council has been appointed to work for
God (the dominant D of G minor turns into the tonic of
D minor for Ex. 59, then Ex. 7) and Morone's enthusiasm
and fervour are clear to all. He goes on to refer to the heretics;
Budoja interrupts to pray for their enlightenment, but the
spirit of the Council is that they should be cursed and cast
down into darkness. Amid the strength and nobility of
Morone's music Pfitzner is keen to remind us that the Council is not, in his symbolism, a force for good. For all that
Budoja is the buffoon of the Council, he stands closer to
present-day liberalism than do most of the other delegates.
The shouts of condemnation give way to more civilised
thoughts from Morone. Ex. 78 is introduced by the same
chords as before, but now transposed so as to lead from the
disruptive 'Council' key of E flat to the A major of the angels,
and this time the trombones double the theme. Pfitzner
refuses to repeat any idea literally if he can help it.
    It is followed by Ex. 56a in augmentation in the horns.
Morone's striking metaphor

> Auf dass der Windhauch schwellender Gelehrsamkeit
> Des Redeschiffleins allzuleichte Segel
> Der Demut stillem Hafen nicht entführe![91]

is accompanied by Ex. 7 (flute) and Ex. 79 (horn), starting in
F major and returning to A.
    Budoja interrupts once more to make mock of this high-
flown language to Theophilus (Ex. 74). But he is suppressed
by Severolus (we have a suggestion of the Master of Ceremonies' sense of his own importance), and Morone can
continue with Ex. 79 and a report of his visit to the Emperor

---

[91] 'So that the rising winds of erudition
    Won't blow the ship of Rhetoric away
    From its true haven of humility!'

Cf. p. 253, below.

*The Vienna State Opera production of 1969: Act Two, Scene Five
(photograph by Helmut Koller, Vienna)*

(Ex. 29, in C, of course). The rising fifth at 'und friedbereit' sends thoughts to Ex. 52. The music here is of a gloriously Romantic richness complete with harp arpeggios, the passage appearing almost unchanged in C major after its initial appearance in A. Luna, concerned with the reservations about the honour of the Pope, interrupts (Ex. 61, but with significantly angry sevenths in the voice part). Morone, however, is now interested only in securing agreement to the proposals he has brought. Are the Holy Fathers happy to agree in principle to the Emperor's 42 propositions and leave the details to be decided on by the Pope? Morone asks this to a repeated-note 'voting' figure, Ex. 80; this is Morone as diplomat and President of the Council, and the theme punctuates the debate which follows, appearing four times, always in G flat. It turns the scene practically into a rondo.

Ex. 80

Yes, everyone is happy to pass by these difficult problems with so little effort – 'Placet, placet',[92] everybody cries (Ex. 68, in a naive G flat). Avosmediano's 'Non placet' (Ex. 81, with the major seventh of Discord) changes the mood suddenly; perhaps they were not expecting disagreement.

Ex. 81

Non pla-cet!

Avosmediano feels that the Synod is there to discuss questions, not to pass the buck. The inversion of Ex. 56a is

[92] The use of this Latin form of assent – literally, 'it pleases' – survives today in the degree ceremonies at Oxford and Cambridge.

developed here in combination with the major seventh with a symphonic determination. Lorraine suggests that each individual point should be voted on, and there are no dissenting voices when Morone puts this to the Council, the Placets this time in G major. Yet Ex. 56*b* tells us that things are still being hurried. The first point is that of church music. Morone quotes Ferdinand's words that we have already heard from Borromeo in Act One (Ex. 32). The keys are the same, but the orchestration is ennobled by a solo trombone doubling Morone's vocal line an octave higher. The chorale has again put a stop to the motion; this time the music is restarted in a different way, by the voice alone. The Pope has agreed with the Emperor's view, but Avosmediano's previous dissent has woken up the Council to a more argumentative spirit, and there is fierce disagreement now. All the Italians are in favour, but 'Non placet' is heard from everybody else, and Avosmediano stands up as spokesman, to Ex. 56 inverted. There has been too much 'if-ing and but-ing', he says. Meanwhile Budoja, uninterested in the discussion, has noticed that the Patriarch of Assyria has fallen asleep (Ex. 76). Novageriq and Borromeo consult. After a hint of Ex. 69, the music pauses on a dominant ninth in G flat minor, apparently uncertain as to which way to resolve itself. With easy mendacity Borromeo resolves it into G flat major and collectedly informs the assembly that the trial Mass is being written. The legates remind one another that someone or other in Rome – Palestrina, the name was – is writing it; they are in a hurry to move on to the voting now, and Ex. 56 is heard in the lower strings. After their rather offhand 'Placet's Morone returns to G flat and passes on to the question of using the vernacular in the service.

A theme from the First Act, Ex. 28, returns. But now Brus interrupts, to Ex. 58. He feels that the points are not being dealt with in the right order, and that first should come the important question of the Eucharist. His words ('Das Abendmahl in beiderlei Gestalt'[93]) are set to a slow $\frac{6}{4}$ paraphrasing the Eucharistic recitative from the *St Matthew Passion* (Ex. 82).

[93] 'Holy Communion, in both of its forms.'

Ex. 82

A Spanish bishop shouts that it's only Brus who is bothered about it (Ex. 61) and falling major sevenths in the orchestra (Ex. 81 again) speak of more disagreement. We have reached E flat minor; the orchestral figuration that follows is that of the Prelude, and the impression gained is that musically we are now in a freely expanded and long-awaited recapitulation. Novagerio says that discussion of the sort suggested would take far too long, but now Luna, to the sound of Exx. 61 and 56, takes a hand. He insists that everything should be discussed as fully as possible. Perhaps this is deliberate provocation; but there is no doubt of it when, in answer to Lorraine's attempted cooling reply (including Ex. 79) Luna tells Lorraine that his opinion wasn't called for. The music shifts back from A to C minor with Ex. 61, now heard extensively. Lorraine's anger becomes personal now, for he recalls that Luna has been given a special place of his own whereas Lorraine should take precedence over him (we are

reminded by Ex. 60 of the opening scene).[94] Tempers rise on
both sides, with rising sevenths everywhere – but now Budoja
interrupts for the third time. He speaks of sorrow at this out-
of-place bickering, but his manner is so exaggerated, the
orchestral accompaniment so unusual (trombone vibrato and
glissandi, for example), the vocal range so extreme, that all he
achieves is a 'Parody of the Prophet'.[95] The glissandi destroy
the C major tonality and Budoja moves from a sort of F to his
usual key of D before rising chromatically to a top B flat.
Severolus, reminded by Ex. 60 of his initial instructions, cuts
him short. This is a pity, because Budoja was doing something useful: helping to reconcile the arguing parties by giving
them a common target for scorn.[96] In any case, peace is now
restored as Morone returns again to G flat and normal business (Ex. 80 spaced out in the horn, combined with Ex. 60 in
cellos and basses *pizzicato*: Ex. 83).

Ex. 83

He asks for a vote on the question of Mass and breviary, but
the disagreements are as violent as before, again with the
Italians in favour and everyone else against. The figuration of
the Prelude and Ex. 56 inverted are again heard beneath the
uproar, the bass rising by semitone steps. Avosmediano
insists on his own way; if the discussion is not as full as he
would like, he will protest formally at the closing Session and

[94] The wholly unbecoming nature of this dissonance between events and
context is closely paralleled by St Luke 22, 24–26. It is easy to imagine this
passage being at the back of Pfitzner's mind.

[95] Rectanus, *Leitmotivik und Form*, p. 129.

[96] *Cf.* Shakespeare again: *Julius Caesar*, IV, iii; the Poet plays the same
role.

thereby ensure prolongation. The Italians are furious, and to ever-more-violent sevenths call Avosmediano a schismatic. But now Severolus stops the argument for another delegate's view (we hear Ex. 59 as well as Severolus' music, the violin line carefully portraying the gradually rising tempers as its intervals widen).

Budoja will not be kept quiet. Having made no headway with his last interruption or, a more charitable view, hoping to break up this argument as well, he has prompted the Patriarch Abdisu (who has slept through most of the preceding debate) to stand up and give his opinion on the last question he heard, that of church music. (This is Pfitzner's reminder of the context in which we must view what is happening.) Abdisu's comments are again accompanied by the other-worldliness of his music (Ex. 76 in its original B minor), and he has to be prompted further by Budoja as to Palestrina's name. As he gets it wrong, Ex. 4 is heard with the fourths augmented and the whole thing inverted: Ex. 84.

Ex. 84

None of the other Palestrina motifs is heard; this has nothing to do with music. Budoja is enormously amused, but if there ever was a time to avoid stupidity this was it. The Council's mood has become thoroughly dangerous. Luna calls out that all the world wants the debate prolonged (Ex. 61 again), but the Italians mock him: Spain isn't the whole world, and if he thinks it is, he should read Ptolemy. Budoja relishes saying this, on a high C. This is the last straw. Luna shouts that he will invite the Protestants to the Council, and what is practically a free-for-all breaks out. Everyone is on his feet and shouting, and even Abdisu is woken up. A massive orchestral *tutti* accompanies this chaos – through it Severolus' theme (clarinet, trumpet, trombones) tries to make itself heard, and

Ex. 61 is also buried in the texture. Abdisu is there, with Ex. 73 in deep woodwind and trombone, and so is Theiphilus (Ex. 68, on flute, oboe and clarinet). The music of the Prelude runs through the passage, and underpinning it all are the twelve strokes of a deep bell on F sharp and C: noon is striking. Incidentally, Budoja's high C and Luna's succeeding G flat (calling in the Protestants) anticipate this tritone. The whole passage is a remarkable display of contrapuntal and orchestral skill; and it exactly mirrors the bell climax at the end of the Dictation Scene of Act One, where the tritone was A-E flat.

Technically it makes an interesting contrast with the riot at the corresponding point in Act Two of *Die Meistersinger*. There the tumult is in the myriad of different voice parts – Sachs, Beckmesser, David, Magdalena, Pogner, Walther, neighbours, apprentices, journeymen, women, masters – all singing individual lines, while the orchestra keeps up an ostinato on a single figure. Pfitzner, making the music purely orchestral, leaves the singers to get on with their own stage business – a far easier task for producer and conductor to co-ordinate. Perhaps the result is still partially under control, with the different strands clearly audible in the orchestra; but then, as this is only a preliminary to the fatal happenings with which the Act ends, it is doubtless part of the general scheme. When at the end the servants fight, the musical content is far simpler, being merely a return to the figurations of the Prelude.

How is such a scene to end? Wagner reintroduces the Nightwatchman; Nuremberg clearly has respect for authority. The 'controlled' element of Pfitzner's riot is emphasised by the fact that in *Palestrina* the noise dies down more or less of its own accord, and Morone is able to restore an unwilling order. To a mixture of Ex. 56*b* inverted and Ex. 56*a*, he adjourns the Congregation until two o'clock. The same modulation as originally takes us from D minor to A flat and Ex. 78, followed by Ex. 59 in F minor. Musically this ends the vast section that the same music had initiated, at the start of Morone's address. Morone says that the debate must finish today. He asks everyone, and especially Luna, to behave peaceably (Ex. 79 in A major), and he dismisses them.

Scene Six

The assembled company breaks up, still arguing, gesticulating,
threatening. The Spaniards leave first, in a tightly knit group.
Some of the Italian ecclesiastics, including Budoja, still hang
around in the background.

As they leave, the Prelude's diminution of Ex. 57 breaks out
angrily in E flat minor, slowly dying away. Morone is much
relieved that so explosive a situation has been defused, but he
despairs of reaching agreement in the final Session. Ex. 56
and rising sevenths in the orchestra bass, minor now, reflect
the past conflict. Morone accuses Lorraine of provocation,
but Lorraine is still seething and will not concede any precedence to Luna. When Lorraine says that he will appeal to a
more liberal council we hear Ex. 7 again. In such a context,
reference to the nobility of the Council theme must be wholly
ironical. Morone continues, his words 'ganze Zeremonie',[97]
being set to a variant, Ex. 85, of the 'angels of peace' theme.
At least enough has been said to show that there is still a
possibility of the Council's being brought successfully to a
conclusion – as, of course, was indeed the case.

Ex. 85

All this time Budoja and the D major of Ex. 73 have been
trying to interrupt. Budoja has chosen now of all times to ask
about his travel expenses. Not surprisingly this is too much
even for Morone, who, having been close to achieving reconciliation (Ex. 79), now loses his temper and dismisses Budoja
with anger and contempt. The music sounds like Theophilus'
Ex. 74, shorn of its last three notes and combined with
Budoja's Ex. 73. Theophilus of Imola is not stated as being
among the group of Italians who 'still hang about in the

[97] 'Whole ceremony.'

background', and it seems more likely that this fragment should be read merely as a reference to the impatient music that accompanied Novagerio at 'Auslegung der Beschlüsse' in his conversation with Borromeo in Scene Three. And now Novagerio takes a hand. Modulating to D flat, he invites Lorraine and Morone to dine with him, to the reconciling and calming Ex. 67. Is that to their liking, he asks, to the words and music (Ex. 80) used earlier for voting ('Ist's euch gefällig, Väter?'). For a moment the two antagonists would refuse (a smoothed-out Ex. 81 – 'Non placet'), but then they think better of it, and light-heartedly establishing G flat with Ex. 62 ('Placet' turned into a symmetrical tune) they all depart together, leaving the stage empty.

Scene Seven

We have a moment to reflect on the dangers that have gone by, the conflict that has been defused, and to realise that the Council has been fortunate: a sort of peace has been reached. But only for a moment. The servants of the different nationalities have witnessed the dispute from the wings, and now, furtively, the tonality dissolves as they creep forward onto the stage, ominously accompanied by Ex. 56a rising in chromatic sequences. The Spaniards are angered by the insults to Luna and Avosmediano. They call the Italian servants 'dogs', repeating the insult more boldly. They are not only rushing the Council to a conclusion, they are also rushing to their own damnation.[98] The short, angular vocal phrases are based for the most part on intervals of a fifth or a tritone, drawn from the figuration of the Prelude. The Italians remind one another that they have been warned not to fight, for this is presumably how previous scuffles began. Rising sevenths and more intense orchestration mirror the rising tempers, the two sides come down to shouting insults at one another, with a shout the Spaniards draw their daggers – and suddenly we are in the midst of a full-scale battle. At this moment the tonality has at last taken shape as E flat. Amid all the presumed noise from the stage, the orchestra has returned to a full repeat of the

[98] *Cf.* p. 100, above.

opening Prelude, expanded and elaborated in orchestration. Now, though, to the same chord of C as in the Prelude, Madruscht has appeared at the head of a troop of soldiers. 'Shoot to kill' is the order; a volley of shots is fired; many fall dead; and those that are left are taken to be tortured. The interval of a major seventh, so often associated throughout the Act with the threat of force, is compressed into a single grinding dissonance.

Ist das der Sinn des heiligen Konzils?[99]

The Council theme accompanies these last words of Madruscht. But the G minor is wrenched back to E flat; and in seven bars the motif of haste which has dominated the Act, combined with the opening of Ex. 7 in the bass, brings it to its conclusion in the key with which it began.

In such a way does the Prelude round off the riot as well as resolving the tension built up with the same music when the priests were at the height of their earlier argument. In the same way the resumption of the bell music, suddenly pulled back into the main tonality, had rounded off the final scene of Act One as well as resolving the earlier, dissonant, bell climax.

The shooting of the rioters is a scene of horrifying brutality, as much so as anything in opera – not merely for the utter ruthlessness with which the servants are mown down but in the blatant hypocrisy which is felt the more strongly by its proximity to the almost identical pandemonium among the delegates in the Council. Only the dress and weapons differentiate between cardinal and servant. Only now, in this dreadful aftermath, is the blasphemy of the scenes in the Council felt for what it is.

We like to think that our anger, like that of Lorraine or Luna, is something we can explain away when called to defend man as a civilised animal. The riot scene shows that we are fooling ourselves; the border between man and animal is never far away.

---

[99] 'Is this the meaning of the Holy Council?' Bernhard Adamy points out (*op. cit.*, p. 36) that the emphasis in the word 'Sinn' recalls the 'meaningless' nature of Ighino in Palestrina's view; *cf.* p. 158, above.

Both musically and dramatically the whole Act is a master-piece. Held on the tightest rein by the unifying presence of Ex. 56, the dramatic power of tonality is illustrated with overwhelmingly effect as E flat gradually annihilates all the other keys. Without any reliance on pre-existing forms Pfitz-ner has constructed a musical span which sustains the Act throughout its eighty minutes and perfectly reflects and mag-nifies the drama. It also shares formal features with the First Act – the initial key progressions, the conclusion with a double climax in such a way as to give the impression of being an image in a distorting mirror. Overflowing with invention, it builds from the lightness of its opening through the discussion between Borromeo and Novagerio to the spectacle of the full Council in Congregation, interrupted by a series of cameos with disprove any accusation about the opera's lacking a lighter side; and we sense the storm coming as the Council becomes more heated, until the stunningly theatrical catas-trophe at the end.

Act Three

The Third Act is considerably shorter than either of the first two, and even more than the others it seems to grow naturally from the Introduction. The whole atmosphere is strange, not unlike the wanderings of the Prelude to *Parsifal*, Act Three, or even the desolation of *Tristan*, Act Three, if without its pained intensity. Indeed, the whole Act seems to me to have some-thing in common with *Tristan* – the recuperating hero with his faithful friend or friends, anxiously awaiting news from out-side. Palestrina is not in a state of delirium, but he is wholly bewildered; the stage directions[100] speak of the 'calm of the sick-room', and the whole situation suggests that he has gone through a severe mental trial. One has only to remember the extraordinary dissonance of the bell climax to Act One which described his reaction to the stress of the night, and the mentions of imprisonment in Act Two, to recall how severe that trial was.

---

[100]*Cf.* p. 207, below.

The music is unmistakable Pfitzner. The first sound we
hear is Ex. 86 in muted violas (instruments which are prominent throughout the act), and from it is built the whole of the
Introduction. Helmut Grohe has suggested[101] that the theme
represents Palestrina's 'submission to destiny'.

Ex. 86

The three repeated crotchets toll like bells again and again in
this Act. The key is at present B flat minor, a key which has
until now only been of importance in Palestrina's Act One
soliloquy. His mind is far removed from thoughts of creativity
or of the Council; it is the other side of the coin from the B flat
major of 'highest joy' at the end of Act One. The music
evolves seamlessly; the third phrase begins between the end of
the third bar and the beginning of the fifth, but it is impossible
to tell exactly where.

The music reaches a chord of C flat, over which a new idea,
Ex. 87, enters, repeated 'at an angle' over a first inversion of E
flat minor.

Ex. 87

The tolling crotchets return twice, moving back to the tonic,
where a solo oboe is followed by a brief silence. The music
begins again in the same key but this time there is an interrupted cadence to G flat before another new idea, Ex. 88,
emerges from a half-close on the home dominant.

---

[101] 'Wunder ist Möglichkeit', notes from the Deutsche Grammophon
recording, 1973.

Ex. 88

Strings extend a line derived from Ex. 86, leading to E flat
minor harmonies. Ighino is present, and a clarinet plays his
motif, Ex. 15; it is in D flat, one of the most prominent
appearances of this theme with major-key harmonisation.
Ex. 15 is repeated at once in E major (= F flat). The tolling
crotchets accompanied by a horn motif in the rhythm of
Ex. 88 move the music down to an unequivocal C sharp
minor. Woodwind quavers lead to Ex. 86 in the trombones,
now on the dominant of C sharp, and distant bells are heard.
A climax is built up, at the top of which we have not the local
tonic C sharp but a chord of F sharp minor over an F natural
in the bass. Trombones remind us of the theme of Borromeo's ruthlessness, Ex. 69; but there is a rapid diminuendo
and we are soon back in B flat minor with Ex. 86 and the
tolling crotchets, and an almost – but not quite – exact
repetition of the first three phrases. It is surely significant that
the two main keys of this Introduction – B flat minor and
C sharp minor – are a minor third apart, just as were each of
the main keys of the preceding Act; and in their contrast it is
possible to detect a sonata structure. (The 'classical' key for
the second subject of a movement in B flat minor would be
D flat (= C sharp) major.)

Scene One

*Palestrina's house, as in the first Act. It is early evening. The bells
of Rome can be heard ringing. There are five young choristers from
the Church of Santa Maria Maggiore in the room. Palestrina is
sitting in the chair; he is leaning back, his eyes closed, his arms
resting on the chair-arms. He seems to have aged. Ighino kneels by
his side, his head and hands leaning on Palestrina's left hand.
Behind the chair stands Giuseppe, Palestrina's frail old servant,
ready to give assistance if need be. There is an air of expectancy over
all, and at the same time the calm of the sick-room.*

We are in B flat minor again, and the bells are heard as the curtain goes up, along with Ex. 86. As one of the singers sings the first words, horns echo Ex. 87 to a slightly different rhythm. The singers' varying thoughts move the tonality to D flat and then G minor, reaching E flat minor for the Rome motif, Ex. 12, heard through a harmonic haze – the bells of St Peter's are ringing. The anticipated move back to B flat minor is again interrupted by G flat.

Palestrina gives his first indication of consciousness – who are these men? – and an oboe hints at Ex. 2. With an oboe solo Ighino, explaining that the Mass is being performed at the moment, moves towards D, but not for long as Ex. 86 restores the tonic. But the next reflections take us further, via G and E minor to an almost motionless A major when Palestrina enquires about his singers. A major drops to A flat minor, and the movement is slowly resuscitated with a version of Ex. 88 heard in the Introduction. Pfitzner's ability to sustain and control the slowest pace and to begin motion again without losing the overall mood is seen at its best here. An oboe and a flute refer to Ex. 12, reaching B flat; the rhythm continues in the lower strings. Woodwind and trumpet remind us of the Christe and Kyrie (Exx. 49 and 45) respectively, turning unexpectedly and with memories of the angels to A major. Palestrina recalls that he wrote the Mass in a single night. But all that he remembers of it is the loneliness of Ex. 39 (in C sharp minor as before), and, very distantly, the pain of imprisonment (trombones alluding to Ex. 69). He does not remember the music at all, for that was conceived and written down in the total absence of self-consciousness. The themes of the Mass are heard only when Ighino is speaking.

Ex. 86 recurs in several distantly related keys but it eventually returns to B flat minor, and here most of the rest of the scene stays. Ighino tells Palestrina of his emotions when his father was taken and put into prison. At the words 'nicht hab' da die Welt ich verstanden'[102] Ex. 86 is combined with a variant of the Council theme, Ex. 7, on the oboe. Ex. 88 is heard again. Ighino was concerned about the Mass (Ex. 15 on the oboe and Ex. 44 on a solo violin turn the tonality to

[102] 'I couldn't understand a world [in which such a thing could happen].'

D major), but his father was in prison, and now Ex. 71 returns in the strings to dominate the next few pages, moving sequentially back to the tonic. But now Ighino's father has been returned to him, and the sincerity of his joy is expressed by Ex. 15 in flute and clarinet, changing beautifully to the tonic major and with rich inner parts. The Christe theme, Ex. 49, appears in the second horn at the words 'die Messe durchklinget die Welt'.[103] With further fragments of the Introduction and with Ex. 4 Ighino finishes, and everything dies away almost to silence and stillness. The B flat minor which has never been absent for long in this scene and which proves how little spiritual energy is left to Palestrina now moves slowly in the direction of C major with A in the bass.

Scene Two

Suddenly in the distance and in the simplest C major mandolins are heard, accompanying distant voices. 'Evviva Palestrina! Long live the Saviour of Music!' are the words, all on the tonic chord of C. Here the C major of Silla's song is reconciled with the C major of the Pope, linked by the outdoor liveliness which introduces the latter. Some of the singers from the papal chapel burst in and confirm at once that the performance has been an enormous success, and the Pope is delighted. So full of enthusiasm are they that they have to start talking about their own part in the affair: 'We showed it off to its best advantage – truly, the performance makes all the difference!' This is where Pfitzner rather naughtily sets the line 'one could hear each word quite clearly' in such a fashion that the words are wholly inaudible. Musically, the scene develops on simple tonic-dominant lines, the chorus in $\frac{2}{4}$, the orchestra in $\frac{6}{8}$, not unlike the offstage mandolin music; the C major tonic remains almost unaltered apart from a couple of flatwards diversions. Eventually Ex. 89 emerges as the melodic basis. This appears just before a second group of singers enter to tell everyone that the Pope himself is coming to visit Palestrina in person. All at once Ex. 70 wells up in the orchestra, the Pope's train comes in, and

[103] 'The Mass rings out through the world.'

Ex. 89

finally Pope Pius IV himself. (The fourth and fifth in the
Pope's theme proclaim its family resemblance to Ex. 1.) The
Pope's beautiful words, which, it will be remembered, are
said to have been pronounced by him after hearing the Mass
in July 1565, should be quoted in full:

> Wie einst in himmlische Zion Johannes der Heilige hörte
> Singen die Engel der Höhe, also lieblich und hehr
> Tönte im Ohre mir die Messe eines andern Giovanni.
> Bis an dein Ende nun bleiben, Pierluigi, bei mir;
> Fromm die Sixtina mir leite, wie weiland dem heil'gen
> Marcellus.
> Fürst der Musik aller Zeiten! Dem Papste Diener und
> Sohn![104]

A few bars of complex orchestral accompaniment involve
flute, trumpet, harps, celeste and solo strings, including the
viola d'amore which has been silent since its one previous
appearance several hours ago and which is no more audible
now than then. There follows the motif of happiness (Ex. 52),
and the theme of the Mass itself (Ex. 51), both this time in
A major, as well as Ex. 69. As the Pope leaves, the repeated
notes of Ex. 86 have accumulated a rising scale which seems
to reconcile it to Ex. 70. By this time the tonality has sunk
back to F. But it does not relapse into B flat minor, and we
move sideways, as it were, towards A. Meanwhile Pfitzner
demonstrates in the melodic line (violins and flutes) the close
relationship between Ex. 70, Ex. 86, and – for reasons about

---

[104] 'As once in celestial Zion St John the Divine
Heard the voices of angels on high, just so was
My ear ravished by the celestial beauties of a Mass by another
Giovanni.
Stay with me now, Pierluigi, until the end of your days;
Lead for me the Sistine choir, as once for the holy Marcellus.
Sovereign of music through all the ages! Servant and son of the Pope.'

to become clear – Ex. 33, the theme of Borromeo's plan. The
music dies away in fragments, lower strings once more pre-
saging the first theme (Ex. 35) of the next section.
Borromeo has come, to make his peace with Palestrina.
(Well may he afford to do so, for his whole plan has been
vindicated.) Borromeo is contrite but nonetheless full of joy at
the beauty of the Mass – Ex. 45 in the cellos at the words 'die
Messe, süsses Licht!'[105] From stuttering beginnings in F sharp
or thereabouts, vividly pictured in the orchestra, the confidence of Ex. 52 and the angels' key of A are reached,
although with unexpected harmonies.

Both men's emotions at this time are too deep and complex
for speech to do them justice. Palestrina speaks of the 'breath
of love' coming from the shattered fragments of the vessel that
both men are. Ex. 52 in A, differently harmonised, and then
in B flat is succeeded by Ex. 51, first in that key and then,
significantly, in D minor. Borromeo can only repeat his
friend's name; the last time a distant echo of Palestrina's last
words in Act One ('den Frieden'), accompanied by the outline of Ex. 4. After the rising scales of fifths, Ex. 51, the music
comes almost to a halt with Ex. 4 on the dominant of
C minor; Ex. 34 returns in that key as Borromeo leaves, and
again the music slows down, this time on a second inversion
of B flat. Again nothing has really changed Palestrina's mood,
and another ABA section has been completed.

In B flat major, Ighino now comes forward, to the lively
music of the opening scenes of Act One, and of course his own
theme, Ex. 15. But it is now in D flat and harmonised much
more diatonically and 'obviously'; Ighino's warmth of understanding does not extend to his father's feeling now. His
father is the most famous man in the world (the fame and robe
themes, Exx. 20 and 19 from Act One shifting sequentially to
D flat) – the Pope himself has said so (Ex. 70). But Ex. 22
reminds us that fame is not everything to Palestrina. Ighino
realises one profound truth, however: his father must 'live
again', his composition must continue, and Ex. 15 recurs in
yet another new harmonisation, tenderly in B flat minor. But
Ex. 36 implies that maybe this is now the end of Palestrina's

---

[105] 'The radiance of the Mass!'

212   *The Music of the Opera*

inspiration, its juxtaposition to Ex. 15 confirming the link between them. He asks about Silla, and from Ighino's hesitant reply, voice and strings dovetailing to outline Ex. 9, he realises that Silla has indeed left to go to Florence (Ex. 10, a literal restatement in the original B major, though with subdued orchestration and much slower than at first). Ighino, however, will stay with his father. Again, though from a different direction, the voices crying 'Evviva' interrupt from outside in a contrasting C major, so Ighino, to a perky version of Ex. 15, begs to go and join those who are shouting his father's praises. This theme has gone through many changes of character since the beginning of the opera. Palestrina lets him go; for all Ighino's love and sensibility he is not a creative artist and he cannot understand his father's emotions and requirements at this moment.

Palestrina is again left alone; but this time he is not lonely. His life has achieved fulfilment and he knows that his work will stand more firmly as his achievement than all the world's praises can now tell. He can reject the world and live in pure contemplation. The unbroken C major gives way via G and B flat to B minor, where the 'music of the past', Ex. 32, richly and beautifully orchestrated, is recalled and is joined by Ex. 1a in its original D minor in the woodwind. Ex. 32 makes only three appearances in the entire opera, one in each act, but it is so large an inspiration, in every sense, and occurs at such important moments that each appearance is a major event in the work. Strings throw in the rising octaves of Ex. 7 as a very distant memory of the Council. Evening is falling over Rome; a solo violin outlines Ex. 12, and, as Palestrina's thoughts turn to memories of his wife, the strings give out a long-drawn version of Ex. 21, a solo violin echoed by a solo cello. We had expected the same interruption with a chord of G that had occurred in the Introduction to Act One; but the interruption is in fact in F sharp minor, duly turning to A major for the last time in the work. This was the most vital inspiration of all. The effect is of a drawing-together of elements, a musical recapitulation in brief; but one thinks, too, of Strauss, and the 'Hero's Works of Peace' in *Ein Heldenleben*. There, too, are memories of the past similarly reviewed in tranquil procession, though the context is far more profound here.

Trombone, tuba and double-basses play the Masters theme, Ex. 25, while simultaneously oboes, cor anglais and clarinet play its inversion. The circle is complete. In tones of subdued but almost mystical exhilaration, Palestrina sings his final lines.

> Nun schmiede mich, den letzten Stein
> An einem Deiner tausend Ringe,
> Du Gott – und ich will guter Dinge
> Und friedvoll sein.[106]

It is at this statement that the whole of the opera has been aiming; Palestrina's expression of his fulfilment is the fulfilment of Pfitzner's own conception. First the 'forging' motif (Ex. 44) is heard, then the full version of Exx. 2 and 4 as they appeared in Act One as the music makes its way from B flat back to the inevitable D minor. Ex. 5 returns in the flutes and clarinet. Palestrina plays a few bars on the organ, outlining the harmonies of Ex. 5, twice interrupted by ever more distant cries of 'Evviva', still in C major, from outside. The first organ phrase ends with a rising five-note scale reminiscent of the Mass theme, Ex. 51. On the second occasion the organ notes outline Ighino's Ex. 15, and finally the notes coalesce into Ex. 4. Two final 'Evviva's from very far off are heard; and woodwind and strings play the concluding motif of the opera, Ex. 6, ending in the same D minor in which the opera began with the 'letzte Stein' cadence. The last sound heard is a single sustained D on the organ as the curtain falls.

It is one of the subtlest and least conventionally 'dramatic' curtains in the whole of opera; for it is the expression of one of the most restrained and inward emotions which any composer has expressed. The sustained beauty and quiet intensity of these concluding pages are as moving in performance as many a more spectacular ending.

The differences between this Act and the two others are

---

[106] 'Now fashion me, the final precious stone
On one of your unnumbered rings,
Thou God! And I will be of good heart
And live in peace.'

obvious, and the fact that almost all that takes place passes without making any lasting impression on Palestrina is proved by the way in which the tonic B flat minor is hardly ever left for long enough to allow the real establishment of another key. The separate scenes pass statically in sequence. Only the recollection of Lucrezia is able to prepare the final resolution into D minor; and thus, thematically and tonally, the work is brought to its end with perfect quiet logic.

VII

THE HISTORICAL BACKGROUND

Palestrina and the Mass

The composer Giovanni Pierluigi da Palestrina is universally considered to be one of the greatest figures in the history of music. His reputation could almost be described as legendary: for every ten people who know of it, perhaps one knows his music. His reputation as the quintessential composer of Renaissance sacred polyphony is to some extent a product of the music historians and theorists who followed him. Even today the music student is taught to write strict counterpoint 'in the Palestrina style', according to so-called 'rules' which have been inferred from Palestrina's own practice; and in many cases the student will have only the most cursory acquaintance with the music he is supposed to be imitating. The legend embodied in Pfitzner's opera, that Palestrina was 'the saviour of church music', added to the aura surrounding this mystic figure.

He was born in 1524 or 1525 in the town of Palestrina in the Sabine hills near Rome. As a boy he studied singing in Rome, where his teachers included the Frenchman Mallapert and possibly Arcadelt, and in 1544 he returned to Palestrina as organist and singer. In 1547 he married Lucrezia Gori who bore him two sons: Rodolfo, born *c.* 1549, and Angelo, *c.* 1551. Pope Julius III now appointed him as *maestro di cappella* at the Julian Chapel in Rome, and in gratitude Palestrina dedicated his First Book of Masses (1554) to him. And on 13 January 1555 the Pope appointed him to be a singer in the Pontifical Choir. It is said that his tenor voice was not a good one; in effect he was composer to the Papal Chapel.

When Paul IV succeeded to the Pontificate in 1555, following the death of Marcellus II after a mere three weeks in office, he continued the reform of the Papal Chapel, its music and its singers, begun by his predecessor. He excluded married men from the Choir, and so Palestrina had to seek another post. He was appointed successor to Lassus as *maestro di cappella* at St John Lateran. His son Iginio was born in about 1557. The next few years saw him moving through a number of different ecclesiastical appointments, before returning to the Julian Chapel in 1571, and at the same time he was making the acquaintance of various important noblemen who acted as his patrons. His name was obviously familiar in widely spread circles: in 1567 he was nominated for the post of music director to Maximilian II in Vienna, but apparently he demanded too high a salary. At the time at which Pfitzner's opera is set, 1563, he was *Maestro di Cappella Liberiana* at another Roman church, S. Maria Maggiore.

Between 1572 and 1580 deaths from bubonic plague in Rome reached epidemic proportions; among those who succumbed were Palestrina's two eldest sons, his brother Silla and finally, in 1580, his wife. He thought of joining the priesthood; his musical output declined in quantity and he published nothing between 1575 and 1581, although in 1577 he and the composer Annibale Zoilo were appointed by Pope Gregory XIII to examine the chant books issued after the publication of the Breviary and Missal by the Council of Trent. But within seven months of his wife's death he remarried and his compositional fluency returned. Pope Gregory named him 'Prince of Music' in 1584. He lived in Rome for a further ten years before his death on 2 February 1594.[1]

Gustav Reese writes that 'Although Palestrina was a good composer of madrigals and a superior one of motets, it is as a composer of masses that he particularly excels'.[2] The *Missa Papae Marcelli* is his most famous mass; its being singled out from the many masses he wrote must inevitably owe much to

---

[1] Adapted from Gustav Reese, *Music in the Renaissance*, Dent, London, 1954, chapter 9.

[2] *Ibid.*, p. 469.

*Giovanni Pierluigi Palestrina: engraving after an original in the
archives of the Vatican Museum
(courtesy of the BBC Hulton Picture Library)*

the reputation surrounding it which was developed by the 'legend' told in the opera. The Mass rapidly became the most famous of all Palestrina's compositions, to the extent that 'pirated' versions became popular. For instance, Francesco Soriano, one of Palestrina's own pupils, wrote a paraphrase of the six-part original for two four-part choirs, with various Baroque chromaticisms added. The problem of the exact date of composition of the *Missa Papae Marcelli* and its relationship to the Council of Trent is one of some difficulty. An excellent selection of documentary evidence on the question accompanies Lewis Lockwood's critical edition of the Mass[3] and I shall do no more here than summarise it.

Because the Mass bears the name of Pope Marcellus II, the natural assumption is that it was written in response to an event of Good Friday 1555. The Pope, according to the diary of Angelo Massarelli, Secretary to the Council of Trent, was displeased at the apparent joy occasioned by the singing of the mass on that day, and 'enjoined on them, that whatever was performed on these holy days [...] should be sung with properly modulated voices, and should also be sung in such a way that everything could be properly heard and understood'.[4] There had already been objections to the use in church of mass settings incorporating secular elements and requests that an appropriate use be made of the available modes,[5] but this seems to have been the first occasion on which mention had particularly been made of the intelligibility of the words. The *Missa Papae Marcelli* as it stands is notable for fulfilling these demands in two ways: first, it is based wholly on original material, without quotation from any secular or sacred external sources (the most important melodic elements of the work are used by Pfitzner), which is true of no more than one in thirteen of the total number of Palestrina's masses.[6] Secondly, and even more significantly, it is written with particular attention to the audibility of the

[3] Palestrina, *Pope Marcellus Mass*, ed. Lewis Lockwood, Norton Critical Scores, New York, 1975.

[4] Translation in *ibid.*, p. 18.

[5] *Ibid.*, pp. 10 *et seq.*

[6] *Cf.* Reese, *op. cit.*, p. 470.

*Pope Julius III receives Palestrina: woodcut
(courtesy of the Bavarian State Opera)*

words. The use of an elaborately contrapuntal style inevitably means that the underlay of the text varies widely between the different voices, which will often be singing different syllables at the same time. This makes it hard to hear the words, and in the *Missa Papae Marcelli* it is very readily noticeable that Palestrina restricts his use of such a style in those movements where the text is complex. There is no problem with intelligibility in, for example, the Kyrie or Sanctus, for these texts are very short and simple. But in the Gloria and Credo in particular Palestrina makes much use of chordal or 'note-against-note' writing, in which all voices sing the words together in the manner of a hymn. In an attempt to give numerical support to this view, Jeppesen[7] analyses the Gloria

[7] Knud Jeppesen, *The Style of Palestrina and the Dissonance*, Oxford University Press, London, 1946, p. 43. The other Masses are the *Missa ad fugam*, the *Missa Brevis, Ut re mi fa sol, Beatus Laureatinius* and *Assumpta est Maria*.

of six masses according to three different types of vocal entry.
The resulting table of percentages shows a significant difference between the *Missa Papae Marcelli* and the other settings,
in favour of increased word-intelligibility in the former. Such
figures never tell the whole story, but at least in this case they
confirm listening experience: the words in the most complex
sections – the Gloria and the Credo – are clearly audible in
any adequate performance.

So it seems that we are on moderately safe ground in
asserting that intelligibility of the text was a significant pre-
occupation of Palestrina in writing this Mass, more so than in
some of the works which followed. (All but one of the other
Masses analysed by Jeppesen were published later than the
Missa Papae Marcelli, which is a comparatively early work.)
What does this tell us?

In isolation, of course, it favours neither the supposition
that it was written in response to a comment from Pope
Marcellus in 1555 nor the plausible alternative that it was
written in response to the Canon of the Council of Trent on
Church Music published in September 1562. This called for
reform of music rather than the wholesale destruction of
polyphony. The first suggestion that the Mass was responsible for the preservation of church music is thought to be in
Agostino Agazzari's *Del sonare sopra il basso con tutti gli stru-
manti*, published in 1607:

> Music would have come very near to being banished from the
> Holy Church by a sovereign pontiff had not Giovanni Pales-
> trina found the remedy, showing that the fault and error lay,
> not with music, but with the composers, and composing in
> confirmation of this the Mass entitled Missa Papae Mar-
> celli.[8]

It will be noticed that this passage makes no reference to the
Council of Trent, nor does it make clear which Pope was
meant. Lodovico Cresollio, in *Mystagogus*, a collection of
essays on various 'sacred and erudite' subjects, published in
Paris in 1629, tells the story much as it appears in Pfitzner,
referring to Pius IV's determination 'to set the question of
banishing sacred music from the Church before the Council

[8] Translation by Lockwood in his edition of the Mass, p. 28.

of Trent' and Palestrina's setting himself 'to compose some Masses in such a way that not only should the combination of voices and sounds be grasped and remembered by the listeners, but that all the words should be plainly and clearly understood'. He says: 'This was told by Palestrina himself to a certain member of our society, from whom I heard it'.[9]

The story gained wide currency, and by 1828 we have practically the full version of it, including the commissioning by Borromeo, in Giuseppe Baini's *Memoire storico-critiche della vita e delle opere di Giovanni Pierluigi da Palestrina*. This first major figure in Palestrina study therefore dates the Mass to 1565, though he has more to go on than mere reportage. He cites an entry in the Diary of the Papal Chapel, Saturday, 28 April 1565:

At the request of the Most Reverend Cardinal Vitellozzi we were assembled in his residence to sing some Masses and test whether the words could be understood [. . .].[10]

These words give no indication, of course, as to whether the *Missa Papae Marcelli* was one of the works performed nor, if it was, whether it was written expressly for the occasion. But it is known that it was performed on 19 June 1565 at a High Mass celebrated by Borromeo before Pope Pius IV, and it is said that the Pope expressed his admiration of the Mass in words which Pfitzner put into the Pope's mouth in Act Three of the opera.[11]

Further evidence cited by Baini includes the fact that the Mass was entered in the archives of the Papal Chapel with two other Masses, one of which is known to have been entered in 1565; and that Palestrina's stipend was raised in June of that year.

On the other hand, F. X. Haberl, in 'Die Kardinals Kommission von 1564 und Palestrinas Missa Papae Marcelli',[12] challenges the palaeological evidence of the Papal archives

[9] *Ibid.*, p. 30.

[10] Quoted in *ibid.*, p. 21.

[11] *Cf.* p. 210, above.

[12] *Kirchenmusicalisches Jahrbuch*, 1892.

*Copy in Pfitzner's hand of the beginning of the Kyrie
of the* Missa Papae Marcelli
(courtesy of the Sammlung S. Kohler)

cited by Baini and opts, with some reliance on Massarelli's
diary entry, for a date of 1554 or 1555. This view has the
advantage of relating the date of the composition more
directly to its title. But there is no reason that Palestrina
should not have given the name of Pope Marcellus to a work
written later, bearing in mind that Pope's known views on the
subject of intelligibility which is so important a technical
feature of the work. In any case, the work was published
under its present name as part of the second volume of
Palestrina Masses, in 1567.

On the documentary evidence, therefore, the controversy is
undecided. Jeppesen[13] denies both Baini's and Haberl's views
on the Papal Archives manuscript; but he goes on to examine
the internal musical evidence and infers that the *Missa Papae*

[13] *Op. cit.*, pp. 99 *et seq.*

Marcelli was written after the *Missa Benedicta es*. The 'Christe' of the former is derived from the 'Qui tollis' of the latter, and as the 'Qui tollis' music is itself derived from the main theme of the *Missa Benedicta es*, it seems likely that the quotation is that way round – especially as the *Missa Benedicta es* contains several stylistic features which mark it as an early work and these features are not to be found in the *Missa Papae Marcelli*. And the *Missa Benedicta es* is known to date from 1562. Jeppesen then says:

> The *Missa Papae Marcelli* is to be seen as a composition for a particular occasion. [...] its probable date of composition would be between the twenty-second and twenty-fourth Sessions of the Council of Trent.[14]

Yet in saying this Jeppesen makes it clear that he has not provided conclusive proof; it is merely that this sequence of events seems the most likely. Whatever the truth, it is hard to doubt after considering the numerical evidence that Palestrina wrote the *Missa Papae Marcelli* with special concern for intelligibility of the words, and easy to believe that the reason for this was Pope Marcellus' expression of his views, or the decrees of the Council of Trent, or both. The most plausible reason for choosing the 1555 date is the name of the Mass; but if this aspect is overlooked, much is explained and made plausible by taking the date to be 1563 – most apparently the beginning of the evolution of the legend.

Pfitzner was well aware that the story he was using might easily be invention not only in detail but in essence. Ambros himself, Pfitzner's source, undoubtedly felt that the *Missa Papae Marcelli* was written specifically to make a technical point. Nevertheless Pfitzner's paraphrase of 'Iginio' to 'Ighino' for Palestrina's son, and the use of Palestrina's brother's name of Silla for an unrelated pupil in the opera are two examples of his readiness to alter details for his own ends; other examples will appear later in this chapter. As with any opera based on historical events, we must be cautious in assuming that any detail of Pfitzner's plot is historically exact.

---

[14] *Ibid.*, p. 129.

The Florentine Camerata

The story of the Florentine Renaissance is probably the most often told and the most important in the history of western Art. In Italy native pride in its artists from Giotto and Dante on grew steadily and comparisons were made with the glories of Ancient Rome. The year 1401 marked an important moment: in that year the Signoria (the City Council) and the Cloth-merchants' Guild of Florence promoted the competition for the making of the North Doors of the Baptistry, a competition won by Lorenzo Ghiberti who subsequently created the East Doors, the 'Gates of Paradise', as well.[15] There could be no doubting the difference of the new style as it swept through Italy in the fifteenth century, with its lucid use of Roman forms in architecture and its concentration on individual personality and unity of light and perspective in painting. The change from Gothic to Renaissance was accomplished swiftly and definitively.

No comparably strong caesura divides the music of the Renaissance from its immediate forerunners. With Dunstable, Dufay and their successors had come a new smoothness and balance in contrapuntal writing, more subtle harmonies with more emphasis on the third of the chord, and an increasing use of secular texts. The tendency was gradually towards a feeling for tonality as opposed to modality, but the latter was still strongly dominant. The text still plays a smaller part than the music in word-setting. The differences between Machaut and Palestrina are matters of increased balance, smoothness and refinement rather than the speaking of a new language. In Italy the musical Renaissance had a far less significant effect than in the visual arts.[16] The decisive change of direction arrived, as is usual in music history, much later than in the other arts, in this case nearly two hundred years later; but it was equally a consequence of classical influence.

In Florence between the years 1573–87 there assembled around the dilettante and intellectual Count Giovanni de'

[15] *Cf.*, for example, Vasari's 'Life of Lorenzo Ghiberti', *Lives of the Artists*, Penguin edition, Harmondsworth, 1965.

[16] For the reasons *cf.*, for example, Alec Harman and Wilfred Mellers, *Man and his Music*, Barrie and Rockliff, London, 1962, pp. 226–27.

Bardi a small circle of like-minded artists. They included the classical scholar Girolamo Mei, the poet Ottavio Rinuccini and the musicians Giulio Caccini (known as Giulio Romano but not to be confused with the Mannerist architect of that name), Vincenzo Galilei (father of the astronomer Galileo), and Pietro Strozzi. They shared a dissatisfaction with the treatment of words current in polyphonic music; often words were set to false rhythms or lost their expression in the contrapuntal whole. They complained, too, that often the words were inaudible, a complaint which was also being made with increasing persistence by the Roman Church. Mei had concluded that the music written for the Greek tragedies of ancient Athens had been devoid of polyphony and even, perhaps, of harmony, and as his fundamental interest was in literature he was quick to draw on this opportunity to advocate a style in which a truer value could be given to the words in vocal music.[17] He subscribed, too, to the theories of Plato, at any rate as followed in the then fashionable school of Neoplatonism,[18] and he fastened on one particular passage in *The Republic*[19] which implies that priority in song must be given to the words:

> Socrates: Surely the mode and rhythm should fit the words.
> Glaucon: Certainly.

What resulted from this theoretical approach was the new style of monody in which the voice declaimed in notes and rhythms appropriate to the text, supported by an accompaniment which was purely harmonic. As this harmony was found to require an effective bass line the way was open for the adoption of the *basso continuo*, an invention usually said to have made its first appearances in the music of Giovanni Gabrieli and Alessandro Striggio in Florence and Lodovico Viadana at Mantua; and from this technical novelty sprang the entire harmonically based style of the Baroque. Indeed, it

[17] Robert Donington, *The Rise of Opera*, Faber, London, 1983, p. 81.

[18] *Ibid.*, pp. 21 *et seq.*

[19] Plato, *The Republic*, III, 398d; translated by Desmond Lee, Penguin, Harmondsworth, 1955.

is hardly too much to claim that this was the beginning of a musical language which in essence developed continuously for three hundred years.

The first known work in the monodic style was Vincenzo Galilei's *Dialogo della musica antica e della moderna* of 1581; Galilei also set the *Lamentations of Jeremiah* and, from the penultimate canto of Dante's *Inferno*, the story of Count Ugolino. The results had a mixed reception.[20] From these beginnings, unfortunately now lost, Caccini began to develop the so-called 'solo madrigal', or song in *arioso* style.

Attention now shifts to a rival group to Bardi's, led by Jacopo Corsi. The two circles were certainly in contact as well as competition with each other. Corsi's principal composer was Jacopo Peri, and it was his development of what Donington calls a more 'open-ended structure'[21] that was the origin of recitative. Donington goes on:

> Recitative was quite certainly the innovation in and through which opera arose [. . .]. It was the flexibility and adaptability and open-endedness of early recitative which enabled it to solve the central problem of opera: the problem of declamation.

All the ingredients for the composition of opera were now prepared; it was required only for them to be put together. For the carnival celebrations at Florence in 1598[22] Corsi produced a setting of the familiar story of Daphne to a poem by Rinuccini. It was set to music by Peri, with additions by Corsi himself, and Peri's *Dafne* is generally granted to be the first opera. Unfortunately, again, the music is lost. The earliest opera known to us today is also a setting by Peri of a poem by Rinuccini, this time on the subject of Orpheus and Eurydice; it was written for the celebrations in Florence in 1600 of the marriage of Maria de' Medici and Henry IV, King

[20] Manfred Bukofzer, *Music in the Baroque Era*, Dent, London, 1948, p. 26.

[21] *Op. cit.*, p. 88.

[22] Modern dating is followed throughout. The complications produced by calendar changes at this time are too complex to discuss here. Robert Donington devotes an appendix to the problem (*op. cit.*, pp. 307 *et seq.*).

of France (who was represented by proxy[23]). Some of the music was provided by Caccini. Not content with this, Caccini wrote a complete setting of Rinuccini's text himself, incorporating the music he had written for Peri's work.[24] In dedicating his *Euridice* to Bardi, Caccini, referring to the circle whose ideas had influenced his work, used the term 'Camerata'.

The novelty of these works can still be appreciated today. The emphasis remains very much on poetic diction. For instance, it takes Rinuccini's Dafne 33 lines of florid Italian to announce to Orfeo the death of his wife. Musically the results are ascetic and often, frankly, dull, although for a listener in a suitably patient and Olympian frame of mind the classical restraint can be genuinely beautiful and involving. In the same way we have to adjust our impatient minds to the slower and wonderfully ritualistic pace of the greatest Greek tragedies. But it is also abundantly clear that this was a new and naive art, and it was not long before the need was felt for a more interesting bass and a more tuneful melodic line. The limitations of Peri and Caccini are highlighted by the emergence within a decade of an operatic composer of genius. Monteverdi's *Orfeo* was first performed at Mantua in 1607, and at once it can be seen how superior are the results when poetic diction is permitted to be subservient to vocal melody and dramatic expression. Within fifty years of the first opera the new art-form had been shown in Monteverdi's output to be capable of a range, variety and subtlety quite undreamt-of by the intellectual amateurs of Bardi's and Corsi's circles.

Yet the style could not have come to be without the work of the Florentines, and Monteverdi knew as well as anyone how significant had been the change. In an appendix to his brother's *Scherzi musicali* (Venice, 1607) he wrote of a *prima prattica* and a *seconda prattica*,[25] the 'first practice' or *stile antico*

[23] This practice seems to have been common enough at the time not to call for special explanation. (The Rev. Hugh Mead has suggested to me that it enabled the marriage to be annulled more easily if it were later necessary to do so.)

[24] Donington, *op. cit.*, pp. 130 *et seq.*

[25] *Ibid.*, p. 93.

corresponding to strict counterpoint after the manner of Palestrina and the 'second practice' or *stile moderna* for the new method based on monody and the *basso continuo*. In *stile antico* the smoothness of the overall sound was of more importance than expression of the words, while in *stile moderna*, initially at any rate, the priorities were reversed. ('Prima la musica, doppo le parole', or vice versa? – this question is the subject, three-and-a-half centuries later, of Richard Strauss' *Capriccio*.[26])

Never before had there been so consciously felt a division between two techniques of writing music; nor was there again until the twelve-note revolution of the early twentieth century, when once more a new, theoretically based, method of writing music was the centre of discussion by artists and cognoscenti. So, at any rate, Pfitzner felt; he could not have picked a closer historical reflection of the state of music as he saw it in his day than the conflict between Palestrina's style and the *stile moderna*, even though he had to dislocate his dates somewhat to have the Camerata meeting in 1563. For Pfitzner, the Camerata stood at a crossroads in artistic history of an importance out of all proportion to their musical qualities.

Today, however, the role of the Camerata is perceived by some as being more marginal. Nino Pirrotta[27] has drawn attention to the development of the monodic style from, on the one hand, pastoral plays with music (of which the fundamental work is Angelo Poliziano's *Orfeo* of around 1480) and, on the other, the *intermedi* composed for the intervals between the acts of plays, a form developed by the Florentines for the many celebrations marking weddings of members of the

[26] 'Prima la Musica, poi le Parole' is the title of a libretto by the Abbé Cesti, written for, and set to music by, Salieri. The title formed the starting point for Clemens Krauss' libretto for *Capriccio*, as described by Norman del Mar in *Richard Strauss*, Vol. III, Barrie and Jenkins, London, 1972, pp. 180 *et seq.*; Krauss changed Cesti's 'poi' to 'doppo'.

[27] Nino Pirrotta and Elena Povoledo, *Music and Theatre from Poliziano to Monteverdi*, Cambridge University Press, Cambridge, 1982 (*cf.* particularly pp. 221–48); Nino Pirrotta, 'Temperaments and Tendencies in the Florentine Camerata', *Music and Culture in Italy from the Middle Ages to the Baroque*, Harvard University Press, Cambridge (Mass.), 1984. I am indebted to Dr Dennis Fallows for drawing my attention to these works.

ruling Medici family. For example, the marriage of Ferdinando de' Medici and Christine of Lorraine in 1589 was accompanied by performances of Girolamo Bargagli's play *La Pellegrina*. The intermedi were composed by a variety of musicians, including Peri, Caccini and Bardi (who was also in charge of the celebrations) but also Luca Marenzio and Emilio dei Cavalieri, the latter the Superintendent of all the musicians of the Medici court. It was in the work of practical musicians such as Cavalieri and his team, rather than in the theories of amateurs, that we should now look for the immediate harbingers of opera.

The Council of Trent

It is neither easy nor helpful to put an exact date to the start of the Renaissance. But the Reformation is conveniently said to have begun on 31 October 1517, the day on which a local professor of theology called Doctor Martin Luther nailed a list of 95 theses to the door of the Castle Church, Wittenberg. This was a normal method of proposing topics for debate, but the content of these theses was to have enormously far-reaching consequences. Germany at the beginning of the sixteenth century was an unhappy country. The commoners were increasingly being pressed by the demands of their landlords, a result of a diversity of economic effects which bore heavily on the lower classes. The situation was not helped by the fact that the Holy Roman Emperor, Charles V (b. 1500, Emperor 1519–56), had inherited a large number of other territories apart from the Holy Roman Empire; these included the whole of Spain (and hence its newly acquired American possessions) and parts of Italy and Hungary. The political requirements of this huge empire caused him to be absent from Germany for long periods and in consequence he was not on hand to exercise a strong central rule.

In this increasingly messy society the Church was suffering severely, for it was failing to provide the spiritual consolation which should have been the reason for its existence. The clergy were becoming increasingly corrupt and worldly, while higher echelons were often filled by mere nepotism. In

Germany bishops were particularly criticised for their tendency to live the life of secular princes rather than spiritual
guides, surrounding themselves with pomp and spectacle,
while elsewhere, and particularly in Italy, the question of
episcopal residences posed another problem. Bishops would
live in Rome, installing deputies in their dioceses, while
drawing on the resources of the Papal court. They would hold
several bishoprics at once. In short, they were not fulfilling
their pastoral responsibilities. The whole question of the
obligation of ecclesiastical residence was at the centre of the
debates on reform at Trent. The Church was very wealthy –
another source of envy – and some of its riches had been
raised by the controversial practice of 'selling indulgences': in
return for a sum of money the Church would give the suppli-
cant a blessing which would show that some of his sins had
been forgiven, so reducing his time in Purgatory. It was
recognised that this practice could appear disreputable, but
since it was a major source of revenue, successive Popes – who
were as nepotistic as anyone else when it came to appointing
cardinals – were unwilling to do anything about it.

   This practice was one of the major targets of Luther's
theses. As a theologian he had worked out a doctrine that
salvation could come 'through faith alone' (*sola fide*), that one
must abandon oneself to the Word and that the services of a
priest were unnecessary to receive salvation. Thus the whole
idea of partially 'buying' salvation was to him a sin, and the
granting of indulgences, while not affecting the recipient's
state of grace, smacked somewhat of this worldly scheme.
Unsurprisingly, these revolutionary ideas caused Luther to be
considered an important heretic and his case was referred to
Rome. If the Church had had any foresight, he would doubtless have been burned at the stake, but his case came before a
liberal-minded cardinal, Cajetan, and was merely referred to
the Diet set up at Worms in January 1521. (In not challenging
this lenient view, the Pope ensured that he did not offend
Frederick the Wise, Elector of Saxony.) Although it put
Luther under the ban of the Empire, this prevarication saved
his life; he had received a safe-conduct to appear at Worms
and, before this guarantee could be recanted, friends kid-
napped him and hid him in the castle of the Wartburg. By

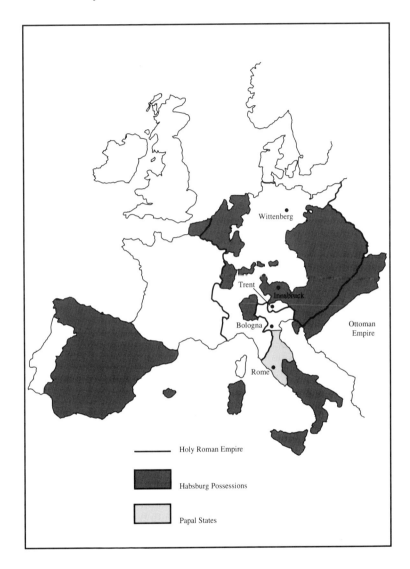

Western Europe in 1550, after Geoffrey Elton,
Reformation Europe 1517–59, *Fontana, London, 1963*

now he had become famous throughout much of Europe. His
ideas spread, helped by the printing press, and were taken up

by a number of German princes who in 1531 brought about a palpable split in Germany by their formation of the League of Schmalkalden. Progress was helped by the absence of the Emperor, who between 1521 and 1529 was fighting the French for control of parts of Italy, and because the Vatican had not yet realised the gravity of the problem.

When at last Charles V could give any real attention to the religious split in Germany, his attempted means of reuniting the country was to call a General Religious Council to discuss the differences and agree on compromises. This drift towards a Council was helped, too, by a tendency in the Church to think of the decisions of a General Council as taking precedence over the Pope's rulings. His plans might be called, therefore, those of Counter-Reformation. There was pressure for a General Council, too, from the Pope (Paul III, 1534–49), but his reasons were different. He wanted to be able to create a united Christian front against the infidel Turks who had been making warlike noises on the Empire's eastern border in Hungary, and also in the Mediterranean. A Council was convened and met in Vicenza in April 1538 but so few bishops attended it that the Pope adjourned it indefinitely.

Charles V's attention meanwhile continued to be distracted by, for example, the Ghent uprising of 1539 in which a popular government was set up, rebelling against an order which had apparently supervised the decline of the Flanders cloth trade. But he was able to achieve a conference of both Church parties at the Diet of Regensburg of 1541. Problems of unity were discussed but, with the Protestants refusing categorically to recognise the Pope, it was inevitable that no conclusions would be reached.

Meanwhile the Pope was beginning to do something about making good some of the problems of the Catholic Church in the so-called Catholic Reformation. There had been sporadic attacks on abuses even before Luther, but it was 1536 before any determined action was taken, when Paul III appointed a commission to recommend remedies. Results were slow. Bulls were issued but were simply ignored. A further cause of concern was that, if the Pope and the Curia were subject to too stringent a reform, they might lose so much power that they would lose control of the Church. It would be hard to steer a course between the extremes. After the report of his commission Paul III wanted to call a new General Council to make dogmatic rulings on many debatable problems of the Catholic religion. Yet Charles V still had his eye on repairing the Schism by means of a General Council, and so when the Council did eventually convene at Trent, in 1545, it was against a background of tension between Papal and Imperial views. As it was, the conflict was bound to go in the Pope's favour. Without the Pope's approval, the Council could not meet; the Lutherans would not acknowledge any council which had any Papal authority behind it; and without the Lutherans the reuniting of the Church was unlikely to be successful.

Why Trent? The venue had to be more or less neutral ground between Pope and Emperor, as well as being acceptable to the other nationalities. Ideally an Italian city in the Empire was required. Mantua, Ferrara, Modena and Cambrai were all suggested, Trent initially being thought too small and inconvenient. In 1542 Giovanni Morone was sent as Papal Nuncio to Germany to sound out views on the convening of the Council and managed, by some very skilful negotiation, to have the venue agreed – and the only way of agreement was to choose Trent.[28]

The purpose of the Council, then, was two-sided. The Pope's intention was to bring a unification and strengthening of the Catholic Church by defining fundamental Catholic dogma. This would decide which were the articles of faith as opposed to mere opinion. The Emperor saw it as an element in his grand plan for reuniting Germany. If the Council could bring about the reform of some of the abuses, a military victory of Imperial forces over the rebel German Estates could lead to an acceptance of the new Catholic Church by all

---

[28] The material so far in this chapter has been summarised from: Geoffrey Elton, *Reformation Europe 1517–1559*, Fontana, London, 1963; and Hubert Jedin, *The History of the Council of Trent*, Vol. I, translated by Ernest Graf, Nelson, London, 1957, especially pp. 16–29, 41–89 and 54–81. In subsequent footnotes, the first two volumes of Jedin's work will be referred to as 'Jedin, *History*' and the third and fourth volumes, which have not been translated into English, as 'Jedin, *Geschichte*'.

parties. The last thing that the Emperor wanted was a series of dogmatic definitions which would prevent any possibility that the Protestants might return to the fold. So to the two major powers of the day the Council was to some extent a political football. Its eventual achievements seem little short of miraculous when seen against this background, bearing in mind too that on many of the matters discussed individuals could be expected to hold strong and divergent beliefs as a matter of conscience. The start was at the very least inauspicious. Only a handful of prelates were present at the first General Congregation[29] on 18 December 1545; the French party, for example, had not made up its mind whether to recognise the Council. No agenda or constitutional structure had been arranged, so at first discussions involved only such things as who should have the right to vote (proctors of absentee bishops were to have 'not a decisive vote but a consultative one',[30] for example) and who was to sit where. Since the Emperor insisted that priority be given to discussion of reform and the Pope equally strongly on the priority to dogma, the Council had no choice but to agree to discuss the two aspects in parallel.

It was perhaps inevitable by its nature that the problem of reform should be almost completely pushed aside, and in the event all the significant decrees of the Council in this first period were on dogma. This outcome was not precisely because those present, being predominantly Italian, were biased in favour of preserving a system which was to their own advantage, but because, however good might have been their intentions in pronouncing reform decrees, no one could see how they would be enforced. At the back of many minds was the feeling that true reform could not come without an energetic lead from the Pope himself. With this in mind, the

---

[29] A 'congregation' was a meeting of some or all of the prelates in debate, under the direction of the President and legates. When a decree was completed, it was then voted upon at a 'session', a ceremonial occasion including a Mass and a sermon, at which no further conciliar business was carried out. Prelates voted by writing 'Placet' or 'Non placet' on paper, and could qualify their votes by written additions.

[30] Jedin, *History*, Vol. II, p. 20.

three legates, del Monte, Cervini and Pole (who were in charge of the proceedings, del Monte being President), deferred reform as long as possible, although most sessions contained at least a token decree on reform. The principal bone of contention was the problem of the obligation of residence of bishops. A decree on the reform of these abuses was voted upon at Session VI (13 January 1547), but the outcome was unclear – so many affirmative votes had contained qualifications that the legates found it hard to declare whether or not the decree had been passed. In any case, the problem had had no more than its surface scratched. Within two months came the translation to Bologna,[31] putting a temporary stop to the Council's deliberations.

In contrast, the Council had done a vast quantity of work on dogma. The published decrees were all strong in their condemnation of Protestant views, thus completely defeating the Emperor on this front. Whether the members were misguided or not, one can have nothing but admiration for the quantity of work achieved and the quality of intellectual discussion required to forge a unanimous statement of the beliefs of the Catholic Church. The first problem discussed was whether the Church's traditions should be regarded as having equal authority to that of Scripture (the answer was affirmative). The Vulgate was stated to be the definitive text of the Bible (despite its errors); the question of translation into the vernacular gave rise to much disagreement and it was eventually left to individual countries to make up their own minds. Next came the question of who should preach – whether preachers were sufficiently good theologians to present the Church's true views. This issue raised to prominence an underlying conflict between scholasticism – the 'studying of Scriptures in the commentaries of its scholastic expositors'[32] – and biblical humanism, whereby all the clergy should study the Bible itself in the light of modern scholarship. Appearances were in favour of the latter view until the Dominican representative Soto urged that 'Such a blow against

---

[31] *Cf.* p. 237, below.

[32] Arthur G. Dickens, *The Counter-Reformation*, Thames & Hudson, London, 1968, p. 115.

scholasticism would delight the Protestants'.[33] Thus matters
were left very much as they were – on the side of scholasticism. The Council also decided that bishops should hold
personal responsibility for those preaching.

Ahead now loomed the two biggest problems to be tackled.
The first was that of original sin – who contracts it and how?
How is man freed from it? Is he ever freed from it completely?
The answers to these questions were embodied in the decree
passed at Session V on 17 June 1546: the punishments of
Adam touched not him alone, but were transmitted by pro-
creation to the whole human race. Original sin is remitted by
the merits of Christ; baptism removes all sin, but concupis-
cence, which 'had never been regarded as a sin by the
Catholic Church', remained.

The second problem was by far the biggest and most
complicated of the dogmata that the Council had to discuss,
that of justification. Salvation seems absolutely gratuitous;
'can the sinner cross by his own strength the chasm created by
sin between himself and God?'[34] Are good works conditions
for the reception of grace, or tokens of grace already granted?
What is the connection between justification and the sacraments? Can one be certain that one is saved? Has the justified
man need of further justification for his sins committed after
receiving grace? These questions were so fundamental that it
took six months of the most intense work before a decree
could be put before a Session (hence the long gap between
Sessions V and VI). During the course of the debates there
was much heated argument, occasionally becoming personal,
and in particular Cristoforo Madruzzo, Pfitzner's Madruscht,
the Prince-Bishop of Trent and host to the Council, compromised himself seriously by appearing to favour the Lutherans.
He was one of only two Germans present, and he was in the
difficult position of having to attempt delaying tactics to give
the Emperor more time for his negotiations. The Legates
Cardinal Marcello Cervini (Bishop of Gubbio) and Seripando, the General of the Order of Augustinians, put their
utmost efforts into the preparation of a draft decree which was

[33] *Ibid.*

[34] Jedin, *History*, Vol. II, p. 170.

presented at the General Congregation of 23 September 1546. 'Justification must be preceded by an active preparation, proceeding from the concurrence of grace and the human will [. . .]. Faith justifies, of course in conjunction with hope and charity'.[35] Man is made just by faith and by the sacraments. These last two questions above were the subject of much discussion, but for the moment the results already achieved were much admired. On the question of the certainty of salvation views were conflicting and it was omitted from the decree. The second question was eventually answered in the negative, after a debate of remarkable length – on 26 October the Jesuit General Lainez presented a speech that lasted for at least two hours. Ten consecutive days of deliberation were required before the new draft was complete. At Session VI the decree was acclaimed unanimously as an outstanding achievement, the reform decree presented at the same Session took very much a backward place. But the mood of the Council was confident, and a further dogmatic problem, that of the number and nature of the sacraments, was introduced and ran its course with remarkable smoothness. (All seven sacraments were declared to be necessary for salvation, though not all for any one individual.)

But the efforts to prepare the decree on justification, particularly by the legates, had taken their toll. Many were exhausted and feeling old; a number fell sick; all were fed up with Trent. An outbreak of typhus in the city gave the legates the opportunity to bring about, in March 1547, the translation of the Council to Bologna, a move that had been sought for some time. This step was very serious, and one that the Emperor had most strongly opposed at all times, for a Council meeting in a Papal state would never be recognised by the Protestants, while a Council meeting in a city in the Holy Roman Empire might be. With the financial aid of the Pope, the Emperor was making war on the League of Schmalkalden, the Protestant Princes of Germany, and he had just achieved a series of substantial victories. Had he been able to include as part of his offer to the defeated parties the prospect of a united Church governed by the reforms of a universally represent-

---

[35] *Ibid.*, p. 241.

ative Council currently meeting at Trent, it is possible that a reconciliation might have been achieved. As it was, it was too late to repair the Schism. The Emperor ordered his delegation to remain at Trent; and so, although theoretically continuing in existence until September 1549 at Bologna, the first period of the Council was over.[36]

There matters remained until Paul III died in November 1549, to be succeeded by the former legate del Monte as Julius III. He came to terms with the Emperor and reconvened the Council at Trent in May 1551. The most important doctrinal decree to be issued during this second period was that of Session XIII of 11 October 1551, dealing with the important problem of the Eucharist, debates on which had taken place at Bologna.[37] The decree asserted the doctrine of transsubstantiation and condemned the varying Protestant views such as 'mere symbol' as well as Luther's interpretation of 'real Presence'. Also defined, at the next Session, were the sacraments of Penance and Extreme Unction, the latter removing from the soul the remaining effects of forgiven sin. More noteworthy, perhaps, was the fact that a small number of Protestants did attend the later Congregations during this period. They included ambassadors of several German Estates, such as Württemberg and Saxony, as well as from the Margrave of Brandenburg who, although Protestant, had not been a member of the League of Schmalkalden. But, inevitably, their presence produced merely argument: the Protestants wanted all the decisions of the first period, taken in their absence, to be reviewed, as well as insisting that a General Council must declare its lack of subservience to the Pope, while the Papal legates refused to let heretics involve themselves in the Council's business.[38] Results, therefore, were hardly fruitful and the chance was taken to close the Council again in April 1552. The Emperor had been concentrating too much of his attention on Trent to see the dangers

---

[36] Summarised from Elton, *op. cit.*, Dickens, *op. cit.*, and Jedin, *History*, Vol. II, pp. 1–41.

[37] Jedin, *Geschichte*, Vol. III, Herder, Freiburg, 1970, pp. 32–52.

[38] *Ibid.*, pp. 339–59.

threatening him when the Elector Maurice of Saxony forged an alliance with France. The Emperor was forced to rely on the support of his brother Ferdinand, whose forces were fully occupied in Turkey, and when Henry II of France captured Lorraine in March 1552 and Maurice led the army to the Tyrol, the Emperor took refuge across the Alps. At Trent, fearing capture by the nearby Protestant army, the prelates fled.

The Emperor Charles V made one final attempt to recover his lost ground but failed when the siege of Metz was raised in January 1553. Nonetheless, he retained the title of Emperor until January 1556, when he abdicated in favour of his brother Ferdinand, leaving Spain and the Netherlands to his son Philip II. Meanwhile the Diet of Augsburg (February–September 1555) produced a religious peace in which both Catholic and Lutheran Churches were to be tolerated in Germany, each territory following in general the religion of its prince.

Back in Rome, Julius III had died in March 1555 without bringing about the all-important Bull of Reform which he had promised. His successor was Cervini as Marcellus II but, as has been mentioned, his reign lasted for a mere 21 days, and he was followed by Gian Pietro Carafa as Paul IV. In 1542 Carafa had been given powers to set up a Roman inquisition along the lines of that in Spain. Paul III had kept its wilder excesses under control but now the Inquisition was given a free (and sometimes personal) hand. By effectively suppressing free thinking the Inquisition virtually brought to an end the Italian Renaissance, which had relied so much on individual originality of thought. Paul IV also seemed to want to play a leading role in world politics – he intended to drive the Spanish out of Italy, with the help of France. But the small amount of fighting which ensued emerged as a triumph for Spain, and the Pope returned to concentrate his attention on Rome. He died in August 1559, to the considerable relief of many who lived in fear of the Inquisition.

The new Pope was Pius IV, Giovanni Angelo Medici. He had Carafa's nephews, staunch supporters of their uncle's policy, executed. He kept the Inquisition in play, but for the most part his policy was one of gentle diplomacy. With the

240 240 The Historical Background

Treaty of Cateau-Cambresis[39] in February 1559 the dust was
able to settle after the hectic and multi-sided conflicts of the
last years of Charles V, and the Pope saw the opportunity to
complete the Council's business.[40]

With the abdication of Charles V and the Diet of Augsburg
it was clear that the Council was no longer seriously concerned with the problems of Germany. Instead, its political
intention in this final period was concentrated on the
threatened spread of Calvinism in France. If the French had
convened a National Council to discuss the matter, France
would surely have gone the way of Germany, so when such a
National Council was called for January 1561 the Pope took
the only possible course by announcing a General Council at
Trent. Immediately there were arguments about the apparently academic question of whether this was a new Council or
a continuation of the old one. The Emperor feared that a
'continuation' might upset the Augsburg settlement, while
the Spanish wanted a 'continuation' as an implied rejection of
previous decrees might bring further troubles in the Netherlands. The Pope managed to avoid any assertions on the
question, although later historians have always regarded it as
a continuation. The Protestants were again invited to the
Council, but they refused to recognise the Pope and stayed
away.

The Council had been called for April 1561 but delegates
were very slow to arrive, partly because of travel difficulties
and then the summer heat. The opening ceremony did not
take place until 18 January 1562. There were five new legates,
Gonzaga (the president), Seripando, Hosius, Simonetta and
Sittich, and at the solemn opening 105 bishops and eight
abbots were present. (By the close of the Council the numbers
had become 197 bishops, seven abbots, seven generals of
Orders, and nineteen proctors.) It was not long before a
dispute arose over precedence between France and Spain.
The questions of seating position and who was to receive first

[39] Verdians will recall from *Don Carlos* that the ratification of this treaty
included the marriage of Philip II of Spain to Henry II's thirteen-year-old
daughter, Elisabeth de Valois.

[40] *Cf.* Elton, *op. cit.*, Dickens, *op. cit.*, and Jedin, *Geschichte*, Vol. III,
pp. 2–75.

'the censer and the kiss of peace' at the ceremonies were felt to be of considerable political significance, and the entry of the Count of Luna as Orator of the King of Spain brought the problem into the open. His predecessor had avoided a clash, and it became usual for either Luna or the French Ambassador to be absent from the ceremonies, but on one occasion both arrived and the only solution was to omit the liturgical ceremony on that day. The legates soon adopted the seating plan known to us from contemporary engravings, by which Luna was given a special position in the middle, next to the Council secretary Massarelli.

Several dogmatic questions were to be discussed, and some progress was made with that of the 'communion of two kinds' – should the laity receive the wine as well as the bread, and does the communicant who receives both derive more grace than he who receives only the bread? After much argument the majority view was that it doesn't matter (i.e., that Christ is wholly present under either kind of the Eucharist on its own). Following objections the question was referred directly to the Pope, who confirmed this view against that of the Emperor. It was also asserted that the Mass is the sacrifice of Christ. On reform, a deputation set to work to examine the Index of Prohibited Books that Paul IV had drawn up (it did not report until 1564),[41] and another deputation drew up a long list of abuses in the Mass, for Session XXII on 17 September 1562. It was here that the question of church music arose; I have already explained that nowhere is there an explicit mention of a 'ban on polyphony', even when Moroni and Navagerio advocated monophony when the question was reconsidered at Session XXIV.[42]

The centrepiece of the entire period at Trent was the discussion focused on the bishops' obligation of residence.

---

[41] Among the books prohibited were not only all the works of the Lutherans but also those of Erasmus, Heliodorus and Machiavelli, as well as such apparently immoral works as Boccaccio's *Decameron*. I have been unable to find a complete list in a modern study of the Council, but the older libraries hold publications more or less contemporary with the Index, such as *Concilium Tridentinum*, Venice, 1631, which I have used here.

[42] *Cf.* p. 220–21, above.

Yet again the major point of conflict reached was apparently purely academic. Was the duty of residence a law of God or of the Church? The significance of the question was that it bore directly on the standing of the Pope; the duty of residence and the whole of episcopal authority both sprang from the same source. Was that source God, or was it the Pope? Naturally the Italian representatives inclined to the latter view, while the other nations, and in particular the Spanish, were strong in support of the former. The Spanish contingent was powerful – not so much numerically (there were never more than 24) as for their responsibility and unanimity of purpose. All had been selected personally by Philip II. An apparent breaking-point was reached at the General Congregation of 20 April 1562. To the question 'Should the Council declare that the duty of residence was divine law?' the voting was 67 for, 35 against, with 35 referring their vote directly to the Pope. This effective majority of three for the papalists caused such a stir in Rome that the Pope insisted that the debate must be adjourned. The Spaniards threatened to leave in the event of an adjournment, but a personal intervention from Philip II brought about some moderation and the debate was 'briefly' put aside in favour of questions of dogma.[43]

By this time the Council resembled more a party-political parliament, the arguments being conducted between parties of various strengths. Significant in many ways was the arrival at Trent on 13 November 1562 of a strong French party led by the Cardinal of Lorraine. He rapidly rose to be the unofficial leader of the 'opposition' to the papalist side, this opposition now consisting of three parts. The Emperor's supporters wanted the Council suspended because of the difficulty in carrying out the decrees in Germany, or at worst sought concessions in doctrine which would appeal to the Protestants. The French, blaming the Pope for abuses, were interested only in reform, threatening, if they were not successful, to 'appeal to a free Council' or, rather, to set up a National Council at home. The Spanish supported reform but they did not want to encroach on the authority of the

[43] *Cf.* Jedin, *Geschichte*, Vol. IV, i, pp. 116–37, and *Crisis and Closure of the Council of Trent*, Sheed and Ward, London, 1967, pp. 41–50.

*The Council of Trent: engraving by C. Laudy, 1565,
showing clearly the separate chair occupied by Count Luna,
'Orator Regis Philippi' (courtesy of BBC Hulton Picture Library)*

Pope. On the other hand, they were strong in their constitutional demands that they should be able to present for discussion whatever motions they wished, a practice which would undermine the authority of the legates. The arrival of the Cardinal of Lorraine had had the effect of focussing all these problems, and it was easy to foresee what was already a major crisis at Trent turning into a vast political conflict, the Council tearing itself apart in the process. Arguments between Italians and Spaniards grew ever more heated, each side condemning the other as heretics. Rioting among the lay factions supporting the two sides broke out in March 1563; it was quelled only by the co-operation of armed citizens and the local police, which had been specially strengthened on the orders of Ludovico Madruzzo, Bishop of Trent and nephew of Cristofero.[44] That same month, no doubt through mental strain and exhaustion, both Gonzaga and Seripando died, within little more than a fortnight of each other.

The two new legates were Morone and Navagerio. Morone was, says Jedin, 'the most capable diplomatist that the Roman Curia possessed at this time'.[45] As the most senior in rank of the legates he was automatically appointed president, and his first move was to spend four weeks at Innsbruck where he managed to convince the Emperor that the Pope meant business with the reforms. He obtained the Emperor's agreement on most of the controversial points, with only a few concessions.[46] Meanwhile the Pope wrote to Philip II and succeeded in convincing him, too, that he was seriously intent on reform. With these two powerful rulers converted to the papal side, opposition created by their parties at Trent was rendered comparatively impotent. Meanwhile, in Trent, Morone took a firm line in refusing the Spanish constitutional

[44] Jedin, *Geschichte*, Vol. IV, i, p. 270.

[45] *Crisis and Closure*, p. 102.

[46] Clive Wearing has suggested, in a talk on BBC Radio 3 ('Early Music Forum', 10 April 1982), that the Emperor's views on church music may have been influenced by the representations of Cardinal Albrecht of Mainz, and hence indirectly by Orlando Lassus, who was an employee of Albrecht at the time. (*Cf.* Hindemith's *Mathis der Maler*, in which Albrecht is a chief character.)

demands; concession would have slowed business down impossibly. He then dropped hints that Lorraine, who had been disappointed at not being made one of the Council legates, would be offered the legation to France, backing this with a flattering invitation to Rome, reviving Lorraine's hopes of being made a legate and appealing to his vanity. Lorraine's influence was already reduced: in February his brother the Duke of Guise had been assassinated, and the Guise power at the French court, hitherto substantial, was now much diminished. In addition the outspoken Lorraine had recently compromised himself in an over-expressed attack on the Roman Curia. When he returned from Rome with confirmation of his legature, he had been won over to the papal side. On 6 July 1563, Morone held long discussions with French and Spanish representatives and obtained their agreement on decrees concerning residence and ordination, and the Ordination Decree was accepted by a huge majority at Session XXIII nine days later. At the same time the Council passed perhaps its most far-reaching decree, instituting a network of diocesan seminaries for the training of priests. (This gave the whole Church a unified base for ensuring a supply of educated priests.) The Council was back on course.[47]

In September a new text for an article of reform was put to the Council and was discussed for three weeks in general congregations. It proposed that provincial and diocesan synods were to be held regularly; even those who had obtained 'exemptions' (a major obstacle to the authority of bishops) were to be subject to them. Bishops were bound by canon law to visit their dioceses every two years and would be subject to the authority of the appropriate Metropolitan who would ensure that their duties were being fulfilled. For some this decree did not go far enough, the Spaniards in particular demanding 'reform of both the head and the body' – i.e., of both the Papacy and Curia. Count Luna said that the reforming work had only just begun. (Now that the crisis was over, the Pope, of course, wished to finish the Council as quickly as

---

[47] Jedin, *Crisis and Closure*, pp. 101–20.

possible.) But the disagreements were few when the reform decree was passed at Session XXIV on 11 November.[48]

Some questions of dogma remained – marriage, indulgences, Purgatory, the Communion of Saints. Lorraine insisted on a conciliar decision (which would have prolonged discussions beyond Christmas), whereas the legates wanted simply to refer the questions directly to the Pope. A decree was rapidly proposed by a committee under Lorraine himself, but Luna objected to this and demanded full discussion of the remaining points. But he was outnumbered, and the date of a final Session was fixed for 9 December. At this point news arrived that the Pope was seriously ill. The legates saw that the possibility of a new conclave and the wish of the Council to have a say in it (as had happened during the Council of Constance in 1414–18) were good reasons for concluding business as soon as possible, so the Session was brought forward to 3 December. The remaining material was made over to the Pope, who by the time of the close was heard to be recovering. Lorraine gave a moving vote of thanks and the Council of Trent closed in tears of happiness and joy. All those present signed the official statements of the decrees, and on 26 January 1564 Pope Pius IV pronounced the Bull which confirmed them as Church laws.

There can be no doubt of the importance of the Council of Trent to the Catholic Church. In face of the threat of the Protestant movement and the ensuing 'competition for souls', the Catholics had given themselves a clearly defined collection of central beliefs founded on scholastic theology, and thanks to the institution of seminaries they would be better equipped for their task. It is true that some Catholic states, feeling themselves unrepresented at the Council, refused to allow publication of the Council decrees. But not only would bishops, elsewhere, be able to exercise their pastoral guidance from within their own dioceses; thanks to the institution of seminaries, the clergy would be incomparably superior in their education. Above all, the Papacy itself, which had undergone so many attacks during the Council,

---

[48] *Cf. ibid.*, p. 131.

The Council of Trent, painted by Titian (courtesy of The Louvre)

had emerged with its power enhanced, the unquestioned leader of the fight against Protestantism.[49] If in the history of sixteenth-century Europe the Council cannot be assigned so prominent a role, it was nevertheless at the centre of the acrimony which followed Luther, for a period of eighteen years – a period which saw the final frustration of Charles V's grandiose plans and the return of peace to Germany. Every ruler had to take it into account. And within the Council, in the battles that raged and the diplomacy that eventually overcame them, we can see what Hans Pfitzner saw: a microcosm of European politics.

Pfitzner's Council Scene

The picture that I have attempted to give so far of the Council of Trent is, more or less, that of modern scholarship. The opportunity of comparing this picture, that of the works consulted by Pfitzner, and the completed Second Act of the opera, is almost as fascinating as that of, say, comparing the Shakespeare chronicle plays with their sources in Holinshed and elsewhere. I am particularly indebted to the work of Dr Rudolf Kriss,[50] who has identified many of the sources for incidents used by Pfitzner.

In addition to 'the two great Council histories by Sarpi and Pallavicini',[51] Pfitzner was able to draw on the relevant volumes of Ludwig Pastor's gigantic *History of the Popes*[52] and the contemporary documents collected as *Diaries and Acts of the*

---

[49] Adapted from J. H. Elliott, *Europe Divided 1559–1598*, Fontana, London, 1968, pp. 145–74; Dickens, *op. cit.*, pp. 108–27; Jedin, *Geschichte*, Vol. IV, ii, *passim*; Jedin, *Crisis and Closure*, *passim*.

[50] *Die Darstellung des Konzils von Trient in Hans Pfitzners musikalischer Legende 'Palestrina'*, Hans Pfitzner-Gesellschaft, Munich, 1962.

[51] *Cf.* p. 36, above.

[52] Vols. XV and XVI, English translation by Ralph Francis Kerr, Kegan Paul, London, 1928.

Council of Trent.[53] Most of the detail comes from Paolo Sarpi[54] and Sforza Pallavicini[55] but these works form a powerful contrast: Sarpi the anti-papist monk and Pallavicini the Jesuit. Indeed, the title-page of Pallavicini's work says 'in which is refuted a history of the same Council, written under the name of Pietro Soave Polano, or Fra Paolo' (i.e., Sarpi), and it is not surprising that most of the less flattering incidents that Pfitzner incorporates are drawn from Sarpi. Jedin says that Sarpi 'views the Council of Trent as a highly successful deceptive manoeuvre on the grand scale, engineered by the Roman Curia, by means of which it renewed its power [. . .].'[56] Pfitzner, of course, used the German translations of both works. Pallavicini has never been translated into English, but copies of an early translation of Sarpi exist in some of the older libraries. Pastor is readily available in the English translation by Ralph Francis Kerr; the Diaries and Acts are available only in the original Latin.

As well as these works, Pfitzner had recourse, both in writing the opera and producing it in 1917, to a number of paintings and engravings. There are fine contemporary portraits of Madruscht[57] and Borromeo;[58] in addition, there is Titian's famous painting of the Council in Session (in the

[53] Concilium Tridentinum. Diarorum, actorum, epistularum, tractatuum, nova collectio, Görres-Gesellschaft, Bonn, 1901–; translation of excerpts here by Peter J. King.

[54] The Historie of the Councel of Trent, published pseudonymously in London in 1619 under the name of Pietro Soave; English translation published in London, 1620, referred to henceforth as 'Sarpi'. Pseudonymous publication was not uncommon at this time, especially when a book bound to be so controversial was concerned. A further factor in Sarpi's decisions to use a pseudonym, and to publish in London, may have been that his home city of Venice was notoriously antipathetic towards Rome and the Pope. (I am indebted to the Rev. Hugh Mead for this suggestion.)

[55] Geschichte des tridentischer Konzil, op. cit. The translations of excerpts were prepared for this book by Kate Caffrey.

[56] History, Vol. II, p. 578.

[57] Reproduced on p. 260, below.

[58] Reproduced on p. 258, below.

Louvre[59]) and a number of engravings. That made in 1565 by
C. Landy (or Laudy: the signature is unclear), for example,
labels the layout of the seating clearly, and sets Luna's central
position well apart from the others.[60]

Like any good dramatist, Pfitzner was not afraid to sacrifice
factual accuracy to the exigencies of drama. Nonetheless, the
opera-goer without knowledge of the Council will take away
with him a picture which is generally accurate, even if the
emphasis on the disharmony between the prelates is somewhat exaggerated.

The first point to be made is that Pfitzner is not concerned
to follow the historical lines of the General Congregations. At
these gatherings prelates would be asked in turn for their
opinions, which were often in the form of carefully prepared
speeches. Instead of this historically accurate picture, we are
given an open debate much more similar – and no doubt
deliberately so – to a modern parliamentary debate. The
Master of Ceremonies, or Speaker, is in charge, not the Papal
Legates; votes are taken on each point as it arises. One is
tempted to surmise that Pfitzner's Act Two bears a much
closer resemblance to Prime Minister's Question Time than it
does to any congregation of the Council of Trent.

Inevitably, too, the scene as portrayed is very much more
full of interesting incident than any one General Congregation
ever was, and in particular Pfitzner does not restrict himself to
the events leading to the final Sessions of 1563. Even the date
is not absolutely specified, for although the stage directions
talk of 'the last General Congregation before the ceremonial
conclusion' – i.e., 2 December 1563 – and details in the
libretto confirm this, at the head of the score Pfitzner speaks
merely of 'November and December 1563 [. . .]. Between the
first and second Acts is a gap of about eight days, between the
second and third about fourteen'. The reason for this vague-
ness is easy to find: central to Pfitzner's conception (though
not, in fact, taking any significant part in the completed Act) is
the debate on polyphonic music. This was discussed at the
Congregations before the 22nd and 24th Sessions, the latter in

[59] Reproduced on p. 247, above.

[60] Reproduced on p. 243, above.

the light of the Emperor Ferdinand's comments. The date of the 24th Session was 11 November and so by defining the dates as he has Pfitzner enables music to come under discussion without flagrant contradiction. In any case, as Kriss says, 'It was not Pfitzner's intention to present just one sitting, but to give a picture of the tendency of the last Council period of 1562-3'.[61]

Morone's report and the Emperor's views on the question of reform are described by Pallavicini:[62]

> Later the Emperor changed several things in the other Articles, changes that conformed to the Council's feelings, or which had been formerly suggested. For example, in the third Article, where effeminate singing had been forbidden in church, this prince hoped that no one would wish to abandon the polyphonic style of singing which, he said, encouraged piety.

Here are the Emperor's actual words:[63]

> Again, there are some other Articles too, about which we consider that our opinion must be explained to you as clearly as possible. Among these is the last Article of the third chapter, which decreed that the softer melodies of musicians must be rejected, and that a seriousness of tone must be retained in churches, as this is most fitting for the austerity of the church. If indeed this were to be enacted, that contrapuntal music should forthwith be totally removed from the church, we shall not approve, as we believe such a divine gift of music must in no way be pushed out of the church: the minds of men, especially those who are experienced in or devoted to this art, are after all quite often inspired to greater devotion by this very means.

The life with which Pfitzner has invested a wide gallery of different characters, most of them known to us by little more than their names and their part in the Council, is striking. Again, there is some licence involved: Pfitzner describes Borromeo as 'between forty and fifty, a tall intelligent-looking

---

[61] *Op. cit.*, p. 10.

[62] *Op. cit.*, book XXII, chapter v, paragraph 14.

[63] Translated in Pastor, *op. cit.*, Vol. XVI, p. 476, n32.

man with intense eyes',[64] and Palestrina as 'past fifty, his hair greying'.[65] But in 1563 Palestrina was only 38 or 39, and Borromeo 30. This is, of course, a less significant alteration than in, say, the Schiller-Mery-du Locle-Verdi *Don Carlos*, whereby Elisabeth de Valois is turned from a thirteen-year-old girl to a mature woman; but it is nevertheless an indication of the nineteenth-century outlook in Pfitzner's dramaturgy. The ages of the characters are adjusted to fit their dramatic roles.

Let us consider each of these personages in turn, in the order of precedence used by Pfitzner in his list of characters. Cardinal Giovanni Morone was born in 1508, the son of the Chancellor of Milan. His acute observation and grasp of important issues led him rapidly to be appointed Papal Nuncio to Vienna and then to the court of Ferdinand, where he displayed that 'uncommon aptitude for diplomacy which was to make Morone the ablest diplomatist of the Curia'.[66] His experience there aided his task of reconciling the disputing elements of the Council in 1563. In 1541, while travelling on papal business, he stayed in Trent with the newly appointed Bishop, Cristofero Madruzzo; this was doubtless influential in the negotiations which led to the choice of Trent as the centre for the Council. He was appointed Cardinal in June 1542. As we have seen, he became president of the Council in March 1563 and led it to its conclusion. The picture of Morone which emerges from the sources is unanimously that of a great man, dedicated to God and to the just solutions of the problems of the Council called in His name; the same picture emerges from the opera. Kriss makes the interesting point that 'Morone fulfils his function in his own world in just the way that Palestrina does in his'[67] – that Morone, like Palestrina, has to carry out a duty, one concerned with bringing a series of events to its due conclusion, to the glory of God. We are not, of course, shown the spiritual and mental

---

[64] Full score, stage directions, Act One, Scene Three.

[65] *Ibid.*

[66] Jedin, *History*, Vol. I, p. 333.

[67] *Op. cit.*, p. 18.

struggles which Morone surely had to undergo. But if there is a hero in Act Two of the opera, it is he.

The story of Morone's visit to Innsbruck dominates Pastor's Volume XV and is also found in Leopold von Ranke's *History of the Popes*.[68] Certain words of Morone's found their way into the libretto more or less *verbatim*:

Drum, liebe Väter, seid auf Eurer Hut
Auf dass der Windhauch schwellender Gelehrsamkeit
Des Redeschiffleins allzuleichte Segel
Der Demut stillem Hafen nicht entführe![69]

is from his report to the Council on his return, as found in *Concilium Tridentinum*;[70] later on:

So weit es nicht der Ehr' zu nahe tritt
Von Petri Stuhl, und dient zu Gottes Kränkung,
Ist alles Wesentliche ihm gewährt.[71]

is also from *Concilium Tridentinum*.[72]
His final words to the Assembly – 'In Frieden geht!' – come from his closing speech at the very last Session, on 4 December:

Cardinal Morone blessed the Councell; and dismissed them all; saying, that after they had given thanks to God, they might go in peace.[73]

– or, indeed, from the end of the Order of the Catholic Mass. Pfitzner naturally gives added importance to the single scene he is portraying by ending it with the closing words of the whole Council.

[68] English translation by Sarah Austen, Murray, London, 1851; Vol. VI, pp. 321 *et seq.*

[69] 'Therefore, dear fathers, be upon your guard,
So that the rising winds of erudition
Won't blow the ship of "Rhetoric" away
From its true haven of humility.'

[70] *Concilium Tridentinum*, Vol. IX, p. 473, §40.

[71] 'Save where the honour would be threatened
Of St. Peter's throne, God's glory,
He is assured of all he finds essential.'

[72] Vol. IX, p. 473, §29.

[73] Sarpi, *op. cit.*, p. 813.

At one point – but only one – Morone loses his temper, when he says to Avosmediano, the Bishop of Cadiz:

Den, welcher heute nicht von ganzer Seele
Den schleun'gen Ausgang der Verhandlung wünscht,
Den nenn' ich keinen frommen Christen![74]

which echoes a sharp answer given by Morone to the Spanish Bishop of Gerona on 10 November 1563:

The Bishop of Gerona complained, asking why the Fathers were being forced like this to make a hasty pronouncement; the Session ought for this reason to be prolonged [. . .].
Then the President said that a man who dared to speak out against the whole Synod did not deserve to remain in the Synod, as his words were a scandal.[75]

Sarpi[76] and Pastor[77] tell at length of the importance of Morone's mission to the Emperor, but Pfitzner condenses it into a few lines of dialogue between Borromeo and Novagerio in Scene Three: 'Beim Kaiser doch, was tut Morone?'[78] And Kriss[79] reminds us that even the 31-day duration of Morone's visit is not forgotten, being mentioned by Madruscht at the opening of Scene Two.

His suggestion that the debate should continue 'kurz mit ja und nein' so as to make a quick end to proceedings is taken from the Cardinal of Lorraine, quoted in Pallavicini:[80]

a proposal by the Cardinal of Lorraine, who wanted the other matters promptly dealt with after the next Session, by requiring a simple *Placet* or *Non placet* from the Fathers.

Morone is more or less drawn from life, but much less is known of the second Cardinal Legate, Bernardo Navagerio.

[74] 'Anyone who doesn't, from the depths of his soul,
Wish for a speedy end to these proceedings,
I say he's no true Christian!'

[75] *Concilium Tridentinum*, Vol IX, p. 962.

[76] *Op. cit.*, pp. 695 *et seq.*

[77] *Op. cit.*, Vol. XV, pp. 315–27.

[78] 'But what's Morone doing, with the Emperor?'

[79] *Op. cit.*, p. 17.

[80] *Op. cit.*, Book XXI, chapter XI, paragraph 4.

(Why Pfitzner wrote 'Novagerio' is not known.) Jedin[81] tells us that he came from a noble Venetian family, that he studied philosophy in Padua, that he was a chronicler of the relationship between Charles V and Paul IV, that at Borromeo's wish he sought good relationships with the French and the Spanish (hence his conciliation at the end of the Act), and that his sharpness was due to a choleric disposition. Pastor writes:[82]

> Navagerio, too, possessed, in addition to a truly ecclesiastical spirit, great diplomatic skill, of which he had given proofs as Venetian ambassador at different courts, and finally in Rome. It might therefore be hoped that he would be successful in restoring harmony among the legates.

From these few and generally colourless hints Pfitzner was able to create a character from his own imagination, a character described by Kriss as 'the type of cunning, calculating and ice-cold politician'.[83] I am indebted to Gerd Ueckermann for the observation that Novagerio stands in a line of 'scheming clerics' in German literature of Pfitzner's time, a line that also includes Machiavelli, Savonarola and Cesare Borgia.[84] Novagerio is juvenilely humorous to Severolus in Scene One, authoritative to the servants, slimily obsequious to Madruscht in Scene Two, and the single-minded politician for the rest of the Act, culminating in his callous suggestion to Borromeo of sending Palestrina to the Roman Inquisition ('Des alten vierten Paulus' Institut'[85]). He takes little part in the debate, but after the quarrels he is still determined to let no personal feelings stand in his way: 'Ohne Spanien, wenn's denn sein muss: wir müssen und wir werden'.[86] This is from Sarpi on the 24th Session:[87]

[81] *Geschichte*, Vol. IV, ii, pp. 31 *et seq.*

[82] *Op. cit.*, Vol. XV, pp. 280 *et seq.*

[83] *Op. cit.*, p. 19.

[84] *Op. cit.*, cf. also p. 81, above.

[85] 'The ancient Institute of Paul the Fourth'; *cf.* pp. 187 and 239, above.

[86] 'Without Spain if necessary: we must and will.'

[87] *Op. cit.*, p. 781.

And the legates answering, that these matters [concerning the Spanish Inquisition] were already decided, the Count replied, that if they should be proposed, he would not go into the Session, nor would he suffer any of his prelates to enter. Whereupon Cardinal Morone said, that if they would not go into the Session, it should be done without them.

Pfitzner obviously felt that such sentiments were more appropriate in the mouth of Novagerio than in that of Morone. But it is Novagerio who brings about the final reconciliation between Lorraine and Morone by inviting them to dine with him. Carlo Borromeo was the 'historical living embodiment [of the new ideal of a bishop]'.[88] Pastor writes of him at length.[89] He was born in 1538; when young he was a keen huntsman, and although already devoted to the church, where much work was entrusted to him by his uncle Pius IV, it was only later that he became a noted ascetic. The death of his elder brother Federigo at the age of 27 much affected him, resolving him to free himself from worldliness. Following the close of the Council of Trent he led a life of strictness: on one day in each week he would restrict himself to bread and water, and he would perform severe private penances. His life was seen in many ways as a model, and he was later canonised.[90] He represented an ideal of the enlightened clergyman, and he is much the most famous of the prelates at the last period of the Council. But his part in Pfitzner's Act Two is, although not particularly short, of comparatively little significance: he greets Novagerio and Madruscht in Scene Two, and then shares a substantial conversation with the former in Scene Three. But here his role is more or less that of straight man to Novagerio; he tells us little new about himself and is merely held up as a man in contrast to Novagerio's cold, determined statement of policies. Only at

[88] Jedin, *History*, Vol. I, p. 163.

[89] *Op. cit.*, XV, pp. 105 *et seq.*

[90] There are many churches dedicated to St Charles Borromeo. Two of the most famous are the exquisite Roman church of S. Carlo alle Quattro Fontane, built by Borromini between 1633 and 1668, and the Karlskirche in Vienna.

Er war ein Meister – wie beklag ich ihn![91]

does his full humanity emerge (memorably seconded by the orchestra). More of Borromeo is to be found in Act One than here, but this line is, up to this point, his most touching and human response, although his reconciliation scene of contrition is still to come in Act Three.
From there on, Borromeo plays little part in the proceedings. He has, in fact, only two more lines to sing. He is interrupted by Novagerio in welcoming Morone; and, when challenged during the debate, he replies with the simple statement:

Die Messe wird geschrieben.[92]

This is, of course, intended to be bare-faced dissimulation, for he does not know that the Mass is already written. He makes no further contribution to Act Two. Pfitzner drew on his sources here less for incidental detail than for the character himself, the character who dominates the first half of Act One.
Cardinal Cristoforo Madruzzo, Germanised by Pfitzner as Christoph Madruscht, is another strong figure from real life. As Prince-Bishop of Trent he was host to the Council and had much to do with the day-to-day arrangements and running of it. Jedin gives us a full-length portrait of him, describing him as having 'many pleasing characteristics that made him so popular with his contemporaries'.[93] His family background, and his importance in Trent, with its special location, gave him connections with both the Italian and German sides, and high among his many ambitions was to become papal legate in Germany and restore harmony between Pope and Emperor. But he lacked an element of shrewdness and statesmanship, and having had a secular education he was no sophisticated theologian, so it was understandable that he made a number of false steps, both inside and outside the

[91] 'He was a master – how I mourn for him!': Borromeo's words on Palestrina.

[92] 'The Mass is being written.'

[93] *History*, Vol. I, pp. 570–74.

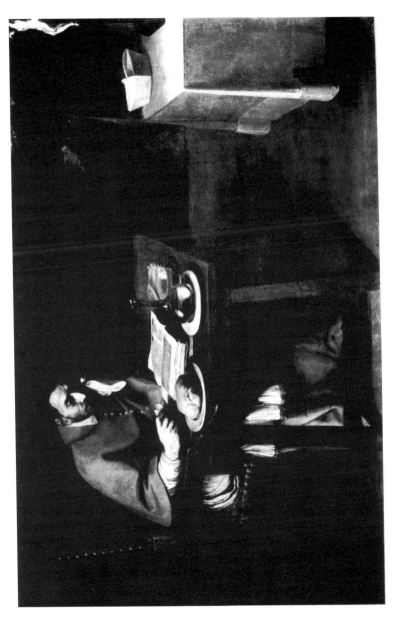

'The Dinner of S. Carlo Borromeo' by D. Crespi (1598–1630)
(Chiesa della Passione, Milan; courtesy of Edizione Alinari, Florence)

Council. On the other hand there was no doubt of his sincerity or of his personal piety. He was a dilettante who found a particular refuge in music at times of stress; he was a generous host who offered hospitality to his fellows of the Council on a magnificent scale, and almost ruined himself by so doing. Pfitzner does not omit the hospitable side of his character, but he gives much more emphasis to the side summed up by the epithet 'the German Bear', as Novagerio refers to him in the libretto. I have been unable to find any source for this epithet earlier than the libretto, and it seems at odds with the picture we have of Madruzzo; it would appear that Pfitzner took as a point of departure for the character of Madruscht the incidents of March 1563 described by Pallavicini[94] and in *Concilium Tridentinum*.[95] Here is the diary entry of Ludovici Bondoni Firmani, Master of Ceremonies of the Council from 1548 until its conclusion, for 12 March 1563:

> On the same day, while the Fathers were in congregation, there was a very fierce fight between the Italians and the Spaniards [. . .].
> On Friday, 12 March, at the nineteenth hour, the Italians attacked the Spaniards, and there was a major battle between them, so great that the whole population of the city was roused to arms; and there was for the whole day enormous confusion and uproar, with many Spanish wounded; two of them I saw with my own eyes being stoned, like St Stephen.[96]

Pallavicini expands this:

> On 8 March a dispute broke out among the servants of two bishops, one French and one Spanish, in which one of the French was mortally wounded. The story ran – whether it were true, or whether it were rumoured only, according to the custom of opposing fashion to fortune – that the Spaniards were guilty of atrocious violence in hurling themselves against the French. For this reason some of the Italians took it upon themselves to join in, to help or avenge the French. The Spaniards, angered by the Italians, began from then on to

[94] *Op. cit.*, Book XX, chapter 8, paragraphs 1, 138–41.

[95] Vol. II, p. 565.

[96] *Ibid.*; Stephen Willink suggested the translation of 'die Veneris' as 'Friday'. *Cf.* Chaucer, *The Nun Priest's Tale*, ll. 521–26.

Cristofero Madruzzo by Titian (1488–1576)
(courtesy of the Museu de Arte de São Paulo, Brazil)

insult every Italian they happened to meet. Frequent scuffles followed, and far from settling anything, each fresh brawl only served to nourish hatred and resentment. It reached such a pitch that the prelates no longer dared to send their servants out of doors, and hardly dared to out themselves, either to mass or to meetings, for fear of fresh disturbances. The two words – often heard in the open street – *Italy*, *Spain*, had the effect of a battle cry on the thoughtless, easily swayed crowds, and became a signal for combat, as though every one felt bound to defend his national honour by joining in the quarrel [. . .] and on 12 March such an affray broke out that it was more like a full-scale battle than a mere street brawl; it left behind many dead and wounded.

The delegates, faced by such a shocking tumult, had recourse not only to the Governor of Trent, D. P. d'Imola, but also to the Imperial Commandant, who was responsible for the protection of the city. He rang the tocsin and assembled a good number of soldiers who, for a time, quietened things down. But when the first fear had passed, the scuffles soon broke out again. This is why the President hastily sent a message to Cardinal Madrucci [. . .] and also to his father, Nicolas, who lived near Trent, asking them to come and control the riots and restore order. But the Cardinal's reply was long in coming, and his father was ill and could not make the journey. On the other hand, the ordinary militia was quite incapable of controlling the mobs, so it looked as though the only way out was to disband them. But this expedient could not at first be put into execution.[97]

Madruscht's loyalty to the Emperor and his disillusionment with the fickleness of politicians, the principal characteristics of his appearances in Pfitzner's Scenes Two and Four respectively, are attested to by Sarpi, for example:[98]

And Madruccio did not forbeare to say, that there was a secret Councell within the Councell, which did abrogate more authority.

But the stroke of ironical genius whereby the rioters are shot down in cold blood in the hall of the Council is entirely

[97] *Op. cit.*, Book XX, chapter VIII, paragraph 1.

[98] *Op. cit.*, p. 658.

Pfitzner's invention. It is enough to stamp Madruscht indel-
ibly in our minds despite his few, generally bitter, words early
in the Act and his almost complete silence during the
debate.

Charles de Guise, Cardinal of Lorraine, is the most important politician present at Trent, a member of the House of
Guise which was becoming the most powerful family in
France. The religious civil war that had broken out in France
in 1562 allowed the Guise family to assert themselves as
guardians of the Crown. But Francis, the Duke of Guise and
elder brother of Charles, was assassinated by a Protestant
fanatic in February 1563. His son Henry took over the duke-
dom and the leadership of the Catholic faction, and he sought
control of the government when Henry III came to the throne
in 1574. In spite of the King's refusal he went ahead with his
plans and as the Duke's power grew the King became increasingly desperate. Eventually he plotted the Duke's
assassination, which was carried out at Blois on 23 December
1588. The King found himself forced by popular opinion to
form an alliance with the Protestant Henry of Navarre but
within a year was killed by a fanatic. Thus the rule of the
House of Valois was ended.[99]

So at Trent it would be fair to say that, more than any of the
other nationalities, the Cardinal *was* his country. For much of
the Council he was an opponent of the Pope; his words in
Scene Six are a memory of this:

Und wäre,
Was ihm geschach, einem Franzosen widerfahren,
Beim ew'gen Gott! Ich reiste ab
Und appellierte an ein freieres Konzil![100]

This is taken word for word from the records of the Congregation of 1 December 1562.[101] But by the time of the last
Congregations he had been won over to the Pope's side ('Der

[99] Elliott, *op. cit.*, pp. 301–38.

[100] 'If a Frenchman
Were to experience what befell him,
By God, I tell you, I'd take my leave and appeal
To a more liberal Council.'

[101] *Concilium Tridentinum, op. cit.*, IX, p. 194n.

Lothringer hielt sich nicht länger mehr',[102] as the Chorus of Spanish Bishops informs us in Scene Four):[103]

> [Lorraine] who having received answer out of France, that he should give the Pope satisfaction in going to Rome, did so resolve so to do in the end of that moneth, so that the Session was celebrated. And he was forced to joyne with the Pope and his adherents.

Lorraine's principal antagonist was the spokesman of the King of Spain, Claudio Fernandez de Quiñoñes, Count Luna. As soon as he arrived at Trent the bickering over precedence, which had been going on for some time, broke out with a vengeance, and so serious did the problem become that there was a real danger that the Council might be torn apart. Most of what we know of Luna is concerned with his attempts to fight for the Spanish wishes, regardless of the consequences to the overall progress of the Council; he takes the precedence struggle not as a personal quarrel but as a trick to allow the question of the obligation of residence to fall into the background. Sarpi is predictably strong on the conflict.[104]

> After that the Pope had given distaste to the Spaniards, in not giving place to the Ambassadors, to appease them again, he gave eare to the instance of Varges, who had troubled him many days together, desiring that as meanes was found that the Count of Luna, the Ambassador of his King, might come into Congregations, so [...] His Holiness would find a way that he might be there also; whereof having considered well and consulted with the Cardinals, he resolved finally that a place, separated from the other Ambassadors, should be given to the Count in the Session also, and to remedy the competency which would be in giving the Incense and the Paxe, he gave orders that 2 Censers be used, and Incense given to the Frenchmen and the Spaniard both at once; as also 2 Paxes to be kissed at the same instant.
>   [...] on the sudden a murrey Velvet Chaire came out of the Vestrey, and was placed between the last Cardinal, and the

---

[102] 'The Cardinal of Lorraine could resist no longer.'

[103] Sarpi, *op. cit.*, p. 746.

[104] *Op. cit.*, pp. 727 *et seq.*

first Patriarch; and by and by the Count of Luna, the Spanish Ambassador, came in, and sat on it; whereat the Prelates kept up a great murmuring, Lorraine complained to the legates of this sudden act, concealed from him [...]. The legates answered that there would be two Censors and two Paxes; wherewith the French were not satisfied [...] the Masse proceeded without Incense or Paxe.

In addition Cardinal Gabriele Paleotti's *Acta concilii Tridentum* tells at length of the struggle.[105] Luna enters with a mocking description of the Italians as

[...] die Boten aus Rom
Mit dem Felleisen auf dem Rücken gereist?
Sie bringen den Heiligen Geist,
Der gibt ihnen dann die Beschlüsse ein.[106]

This is taken from a letter of the French messenger Lansac from Trent, dated 19 May, 1562:

[...] it pleased him to make the propositions [...] free, without prescribing any limits, nor sending for the Holy Spirit in a suitcase from Rome.[107]

Pfitzner makes this an incursion into the chorus of Spanish Bishops, which is a mine of references. Lorraine's 'winning-over' has already been mentioned. Finally, there is the peculiar comment:

Man merkt an der Majorität
Dass die Abstimmung nicht noch der Nation
Sondern nur noch der Anzahl der Köpfe geht.[108]

The question of whether voting at Trent should go by heads or, as at the Council of Constance, by nations, a method Jedin

[105] *Concilium Tridentinum*, Vol. III, pp. 674–79.

[106] '[...] the messengers from Rome
Carrying their baggage on their backs?
It contains the Holy Ghost,
Which will make their conclusions for them!'

[107] Pastor, *op. cit.*, Vol. XVI, p. 56n.

[108] 'One sees by their majority
That the vote will go, not by nations,
But simply by a count of heads.'

describes as 'objectionable',[109] came up in 1545, and both Sarpi[110] and Pallavicini[111] mention it. Here is Pallavicini:

[Sarpi] wrote that the delegates [. . .] requested, among other things, to know whether votes were to be counted by nations or by a poll of individuals. This part of his account is exact [. . .]. He goes on to say that they opposed the former mode, on the grounds that it would help to bring about a coalition between the bishops of each nationality, and make the majority Italian vote powerless. All this is just Sarpi's embroidery. The letter contains only the words: 'We do not know whether they wanted to try counting the votes by national groups'.

On the other hand, regarding the number of Italians present, Sarpi records that the French complained

for that the Pope had lately commanded other Prelates to goe to the Councell, that he might exceed in number.[112]

We see Luna in the opera at first as leader of the Spaniards and enemy primarily of the Italians; later this crystallises into the arguments about 'rushing to a conclusion'. We have seen why the different nationalities came to stand on different sides on this question[113] and Luna did indeed make a formal complaint (put in Avosmediano's mouth: 'protestiere feierlich wider den Schluss!') at the Congregation of 2 December 1563:

Meanwhile, Cardinal Morone had found out, from a sure source, that the Count of Luna was working with all his might to prevent the Session from being held [. . .].[114]

The five and twentieth of this month, the Count of Luna came to the legats, with an instance in writing. He complained that the most principal matters for which the Councell was assembled were omitted, and the others precipitated [. . .].[115]

---

[109] *History*, Vol. I, p. 533; *cf.* also Vol. II, p. 484.

[110] *Op. cit.*, p. 134.

[111] *Op. cit.*, Book XXII, chapter II, paragraph 42.

[112] Sarpi, *op. cit.*, Vol. VI, p. 585.

[113] *Cf.* p. 245, above.

[114] Pallavicini, *op. cit.*, Book XXX, chapter XI, paragraph 4.

[115] Sarpi, *op. cit.*, Vol. VIII, p. 802.

Count Luna, who up to now had not opposed the sitting being held on the appointed day, and the Council being wound up, now began to make open objections, egged on, as people said, by some of his compatriots. He said that the Council should not be dissolved with such speed, and adduced various reasons. He tried this business with Lorraine, the legates, and other speakers; but nearly all disagreed, and instead were amazed that he had put off such a significant discussion until the very last day.[116]

The catcalls about Ptolemy are, predictably enough, from Sarpi.[117]

And the Ambassador saying, that the Councell ought to be held open, because all the world did desire it, the Pope demanded what that world was which would have it open; the Ambassador answered, Spaine would; the Pope replied, Write into Spaine, that if they buy and study Ptolemy, they shall find that Spaine is not the whole world.

In July 1563 Luna had already proposed bringing in the Protestants:

all was upset by a request from the Count of Luna, which was expected, and which increased people's existing suspicions of him. This request was to invite the Protestants again to the Council; he tried to persuade the Pope to agree to it too.[118]

This threat was not as desperate as Pfitzner makes it appear; after all, Protestants had actually been present in the second Council period. In the opera it is as if Luna had threatened to call in the Devil. The near-riot that ensues never happened; the nearest to it occurred not on this occasion but on 1 December 1562, and through wholly different causes.[119]

The Patriarch of Eastern Assyria, Abdisu (Abd Isu, Ebed Jesu) of Mossul was invited to the Council as representative of the Eastern Church, but he never arrived. He travelled only as far as Rome before writing to the Fathers that his advanced

---

[116] *Concilium Tridentinum*, Vol. III, p. 757.

[117] *Op. cit.*, p. 802.

[118] Pallavicini, *op. cit.*, Book XXII, chapter I, paragraph 1.

[119] *Cf.* p. 269–70, below.

age (66) prevented him from going further. Sarpi introduces him.[120]

> The Masse being ended, the letters of Cardinal Amulius were read, who, as Protector of the Orientall Christian Nations, informed the Synod that Abdisu, Patriarch of Muzale, in Assyria, beyond Euphrates, was come to Rome, who had visited the churches, Rendred obedience to the Pope, and received the confirmation, and Cope from his Holinesse [. . .]. Afterwards his letters, directed to the Synod, were read, in which he excused his not coming to the Councell, by reason of the length of the journey [. . .].

Amulius wrote of him:[121]

> This man's outstanding devotion to God, and supreme sensitivity about the true faith we have noticed in several instances, but particularly in the fact that when he was departing he asked most earnestly that we should be sure to have the canons and decrees of this most holy Council conveyed to him.

So the operatic character, whose childlike naivety and sincerity are such a striking feature of the Act (contrasting so powerfully with those around him), is built up by Pfitzner from these few hints. His music immediately marks him as a man from a world apart; Kriss's view that his presence in the opera is 'our good fortune' can only be heartily endorsed.[122]

Anton Brus von Muglitz, the Archbishop of Prague, has no very large part in the history of the Council and he has only a few lines to sing in the opera, but he has an important role. He is the Emperor's spokesman (hence, perhaps, the young doctor's question: 'Prag – liegt das in Deutschland?'[123]), and he asks, in the debate:

> warum nicht nach der Reih
> Und alles einzelne für sich verhandelt wird?[124]

---

[120] *Op. cit.*, p. 572.

[121] *Concilium Tridentinum*, VIII, pp. 957 *et seq.*

[122] *Op. cit.*, p. 22.

[123] 'Prague – is that in Germany?'

[124] 'Why aren't the various points
Dealt with one by one, in their right order?'

This is from Sarpi:

> Prague spoke unto them, and told them, that much time was
> consumed in Councell with doing of nothing; that the legats
> had often promised to handle Reformation, and yet they were
> entertained with speculations, or with promises against small
> abuses; that it was time to make an effectuell instance that they
> would begin to handle important and urgent matters, and that
> if all would joyne in requesting the execution of so many
> promises, made by the Pope and the legats, there might be
> hope to obtaine.[125]

Another of the most striking 'originals' flowering from comparatively pale hints in the source material is Antonio
Chiurelia, the Bishop of Budoja (Budua in Dalmatia, now
known as Budva, and placed by Pfitzner in Italy 'so that the
Italian contingent could have a figurehead'[126]). Tradition
made him the comic of the Council, but Sarpi's description
suggests a different interpretation:

> The Congregation being ended Antonio Chiurelia Bishop of
> Budua, who, in delivering his voyce, was wont to entertain the
> Fathers with some witty conceit, and oftentimes to adde some
> merry Prophecies, which were spread abroad in divers parts,
> did then also deliver one concerning the city of Trent. He said
> in substance; that Trent had been favoured, and elected for
> the city; in which the general concord of Christendome was to
> be established, but being made unworthy of that honour, by
> reason of the inhospitality thereof, would shortly incurre a
> generall hatred, as the seminarie, of greater discords. The
> sense was covered with divers enigmaes, in a Poeticall
> Propheticall forme, yet not so but that it was easily under-
> stood.[127]

What could be a better description of Budoja's 'parody of the
Prophet':

> Weh! Weh! Frieden ist nicht mehr unter den Völken [. . .]?[128]

On the other hand, he took a lively share in debate (as seen in
a number of places in *Concilium Tridentinum* VIII and IX) and

[125] *Op. cit.*, p. 643.

[126] Rectanus, *Leitmotivik und Form*, p. 128.

[127] *Op. cit.*, pp. 698 *et seq.*

[128] 'Woe! Woe! Peace is no more among the peoples.'

was thought 'not only witty but also clever and judicious'.[129] Whatever picture we form of the historical personage, there is no doubt that Pfitzner turned him into a very vivid character – from his exaggerated entry hard on the heels of the Spaniards' disparaging remarks about Italians, followed by his high-handed assumptions about expenses, his determination to be the one to help Abdisu, his frequent and ill-timed interruptions during the debate, and his final failure to get anything out of Morone. His quip about 'französische Krätze und dem spanischen Grind'[130] is perhaps taken from Sarpi's

[Lorraine said] that, with his owne eares, he had heard some Italian Prelates scornfully use that scurrile Proverbe, which was already made common throughout all Trent, that is, That from the Spanish scab, we are fallen into the French poxe.[131]

Novagerio conciliatorily describes Budoja as 'Ein Freihart ist's, ein richtiger Hanswurst',[132] but in truth Pfitzner's character is more of a larger-than-life egotist, so bound up in himself and his own sense of humour that he cannot keep his mouth shut.

Melchior de Vosmediano of Guadix, imported by Pfitzner as Sarpi's 'Avosmediano', and with his see confused with that of nearby Cadiz, is little more than a name as far as the sources are concerned. Pfitzner required an ecclesiastical figurehead for the Spanish contingent and he chose this man whose speech led to the most unseemly happenings in the Council, the nearest recorded to the pandemonium of the opera:

In the Congregation of the first of December Melchior Avosmediano, Bishop of Guadice, speaking of that part of the last Canon, where it was determined that Bishops, called by the Pope, are true and lawfull, said, that the manner of expressing it did not please him, because there were also Bishops not called by the Pope, nor confirmed by him, who notwithstanding were true and lawfull [...]. And there followed a great

[129] Kriss, *op. cit.*, p. 23.

[130] 'Mangy French and scurvy Spaniards.'

[131] *Op. cit.*, p. 640. Both epithets – 'Spanish scab' and 'French pox' – are euphemisms for venereal disease.

[132] 'A jester, that – a genuine buffoon.'

noyse among the Prelates, as well as of whispering, as of feet, partly in offence of the Prelate that gave his voyce, and partly in defence [. . .] the Cardinall of Lorraine said, in presence of many of the Popish Prelats, that the insolency had been great, that the Bishop of Guadice had not spoken ill, and that if he had been a Frenchman, he would have appealed to another Councell more free [. . .].[133]

The last part of this quotation is imported verbatim into Lorraine's speech in Scene Six.[134] Lorraine means to threaten the legates with the formation of a French national council. Avosmediano's role in the opera is as 'mouthpiece of contradiction'[135] or more precisely as the mouthpiece of the *rational* wish to discuss matters fully (as opposed to Luna's merely obstructive tactics). He it is who utters 'non placet' during the voting; his music is the inversion of the 'haste' motif.

Where Pfitzner requires other clerics, for example, during Budoja's exchanges in Scene Four, he continues to use names mentioned in the sources, but that is all they are as far as the opera is concerned: Theophilus of Imola, Dandini of Grossetto, Drakowitz (Georg Droscovitius, Bishop of the Five Churches, described by Ludwig Pastor as 'impetuous and eloquent'[136]), the Bishops of Feltre and Fiesole. None of these men makes a major contribution either to the Council or to the opera. Theophilus, with the grand total of four singing lines and an extra mention by Budoja, is actually named in the list of characters on the title-page of the opera. But all these parts are usually allocated to soloists from the chorus, Drakowitz not even having anything to sing.

Of all Pfitzner's deviations from the sources the most extreme is the investing of Ercole Severoli – Promoter of the Council of Trent and consequently its legal assistant (his advice being 'sought in connection with the legal formulation of decrees'[137]), Prelate of the Curia and author of 'the most

---

[133] Sarpi, *op. cit.*, p. 635.

[134] *Cf.* p. 262, above.

[135] Kriss, *op. cit.*, p. 22.

[136] *Op. cit.*, Vol. XV, p. 295.

[137] Jedin, *History*, Vol. II, p. 511.

reliable diary that we possess, for the first period of the Council'[138] – as Master of Ceremonies Ercole Severolus. In fact, the post of Master of Ceremonies at the Council was held during this final period by that Ludovico Bondoni Firmani whose diary has already been quoted.[139] The duties of the Master of Ceremonies are unclear; during Congregations the order of speaking was under the direct control of the President and the other Legates, so no doubt the Master of Ceremonies functioned during the ceremonial Sessions. To the extent that the formal entrance of the prelates at the end of Scene Four is Severolus' moment and that this is a description of the formal Sessions,[140] the translation of names and duties is perhaps justified. At any rate Pfitzner dignifies Severolus with striking music which conveys both his ceremonial duties and his sense of his own importance.

His reference to Lainez speaking for two hours is also in the sources[141] – but there is no mention of any proposal to restrict the speaking time. Here is Pallavicini:[142]

> [Lainez] presented his paper on 20 October [1546] and it took the whole Session. His discourse was applauded as one of the best ever heard in the Council.

Finally, mention must be made of Angelo Massarelli, Bishop of Thelesia and Secretary to the Council. He is to be envisaged as taking minutes of the proceedings, and his diary, reproduced in *Concilium Tridentinum*, is one of the most significant and reliable of the contemporary sources. The prints of the Council show him sitting at a desk in the middle of the Assembly, and this arrangement is specified in Pfitzner's stage directions, although the character is given nothing to sing. It is interesting to note, by the way, that Novagerio's instructions on arranging the hall include his wish to have 'Massarelli's table as close to me as possible' – as if he had some intention of influencing the Secretary's writings.

[138] *Ibid.*, Vol. I, p. 527.

[139] *Cf.* p. 259, above.

[140] Jedin, *History*, Vol. I, pp. 576 *et seq.*

[141] *Cf.* also p. 178, above.

[142] *Op. cit.*, Book XVIII, chapter XV, paragraph 1.

In considering the contrasts and similarities between events at Trent and Pfitzner's staging of them, I have tried to locate those passages in the sources which are obviously referred to by the opera libretto. Needless to say, this presentation is far from the whole picture of these men that the sources can give us, and a thorough reading of all the material is necessary to decide whether and how Pfitzner was otherwise influenced in creating his characters. The records of the speeches made and votes cast in the Congregations and Sessions are of boundless interest in this context; they are reproduced in Volumes VIII and IX of *Concilium Tridentinum*, and the interested reader may care to examine them in more detail than is possible here.

There is no doubt that Pfitzner's Act Two is a magnificent dramatic achievement. In it a wide range of characters moves on a broad canvas, and all are most convincingly brought to life. Not even any of the minor characters are mere ciphers. (One thinks, for example, of Theophilus' 'Die Ketzer? O Jesus!') At the same time – and this is possibly even more remarkable – what we see is capable of stimulating our understanding of and interest in the Council of Trent itself. Many books have this quality of engendering enthusiasm for a specialist topic (one example that readily comes to mind is Dorothy L. Sayers' *The Nine Tailors*, with its campanological basis), but this is rare with opera. *Die Zauberflöte* on Masonic ritual, *Madama Butterfly* on Japanese custom, *Der Rosen-kavalier* on eighteenth-century protocol – these are comparatively marginal issues (more than marginal in the case of the Mozart, but there in any event very cloudy). Only *Die Meistersinger*, perhaps, and the rules of the Mastersingers can begin to compare with *Palestrina* in this respect. But it must be remembered that, tempting as it is to consider this Act out of context, it must be thought of primarily as the central panel of a triptych, representing the World that is hostile to Art. To some extent that must be self-contradictory; but it is our good fortune that the act whose symbolism is entirely negative should be so full of positive qualities.

VIII

CONCLUSIONS

Whether or not absolute standards exist in attempting to assess a work of art is an open question, and assessment becomes especially complicated when the work under discussion makes few concessions to convention. Such works, from Beethoven's Ninth to Brian's *Gothic* Symphony and beyond, have divided critical opinion; so has *Palestrina*. All one can do is to see to what extent the work achieves the aims of the composer and to what extent these aims are appropriate, bearing in mind all the time that any conclusions reached may be nothing more than personal opinions. The major difficulties of *Palestrina* are a direct consequence of the special nature of Pfitzner's conception, and in consequence it is bound to be misunderstood by anyone who approaches it as just another opera. On the other hand, an opera is not a philosophical treatise, and a composer is not entitled to make excessive demands of his audience for the sake of making a point which is neither musical nor dramatic.

The lack of interest shown in the work outside German-speaking countries resides partly in a built-in prejudice against a highly serious work by a little-known composer, and partly to real or imagined effects of 'national' characteristics. It remains incomprehensible to the English that Elgar's orchestral music, which speaks an orthodox European language with an accent that is more personal than regional, should be rejected by Germans; equally, there seems no reason that the music of Pfitzner, whose language is a tributary of the mainstream itself, should not be heard in a country where concert-halls are packed for the music of Strauss, Bruckner and Mahler.

Palestrina receives a quantity of adverse criticism, whose authors can usually be divided into those who have not taken the trouble to study the work sufficiently, and those to whom any German repertoire from Wagner onwards is anathema, including those for whom philosophy should be kept away from the stage altogether. Neither will *Palestrina* appeal to those whose enjoyment of opera is limited to good tunes and good singing – but then nor does *Tristan*. The most important of the elements which constitute the complete operatic experience is the quality of the music. Like most works of its kind, *Palestrina* requires several hearings for much of the music to 'settle' – and so we have the familiar vicious circle of ignorance and shortage of performances. The position is not helped by *Palestrina* being the work of a composer who is hardly known. Whereas *Die Frau ohne Schatten*, an opera of equivalent complexity, is regularly (if not frequently) revived and is widely discussed as an important work by a famous composer, *Palestrina* suffers from prejudice and over-hasty judgements born of ignorance, although it is much less uneven than *Die Frau* and its symbolism is more readily comprehensible. It is notorious that Bruckner and Mahler were all but unknown in Britain and America up to thirty or forty years ago; the reaction to them then is more or less the same as to Pfitzner now. A public that has come to a real appreciation of the time-scale and spiritual content of Bruckner should have no trouble with Pfitzner. I am sure that the Duo, the Sextet, any of the three Symphonies, the Quartets or either of the mature cello concertos would adorn the popular repertoire, given any sort of a chance.

For perhaps a good many opera-goers the first measure of musical quality is melodic invention. A first hearing of *Palestrina* may disappoint the listener hoping for a succession of big, extrovert tunes; but repeated hearings bring the conviction that almost everything is the right music in the right place, that is inevitably 'thus and not otherwise'. The sheer range of melodic invention, of so many different types, properties and characters, is one of the most extraordinary features of the score. The more familiar I become with Pfitzner's output in general, the more certain I am that he was one of the most gifted and individual melodists of his time. No one who has heard the last movement of the Violin Sonata, or of the Duo, can claim that Pfitzner was incapable of a big, warm, even 'popular' melody. The vast thematic content of *Palestrina* is superficially more restrained; but once assimilated the impression abides of a flood tide of richness. On the first occasion that I saw the complete work in the theatre I was uplifted not so much by the fascination and depth of the drama, or the logic of the musical structure, as simply by the warmth and generosity of page after page of the melodic lines – a response I had associated more readily with *Die Meistersinger*.

Yet there is more to the music than the melodic surface, beautiful as it is. The whole vital progress of the music, judged either as itself or as the expression of the drama, is tremendously coherent and subtle; taken as a whole, the result is a broad expanse of music, profound and full of nobility in its restraint, evolving inevitably and with tireless invention. The technical fingerprints – the harmonies, the direction of the modulations, the whole superb tonal structure, the remoulding of themes as they recur, the interplay of voice and orchestra, the phrase structure, the instrumentation, the overwhelmingly impressive blend of polyphonic and symphonic styles – combine to form a wholly personal musical language of which the composer is absolute master. More than that, each element is handled in a way ideally appropriate for the expression of this particular subject. If *Palestrina* is Pfitzner's masterpiece, it is because the choice of a symphonic opera on a subject blending past and present was perfectly suited to its composer's outstanding and individual musical gifts. The opera's beauties are many and they run very deep; there is treasure here for a lifetime.

As I have come to know *Palestrina* more thoroughly I have come to feel that its single most remarkable quality is the relationship between music and drama. Many operas have musical structures which do nothing but mirror the drama; a few are also satisfying in the abstract, as an independent musical form. It seems to me that *Palestrina* is unique: not only is its musical structure extraordinarily complete and self-sufficient, but that this structure reflects and is reflected by the drama, on the largest as well as the smallest scale, so that each casts light on the other. Wagner's operas concentrate on expression of the dramatic situation, as do most of Strauss'; in Korngold's brilliantly inventive works the abstract structure has not quite the same independent life;[1] more forward-looking composers such as Schreker, Busoni or Berg tended to impose abstract forms on the drama, with results that lead away from vast single spans to an overall design made up of many small cells.[2] Perhaps the operas which come nearest to *Palestrina* in this respect are Strauss's *Elektra* (a near-perfect marriage of music and drama) and the two operas of Franz Schmidt, though none of these approaches the ambitious scope of *Palestrina*. (In any case, the scenario of Schmidt's *Fredigundis* rules it out of serious comparison.) The scale, invention and interrelationships of the two structures of *Palestrina* are a never-failing source of wonder. As Max Hehemann, an early critic, wrote, 'I cannot believe that the Pfitznerian parallel between text and music has been surpassed'.[3]

As far as the dramaturgy of the opera is concerned, the problems posed are rather more serious. Firstly, of course, comes the 'second-act problem', notorious since the work's first performance:[4] the gulf between the outer acts and that of the Council at which the principal character is absent

---

[1] The use of tonality in *Die tote Stadt* makes an interesting comparison with that of *Palestrina*. Korngold uses B flat to represent true values and increasingly sharp keys – especially B and F sharp major – for the false values, the obsession with Marietta, which increasingly distort Paul's judgement. This association of ideas with keys is much closer to Pfitzner's usage than to Wagner's.

[2] In Schreker's *Der ferne Klang* the conflict between E flat and C major, representing respectively the true world of Fritz and Grete and the world of 'low life' into which Grete falls, also has analogies to Pfitzner's tonal structure. But the shape of the scenario itself is more episodic, and the tonal progress of the music reflects this more cell-like structure.

[3] *Allgemeine Musikzeitung*, 1928; quoted by Walter Abendroth, *op. cit.*, p. 321.

[4] *Cf.* pp. 43–44, above.

throughout. Hostile critics have concentrated their fire here; Edward Greenfield calls the plan 'perverse'[5] and Hans Rectanus says that 'no opera text has ever been so misunderstood as that of Act Two of this opera'.[6] Pfitzner felt it necessary to go out of his way to defend its significance and to attack those who wanted to alter the scheme, by cutting or otherwise. He knew well that he was disobeying convention:

> The newspapers would not be sorry to decapitate it, they heard nothing in it and made it formless. To be sure, as the first glance shows, this work does not follow the time-honoured form of drama, which gathers tension as it moves towards the last act. For it is *sui generis* [. . .].[7]

In his essay on the significance of the act, Pfitzner went on to say that:

> The whole work lives or dies with the second act, as it is a living organism [. . .].
> No one under any circumstances or at any time has my permission to alter this second act, omitting it or messing with it in any particular [. . .] the whole work is mutilated if it is thought of without the second act. And I declare that [. . .] anyone who brings about any mutilations or omissions in the work [. . .] is to be taken as a complete philistine and, whatever he may say, artistically coarse.[8]

The unorthodox form is merely one aspect of the unique ethos of *Palestrina*, and its refusal to obey an abstract precept in this respect can hardly to taken as sufficient reason for its condemnation. More probably, those critics who failed to respond to it as a whole seized on its most tangible departure from tradition as the simplest way of voicing their lack of sympathy with the opera. It is more accurate to say that the lack of continuity of plot from act to act is a symbol of the work's special character. It would have been easy to smooth over the irregularities and, anti-historically, bring Palestrina

---

[5] *The Gramophone, loc. cit.*, p. 1596.

[6] *Leitmotivik und Form*, p. 108.

[7] 'Mein Hauptwerk', *loc. cit.*

[8] 'Der zweite Akt Palestrinas', *loc. cit.*

to the Council to defend himself; indeed, as has been seen,[9] an early draft of the libretto intended exactly this development. But Pfitzner's whole conception, the very meaning of the work, turns on the fact that the worlds of Council and artist have nothing to do with each other, and like it or not, we must accept that plan as we have it. For some, no apology is required; others may see it as two different operas juxtaposed. Others still may recognise the theatrical anomaly but be impervious to it regardless of philosophical interpretations. In performance the contrast between the musical styles of the outer and middle acts is the more obvious, and it is possible to wonder whether the desired plan could have worked more successfully in a less extreme way. But the plan cannot simply be condemned as an artistic failure without giving due consideration to the thought that it expresses. There is, after all, no law of nature which says that an opera cannot be successful unless it has orthodox unity of plot, just as there is none which compels every opera to have love-interest.

What cannot be doubted is that the Second Act is, taken by itself, a masterpiece. In it the abstract construction comes to the fore, and its interpretation as sonata form has already been discussed.[10] But in its tingling vitality, cathartic emotional power and wonderfully controlled build-up of tension, it deserves all praise.

I am in no doubt that this Second Act achieves almost flawlessly Pfitzner's aims in his very ambitious plan. Whether he was justified in setting such a plan on the lyric stage is a different question, and a much harder one; ultimately, I believe that there is no objective answer to it. Each individual will have his or her own response, depending on his or her interests in music, drama, philosophical questions, and philosophy itself.

Having come to know *Palestrina* essentially from the score and from recordings, I had doubts about the proportions of the outer acts, and in particular the long and static nature of the Dead Masters scene, placed late in what is already a long act. But as soon as I saw a full staged production (at the

[9] *Cf.* p. 34, above.

[10] *Cf.* pp. 174–78, above.

Bavarian State Opera), the doubts were removed; the audience, which had taken a little while to settle down in the Silla and Ighino scenes, sat enthralled. And the subsequent A major entry of the Angel remains one of my most heart-warming operatic memories. By conventional standards of dramatic pacing the Dead Masters scene is at best a dangerous risk, at worst a dramatic disaster, but in practice I find this music spellbinding in the intensity of its neo-mediaeval harmonies and the almost complete immobility sustained for so long a period. If the right atmosphere is attained one is as little conscious of the passing of time as when listening to a great *Adagio* by Beethoven. I suspect that it is this scene which most arouses the impatience of those who are unsympathetic to the music; but no one in my acquaintance who has become closely familiar with it would describe it as boring. Chris de Souza, producer of the first English performances in 1981, wrote to me: 'In all my recollections of the production it's the scene I come back to again and again'.

The brevity of the Third Act is also a problem connected with the matter of intervals. Clearly brevity is preferable to padding, but as Act Three lasts only half-an-hour or so – less than half of Act Two, less than a third of Act One – the impression of a triptych is weakened. Matters are not helped by the consequent standard practice of having one main interval after Act One and only a brief pause for scene-changing after Act Two. This division increases the impression of the whole opera representing a binary rather than a ternary form. The total lengths of Acts Two and Three combined is virtually the same as that of Act One. On the other hand, that very ambiguity confirms the parallel between the acts of the opera and the classical sonata-form of exposition, development and recapitulation. Scholars remain in disagreement as to whether sonata-form is binary or tertiary, an ambiguity which must be taken as a distinctive feature of the form, in which there is a clear caesura at the double-bar at the end of the exposition but usually no such comparable break between development and recapitulation. Although each act of *Palestrina* is a self-contained musical structure, and the first two acts both have strong elements of sonata-form themselves, the parallels that have been seen between those acts, together with these proportions, tend to confirm in this way a 'sonata-like' shape of the opera as a whole.

Taken on its own, the pacing of Act Three is very satisfying; its leisurely nature contrasts most effectively with Act Two (thereby emphasising further the importance of the idea of 'haste'), and the interruptions by the singers, the Pope and Borromeo are ideally placed, enabling the final scene to move to its necessarily unhurried conclusion. Once again, the ideal must be to approach the work with sufficient lack of haste, so as, in this case, to allow a genuine second interval. Pfitzner condemns impatience in the work itself.

At the end of a good performance one has the sense of having been part of a ceremony, a ritual enactment, rather than a mere evening at the theatre.

Throughout *Palestrina* the characterisation is masterly. No one could deny that just about every one of the seventeen named roles comes vividly to life, the magnitude of Pfitzner's achievement in this respect in Act Two especially being a constant source of wonder. The active characters, such as Borromeo, Madruscht or Budoja, have little difficulty in establishing themselves through the workings of the plot, but it is noticeable that much of the best music in the work is given to the passive or reflective characters; Palestrina himself, Silla and Ighino, the Pope, and, most obviously, the 'character' who does not even appear, the Emperor Ferdinand. John Williamson has pointed out[11] that the way in which Ferdinand is presented by other characters parallels two such examples in Ibsen: Beate in *Rosmersholm* and Captain Alving in *Ghosts*, both dead when the plays start and both explicitly admired by Pfitzner in his essay on Wagner's Melot. It was also a stroke of genius to begin and end the First Act with Silla and Ighino; the light touch which they bring colours our reactions and leads us gently into and out of heavier regions. Their presence diminishes the ascetic nature of the nominally all-male cast, and as much through their humour, spirits and touching immaturity as in the mere fact of their being travesti roles.

[11] John Williamson, 'Pfitzner and Ibsen', *Music and Letters*, Vol. 67, No. 2, April 1986; *cf.* Pfitzner, *Gesammelte Schriften*, Vol. 1, pp. 23–24. *Cf.* also Williamson, *op. cit.*, pp. 138–39.

The amount we know about the real men whom Pfitzner puts onto the stage varies, but for the most part the characters are imaginative extensions of historical fact. We can believe in the politically motivated Cardinal of Lorraine and the obstructive Count of Luna; it is easy to colour in the faint sketches we have of Navagerio and arrive at Pfitzner's oil-painted, scheming Novagerio or to see in Pfitzner's Morone the man who saved the Council of Trent. Apart from Madruscht, only Borromeo is seriously at odds with his historical self. The man who raves at Pfitzner's refusal to write to order and storms off shouting about the stench of sulphur is not the ascetic saint who practised Loyola's Spiritual Exercises and was canonised in 1610.[12] But I think the shade of Carlo Borromeo will forgive Pfitzner that.

The casting of the roles does not make the sort of demands that drive singers to the limits of their endurance in Wagner and elsewhere. There are only two long parts, those of Palestrina and Borromeo, and neither of these is exceptionally heavy. The title-role emphatically does *not* call for a *Heldentenor*, requiring rather an easy lyricism and, above all, the ability to project the character with sincerity. The only top C ('Frieden', at the end of the Dictation scene) elicits a footnote in the score from the composer:[13]

> Only when the singer is able to take the high C quietly and in a transfigured manner should it be sung; otherwise definitely the instructed E [a minor sixth lower], with corresponding expression.

More important than the capacity to make a surprisingly loud noise is the ability to convey Palestrina's inner turmoil during the soliloquy, his exaltation in the dictation scene, his bewilderment at the beginning of Act Three, and the final state of 'pure will-less contemplation'. The list of leading exponents of the part can be left to speak for itself: Erik Schmedes, Karl Erb, Julius Patzak, Max Lorenz, Fritz Wunderlich and, in recordings, Nicolai Gedda and Peter Schreier. The whole ethos is a passive one, a kind of sad yet dignified resignation,

[12] *Cf.*, for example, Pastor, *op. cit.*, Vol. XVI.

[13] Full score, p. 249n.

expressed more by the flavour of the D minor music associated with it than by actions of the man himself. It is about as
far removed from all usual concepts of the 'operatic hero' as it
is possible to be. It was unnecessary, and it would have been a mistake, to
introduce any conventional 'love-interest' into the drama.
When Hindemith shows Mathis in love he increases our
sympathy for his hero. For Pfitzner to have done so would
have negated the integrity of Palestrina's ascetic and 'will-
less' nature; and Palestrina needs no such help. He engages
our sympathy to perfectly satisfactory effect as the opera
stands – a remarkable achievement with so passive a character.

Borromeo's part is more vocally taxing, as he has the long
and almost unbroken monologue of Act One, Scene Three, to
sustain, and does not have the chance to sit out through Act
Two. The other parts are almost all small, but so well written
that they can hardly fail to strike the imagination of the artists
singing them. The biggest difficulty is probably their sheer
number, bearing in mind that in addition to the named
characters there are also parts for the nine Spirits of the Dead
Masters and five Singers of the Papal Chapel. Pfitzner gives
instructions in the score for suggested doublings: Abdisu and
the first Master, the second Master and the third or fourth
Singer, Morone and the fourth Master, Madruscht, the Pope
and the Ninth Master, as well as other possibilities. The
costume department has to work hard here, and also because
the Chorus doubles as ecclesiastics or servants and papal
singers.[14]

The libretto remains a remarkable achievement by any
standards, and for one who had never attempted such a thing
before the result is all but miraculous. Everywhere can be
found beautiful language, telling imagery; the only sufficient
discussion of it would be to quote the whole libretto. But
examples inevitably come to mind: Silla's youthful pretentiousness, Ighino's charmingly naive answers, Borromeo's

---

[14] In the first London production the small numbers of the chorus required
all the non-Italian ecclesiastics to double as the rioting servants, resulting in
an exit, a costume change and an entrance to be accomplished in 81 bars of
music.

conscientious dogmatism, the simple truth of Palestrina's reply and his poetry in the Dictation scene; Novagerio's cold-bloodedness, Luna's irreverence, Morone's piety and fervour; the Pope's striking hexameters, Palestrina's deeply affecting final quatrain. All these are apparent from a first reading of the libretto alone. The only criticism that can be made is that in some places it is over-long, as, for example, in Borromeo's monologue and in the scene of the Dead Masters, where it is as if Pfitzner had misjudged the difference in duration between the spoken and the sung word.

The quality of thought in the libretto, together with the music which expresses it, is all that one would expect from the definitive statement of a profound and intellectual mind. Hans Rectanus calls it a ' "confession opera" [Bekenntnisoper] standing spiritually between *Meistersinger* and *Mathis*.[15] I have already discussed the relationship with *Mathis*[16] but I will repeat that in my view Hindemith produces a beautiful and striking picture of the artist in society which, although it may at once convince, does not go as deep as *Palestrina* before questions start to be left unanswered. More complicated is the case of *Die Meistersinger*. I find Wagner's thought confused and hard to follow in various ways,[17] and in any case I think that the whole problem of whether the composer writes for an audience is not as simple as Wagner would have us think. Occasional works and those written, like the late Beethoven quartets, with no audience in mind at all may equally be masterpieces. (I hasten to add that these strictures hardly detract from the standing of *Die Meistersinger*, whose musical riches are such that they make quibbles of this sort irrelevant.) But the message of both Wagner and Pfitzner is the same: artistic inspiration and progress come by development from within and not by a superimposed system from outside.

Palestrina is occasionally compared with *Parsifal*. Both are long, slow-moving, ascetic operas on subjects of immense profundity, and both are written with much musical restraint.

---

[15] 'Pfitzner als Dramatiker', *loc. cit.*, p. 142.

[16] *Cf.* pp. 74–75, above.

[17] *Cf.* pp. 89–91, above.

Parsifal has to achieve a denial of the will to win back the Spear; in terms of his 'heroic' qualities he is close to Palestrina. But the subject of the two operas have little else in common. The pre-occupations of *Parsifal* with sin and pain, innocence and pity, and the redeeming power of Christ, appeal to a different part of man's spiritual life from the problems of the artist struggling against the world in which he lives and against trends in his own art. It is true, of course, that the arguments of *Palestrina* have answers in terms of Christianity, and the connections of the opera's subject with Christian ritual and the history of the Church encourage such a way of thinking, whatever Pfitzner's own views may have been; but I do not think that that was Pfitzner's intention. Both operas are consistent and convincing on their own terms, but apart from very broad generalities the matters with which they deal and the axioms on which they are based are so different that it is difficult to carry the comparison further.

It must not be forgotten that the whole concept of *Palestrina* contains an element of self-contradiction: its aims of simultaneously extolling unself-conscious composition and of summing up and completing an era of music are ultimately incompatible. The internal philosophy of the work in its different aspects is admirably consistent, and undoubtedly *Palestrina* must be counted among the few outstanding works of art which successfully espouse a reactionary viewpoint, among the seas of consciously progressivist works of all eras. Its philosophy will by no means appeal to all; but it is coherent. It is the definitive statement and summary of all Pfitzner's beliefs; not for nothing did he call it 'my chief work – that is to say, the work of my life'.[18]

The most problematic element of *Palestrina* consists of the balance between its philosophical and its music-dramatic aspects. It is possible that the whole conception was not, after all, suitable for operatic treatment, and that by using the opera house as a platform for philosophy Pfitzner was caught in the same problems as Bernard Shaw when he used the straight theatre for the same ends; but in my own experience, the light cast by Pfitzner's ideas is capable of illuminating

---

[18] 'Mein Hauptwerk', *loc. cit.*

much in art and life, in many diverse fields, some far removed
from early-twentieth-century Germany. It is also true that
Palestrina's demands on the audience, the large number of
principal roles, the huge orchestra, the complex requirements
for Act Two, all mean that it is an expensive work to produce,
and it may be that only special conditions will suffice for its
staging outside Germany. Nevertheless, repeated hearings
confirm *Palestrina* as a work of genius, the product of a
profoundly fertile mind. The realisation of the composer's
hugely ambitious aims is almost completely successful; one
most notable mark of this is that throughout the whole
extraordinary project Pfitzner is never either banal or pre-
tentious.[19] The sheer invention is astonishing; Pfitzner's
enthusiasm as he warms to the details in Act Two is palpable.
Every time I return to the work I find more in it. I would deny
to the utmost that any part of it is boring. Its musical and
dramatic riches may not be for everyone, but they are none
the less real for that. Above all, it speaks with a voice that is
both personal and inevitable – not loud and assertive but
noble, subtle and lasting. It is the product of the sheer
sincerity and belief of a man who could strike inspiration from
the conflict he saw between the art of the past and the world in
which he lived.

The immediate prospects for *Palestrina*, and for Pfitzner's
music in general, are not encouraging. It is not just that at a
time when accountants are as important as artistic directors in
choosing repertoire, an unusual and very expensive opera has
an even poorer outlook than usual. Pfitzner's music makes no
concessions to those who want quick thrills. It requires
patience and careful listening, qualities hard to find when so
few actually listen to the music around them. It may be that,
until better times arrive, the work's survival will depend upon
recordings and a small number of enthusiasts. With such
thoughts in mind, it is only right to end with the words of
Palestrina's first conductor, Bruno Walter. The last letter of
his life was written, by dictation, to Frau Mali Pfitzner on

[19] The apparent banality of such moments as Novagerio's 'what's
indigestible/Must be spat out' (in Act Two, Scene Three – *cf.* p. 187, above)
is, of course, deliberate.

16 February 1962, the day before he died, and it concluded with these words:

> Despite all the dark experience of today, I am still confident that Palestrina will survive. The work has all the elements of immortality.[20]

[20] *Briefe*, Fischer, Frankfurt, 1969, p. 382; translation by Veronica Slater for the DG recording.

Appendix One

PERFORMANCE HISTORY

The first performance of *Palestrina* took place in Munich on 12 June 1917. The Munich company subsequently took the production to Basle (20 November 1917), Berne (22 November) and Zurich (24 November).

Other first productions include Vienna (1 March 1919, with Erik Schmedes as Palestrina); Berlin (11 October 1919, with Josef Mann as Palestrina and Pfitzner conducting); Frankfurt (28 March 1920); Cologne (15 May 1920); and Stuttgart (24 October 1920); as well as many other productions in smaller German, Austrian and Swiss houses. Later Munich productions included two by Rudolf Hartmann: the first, with Julius Patzak, Hans Hotter and Ludwig Weber (Madruscht), was conducted by Clemens Krauss in 1948; and the second, with Richard Holm and Otto Wiener, was first seen in 1962. Heinz Arnold produced it there in 1949, with Lorenz Fehenberger in the title-role and Robert Heger conducting; so did Fillipo Sanjust in 1979, with Peter Schreier and Wolfgang Sawallisch.

Other productions include Berlin in 1939 (Marcel Wittrisch, Rudolf Bockelmann); Vienna in 1949 (Julius Patzak, Hans Hotter, Alfred Poell, Alfred Jerger, Senja Jurinac; the conductor was Josef Krips); Salzburg in 1955 (Max Lorenz, Paul Schloeffer, Ferdinand Franz, Gottlob Frick, Elisabeth Söderstrom; conductor, Rudolf Kempe); Vienna in 1965 (Fritz Wunderlich, Otto Wiener, Walter Berry, Gottlob Frick, Senja Jurinac, Christa Ludwig; conductor, Robert Heger); and Berlin (Deutsche Oper) in 1983.

In Pfitzner's centenary year of 1969 it was given in Berlin, Munich, Stuttgart, Vienna, Zurich, Detmold, Augsburg, Hannover and Mannheim; and there were revivals in 1978–79 to celebrate the thirtieth anniversary of Pfitzner's death, in Vienna, Dusseldorf, Darmstadt, Linz and East Berlin.

A score with reduced orchestration by Hans Zanotelli was performed in Zurich in 1968 and Augsburg in 1969; the first act of this version was given at Mannes College, New York, on 21 May 1970, which seems to have been the first representation of the work in the United States.

In non-Germanic countries there have been productions at Antwerp in February 1939 (by the Cologne company); Paris Opéra, 30 March 1942 (!) in a French translation by Roger Fernay; and Berkeley, California, the first full US production, on 14 May 1982.[1]

The first production in Great Britian was a semi-professional one by Abbey Opera at the Collegiate Theatre (now the Bloomsbury Theatre) in London in June 1981. Antony Shelley conducted (and provided an English translation), Christopher de Souza was tthe producer, and Graeme Matheson-Bruce and Stuart Kale sang the title-role on alternate days. It was through singing in the chorus for this production that I first came to know *Palestrina* and to develop the enthusiam for it to begin this study.

After many plans and rumours of production in various theatres, The Royal Opera mounted the first fully professional British production of *Palestrina* at Covent Garden in January and February 1997, a substantial act of faith in the work, to mark the fiftieth anniversary of the founding of the Covent Garden Opera Company. The cast was worthy of the work:

Pope Pius IV	René Pape
Giovanni Morone	Thomas Allen
Bernardo Novagerio	Kim Begley
Cardinal Christoph Madruscht	Kurt Rydl
Cardinal Carlo Borromeo	Alan Held
Cardinal of Lorraine	Peter Rose
Abdisu	Nicolai Gedda
Anton Brus von Müglitz	Gwynne Howell
Count Luna	Sergei Leiferkus
Bishop of Budoja	Robert Tear
Avosmediano	Stafford Dean
Theophilus of Imola	Alasdair Elliot
Dandini of Grosseto	Timothy Robinson

[1] Compiled from *Kobbé's Complete Opera Book*, Putnam, London, 8th edition, 1969, p. 972; Alfred Loewenberg, *Annals of Opera*, Calder, London, 1978; programmes of Bavarian State Opera productions; and from the researches of the late Harold Rosenthal, to be incorporated in his forthcoming updating of *Annals of Opera*.

Bishop of Fiesole	Robin Leggate
Bishop of Feltre	Jeremy White
A young doctor	Leah-Marian Jones
Bishop Ercole Severolus	David Wilson-Johnson
Giovanni Pierluigi Palestrina	Thomas Moser
Ighino	Ruth Ziesak
Silla	Randi Stene
Lucrezia	Catherine Wyn-Rogers

The conductor was Christian Thielemann, the director Nikolaus Lehnhoff, and the designs were by Tobias Hoheisel and Bertina Walter.

Appendix Two

PFITZNER'S COMPOSITIONS

The following list is adapted from Helmut Grobe, *Verzeichnis sämtlicher im Druck erschienen Werke*, Hans Pfitzner-Gesellschaft, Munich/Leipzig, 1960, and Joseph Müller-Blattau, *Hans Pfitzner*, Kramer, Frankfurt, 1969, pp. 139–41, augmented with details of juvenilia from Hans Rectanus, 'Pfitzners Frühe Werke', *Symposium Hans Pfitzner, Berlin 1981*, Schneider, Tutzing, 1984, pp. 89 *et seq.*

	Geschwind-Marsch (1880)
	Andante, for piano (1880)
	Piece in E minor, for piano (1880)
	Two-part Piano Piece, *Andante* and *Allegretto* (1880)
	Sonatina in C minor, for piano
	Sonatina in F major, for piano
	March in C major for string quartet
	Quartet movement in F minor
	Adagio for violin and piano in B minor
	Andante sostenuto in B minor, for violin, viola and piano
	Minuet and trio in G for violin, cello and piano
	6 *Jugendlieder* (1883–87)
	Trio in B major for violin, cello and piano (1886)
	String Quartet in D minor (1886)
	Rondo for violin, cello and piano (1887/8)
	Scherzo for orchestra (1887)
	Cello Concerto in A minor (1888)
	Der Blumen Rache for contralto, women's choir and orchestra (1888)
	Music for Ibsen's *Festival on Solhaug* (1889–90)
Op. 1	Sonata in F sharp minor, for cello and piano (1890)

Op. 2	*Sieben Lieder* for voice (1888–89)
Op. 3	*Drei Lieder* for middle voice and piano (1888–89)
Op. 4	*Vier Lieder* for middle voice and piano (or orchestra), after texts of Heinrich Heine (1888–89)
Op. 5	*3 Lieder* for soprano (1888–89)
Op. 6	*6 Lieder* for high baritone (1888–89)
Op. 7	*Fünf Lieder* for voice with piano accompaniment (1888–89)
–	*Der arme Heinrich*, Music Drama in three acts (1891–93)
Op. 8	Piano Trio in F major (1896)
Op. 9	*Fünf Lieder*, poems by J. v. Eichendorff (1888–9)
–	*Die Rose vom Liebesgarten*, Romantic Opera in prologue, two acts and epilogue (1887–1900)
–	*Rundgesang zum Neujahrfest 1901* (1900)
Op. 10	*Drei Lieder* (1901)
Op. 11	*Fünf Lieder* (1901)
Op. 12	*Herr Oluf*, Ballad for baritone and large orchestra (1891)
Op. 13	String Quartet in D major (1902–3)
Op. 14	*Die Heinzelmännchen* for basso profundo and orchestra (1902–3)
–	*Untreu und Trost* ('Deutsches Volkslied') (1903)
Op. 15	*Vier Lieder* for voice with piano accompaniment (1904)
Op. 16	*Columbus* (Friedrich von Schiller) for unaccompanied choir (1905)
Op. 17	Music for Kleist's *Käthchen von Heilbronn* (1905)
Op. 18	*An der Mond* (J. W. von Goethe) (1906)
Op. 19	*Zwei Lieder*, poems by C. Busse (1905)
Op. 20	*Das Christelflein*, 'Spieloper' in two acts (1906)
–	'Gesang der Barden' from *Hermannsschlacht* (Heinrich von Kleist) (1906)
Op. 21	*Zwei Lieder* for voice with piano (1907)
Op. 22	*Fünf Lieder* (1907)
Op. 23	Piano Quintet in C major (1908)
Op. 24	*Vier Lieder* (1909)
Op. 25	*2 Deutsche Lieder*, for baritone and large orchestra (1915–16)
Op. 26	*Fünf Lieder* (1916)
–	*Palestrina*, Musical Legend in three acts (1912–16)
Op. 27	Sonata for violin and piano in E minor (1918)
Op. 28	*Von deutscher Seele*, Romantic Cantata on Sayings and Poems of Eichendorff, for four soloists, chorus, orchestra and organ (1921)

Op. 29   *Vier Lieder* (1922)
Op. 30   *Vier Lieder* on poems by Lenau, Mörike and Dehmel
          (1922)
Op. 31   Piano Concerto in E flat major (1922)
Op. 32   *Vier Lieder* for baritone or bass after poems of C. F.
          Meyer (1923)
Op. 33   *Alte Weisen,* eight poems by Keller (1923)
Op. 34   Violin Concerto in B minor (1925)
Op. 35   *Sechs Liebeslieder* to poems by Huch, for woman's voice
          (1925)
Op. 36   String Quartet in C sharp minor (1925)
Op. 36a   Symphony for large orchestra, in C sharp minor (after
          the Quartet, Op. 36) (1933)
Op. 37   *Lethe* (Meyer) for baritone and orchestra (1926)
Op. 38   *Das dunkle Reich,* Choral Fantasy with orchestra, organ,
          soprano and baritone soloists (1929)
Op. 39   *Das Herz,* drama for music in three acts (1931)
Op. 40   *Sechs Lieder* for middle voice with piano accompaniment
          (1931)
Op. 41   *Drei Sonette* for male voice (1931)
Op. 42   Cello Concerto in G major
Op. 43   Duo for Violin and Cello with small orchestra or piano
          (1937)
Op. 44   *Kleine Sinfonie* (Sonatina for small orchestra) (1939)
Op. 45   *Elegie und Reigen* for small orchestra (1940)
Op. 46   Symphony for large orchestra, in C major (1940)
Op. 47   *Fünf Klavierstücke* (1941)
Op. 48   *Fons Salutifer,* choral hymn with orchestra (1941)
Op. 49   Two Male Choruses (1941)
Op. 50   String Quartet in C minor (1942)
          Unorthographisches Fugato, for string quartet ('HABS')
          (1943)
Op. 51   *Sechs Studien* for piano (1943)
Op. 52   Cello Concerto in A minor (1944)
Op. 53   *Drei Gesänge* for male chorus and small orchestra
          (1944)
Op. 54   *Krakauer Begrüssung,* for orchestra (1944) (unpub-
          lished)
Op. 55   Sextet for piano, violin, viola, cello, double bass and
          clarinet (1946)
Op. 56   *Fantasie* for orchestra (1947)
Op. 57   Cantata after Goethe's *Urworten; orphisch,* for soloists,
          chorus, organ and orchestra (unfinished)

Lost works:
Trio in E flat major for violin, cello and piano (1887)
Trio in E major for violin, cello and piano (1887/8)
Concert Waltzes in A minor for piano.

BIBLIOGRAPHY

In spite of the recent publication of John Williamson's impressive book, there is still very little material on Pfitzner in English, and before the publication of the present work no study existed of *Palestrina* which attempted to approach it from the dramatic, philosophical and historical viewpoints as well as the musical. But the quantity of material on Pfitzner in German is almost bewilderingly large. I give here details of works that I have used; more comprehensive bibliographies appear in Williamson (*cf.* 1. below) and Adamy (*cf.* 2. below).

Pfitzner's prose writings are in the course of being republished in a new edition, *Sämtliche Schriften*, by Schneider of Tutzing. Volume 4, edited by Bernhard Adamy, has already appeared (1987); it includes the contents of *Reden, Schriften, Briefen* referred to below. Citations in the present book refer to the earliest editions.

1. General

JOHN WILLIAMSON, *The Music of Hans Pfitzner*, Oxford University Press, Oxford, 1992. The first book on Pfitzner in English, and a worthy one; particularly valuable for detailed technical analysis of elements of Pfitzner's style, and for careful consideration of Pfitzner's relationship with the Third Reich.

Mitteilungen der Hans Pfitzner-Gesellschaft, Munich, 1955–. A vast and growing collection of scholarly articles.

Symposium Hans Pfitzner, Berlin 1981, Schneider, Tutzing, 1984.

The Gramophone, Vol. 51, pp. 1596 *et seq.*, London, February 1974: Edward Greenfield's review of the DG recording of *Palestrina*.

The New Grove Dictionary of Music and Musicians, Macmillan, London, 1980: articles on Pfitzner, Palestrina and the Camerata.

2. Pfitzner and the Writing of *Palestrina*

WALTER ABENDROTH, *Hans Pfitzner*, Langen-Müller, Munich, 1935: the standard German biography, but not politically reliable.

BERNHARD ADAMY, *Hans Pfitzner, Literatur, Philosophie und Zeitgeschehen in seinem Weltbild und Werk*, Schneider, Tutzing 1981: the most authoritative recent biography.

JULIUS BAHLE, *Der geniale Mensch und Hans Pfitzner*, Kulturpsychologischer Verlag, Hemmenhofen am Bodensee, 2nd edn. 1974.

EDWARD J. DENT, 'Hans Pfitzner', *Music and Letters*, Vol. IV, No. 2, London, 1923.

HELMUT GROHE, *Verzeichnis sämtlicher im Druck erscheinenen Werke*, Hans-Pfitzner-Gesellschaft, Munich/Leipzig 1960: complete list of works.

PETER HEYWORTH, *Otto Klemperer: His Life and Times*, Vol. 1, Cambridge University Press, Cambridge, 1983.

ERIK LEVI, *Music in the Third Reich*, Macmillan, London, 1994: an objective study of Nazi policy in music.

JOSEPH MÜLLER-BLATTAU, *Hans Pfitzner, Lebensweg und Schaffensernte*, Kramer, Frankfurt, 1969: brief study of life and music.

FRED K. PRIEBERG, *Musik im NS-Staat*, Fischer, Frankfurt, 1982.

HANS RECTANUS, *Leitmotivik und Form in den musikdramatischen Werken Hans Pfitzners*, Triltsch, Wurzburg, 1967: a thorough musical analysis of all the stage works.

LUDWIG SCHROTT, *Die Persönlichkeit Hans Pfitzners*, Atlantis, Zürich, 1959.

HAROLD TRUSCOTT, 'Pfitzner's Orchestral Music', *Tempo*, No. 104, Boosey & Hawkes, London, 1973.

JOHANN PETER VOGEL, *Hans Pfitzner*, Rowohlt, Hamburg, 1989. A small paperback, one of a series aimed at a wide readership; I bought my copy from a station bookstall in Munich.

ELISABETH WAMLEK-JUNK, *Hans Pfitzner und Wien*, Schneider, Tutzing, 1986: includes important sidelights on the genesis of *Palestrina*.

JOSEPH WULF, *Musik im Dritten Reich, Eine Dokumentation*, Sigbert Mohn, Gütersloh, 1963: a fascinating collection of documents.

GERHART VON WESTERMANN, *Opera Guide*, English translation Sphere, London, 1968: brief comments about the other operas as well as *Palestrina*.

JOHN WILLIAMSON, 'Pfitzner and Ibsen', *Music and Letters*, Vol. 67, No. 2, April 1986.

3. The Dramatic Themes and the Music of the Opera

MOSCO CARNER, 'Pfitzner *vs.* Berg or Inspiration *vs.* Analysis', *Musical Times*, cxviii, London, 1977, pp. 379 *et seq.* (reprinted in Mosco Carner, *Major and Minor*, Duckworth, London, 1980, pp. 253–57): well worth reading.

CHRIS DE SOUZA, programme note for Abbey Opera production, Collegiate Theatre, London, June 1981.

PETER FRANKLIN, *The Idea of Music: Schoenberg and Others*, Macmillan, London, 1985.

HELMUT GROHE, *Wunder ist Möglichkeit*, notes for DG LP recording (2711 013), Polygram, 1973.

STEPHAN KOHLER, *Der Komponist als Opernheld*, Bayerische Staatsoper programme, Munich, 1979.

JÜRGEN MAEHDER, *Die musikalische Aura des Meisterwerkes*, ibid.

THOMAS MANN, *Doktor Faustus*, English translation, Secker & Warburg, London, 1949.

——, *Reflections of a Nonpolitical Man*, English translation by Walter D. Morris, Ungar, New York, 1983.

WOLFGANG OSTHOFF, 'Pfitzner-Goethe-Italien: die Würzeln des Silla-Liedchens im *Palestrina*', *Analecta Musicologica*, No. 17, Cologne, 1976.

——, 'Eine neue Quelle zu Palestrinazitat und Palestrinasatz in Pfitzners musikalisches Legende', *Renaissance-Studien: Helmuth Osthoff zum 80. Geburtstag*, Schneider, Tutzing, 1979.

HANS PFITZNER, 'Mein Hauptwerk', first printed in Hamburg Staatsoper programme, 1979.

——, *Gesammelte Schriften*, three vols., Filser, Augsburg, 1926: the major essays, etc.

——, *Reden, Schriften, Briefen*, ed. Walter Abendroth, Luchterhand, Berlin, 1955.

——, 'Der zweite Akt Palestrinas – ein Vermächtnis und eine Abwehr', first printed in *Mitteilungen der Hans-Pfitzner-Gesellschaft*, Vol. 19, Munich, 1967.

HANS RECTANUS, 'Pfitzner als Dramatiker', *Beiträge der Geschichte der Oper*, Bosse, Regensburg, 1969.

——, *Leitmotivik und Form* [. . .], see under **2.** above.

ARTHUR SCHOPENHAUER, *The World as Will and Idea*, English translation Kegan Paul, London 1883/6.

HAROLD TRUSCOTT, 'The Importance of Hans Pfitzner', *Music-Journal*, Nos. 1 & 2, London, 1947, 1948.

GERD UECKERMANN, *Renaissancismus und Fin du Siècle*, de Gruyter, Berlin, 1985.

MARC A. WIENER, *Undertones of Insurrection: Music, Politics and the Social Sphere in the Modern German Narrative*, University of Nebraska Press, London, 1993: commentary on Pfitzner *v.* Bekker and on Mann on *Palestrina*.

4. Palestrina and the Mass

AUGUST WILHELM AMBROS, *Geschichte der Musik*, Leuckart, Leipzig, four vols. 1862–78: Vol. IV, which concentrates on Palestrina and his contemporaries, was Pfitzner's main source.

GIUSEPPE BAINI, *Memorie storico-critiche della vita e delle opere di Giovani Pierluigi Palestrina*, Rome, 1828.

GUSTAV REESE, *Music in the Renaissance*, Dent, London, 1954.

KNUT JEPPESEN, *The Style of Palestrina and the Dissonance*, Oxford University Press, London, 1946.

LEWIS LOCKWOOD, *Palestrina, 'Pope Marcellus Mass'*, Norton Critical Scores, New York, 1975: contains much useful material in translation.

5. The Florentine Camerata

MANFRED BUKOFZER, *Music in the Baroque Era*, Dent, London, 1948.

ROBERT DONINGTON, *The Rise of Opera*, Faber, London, 1983: indispensible reading on the Camerata and early opera in general.

CLAUDE V. PALISCA, 'The Camerata Fiorentina: a Reappraisal', *Studi musicali*, i, Florence, 1972, pp. 203 *et seq.*

NINO PIRROTTA and ELENA POVOLEDO, *Music and Theatre from Poliziano to Monteverdi*, Cambridge University Press, 1982: the Camerata in the context of threatre-with-music and the Florentine *intermedi*.

NINO PIRROTTA, 'Temperaments and Tendencies in the Florentine Camerata', *Music and Culture in Italy from the Middle Ages to the Baroque*, Harvard University Press, Cambridge (Mass.), 1984: the roles of the individual musicians in the Camerata.

6. The Council of Trent

THEODORE BUCKLEY, *A History of the Council of Trent*, London, 1852.

Canons and Decrees of the Council of Trent, London, 1851.

CHARLES CRONIN, *The Council of Trent*, London, 1910.

Concilium Tridentinum. Diarorum, actorum, epistularum, tractatuum, nova collectio. Görres-Gesellschaft, Bonn, 1901–: a magnificent collection of original source material, in Latin throughout.

ARTHUR DICKENS, *The Counter-Reformation*, Thames and Hudson, London, 1968.

JOHN ELLIOTT, *Europe Divided 1559–1598*, Fontana, London, 1968.

GEOFFREY ELTON, *Reformation Europe 1517–1559*, Fontana, London, 1963.

PETER HELM, *History of Europe 1450–1660*, Bell, London, 1961.

HUBERT JEDIN, *Geschichte des Konzils von Trient*, Vols. I–IV, Herder, Freiburg, 1915–75. English translation by Ernest Graf, *History of the Council of Trent*, Nelson, London 1957 (only the first two volumes have been translated): the standard modern history.

——, *Crisis and Closure of the Council of Trent*, English translation Sheed and Ward, London, 1967.

RUDOLF KRISS, *Die Darstellung des Konzils von Trient in Hans Pfitzners musikalischer Legende 'Palestrina'*, Hans-Pfitzner-Gesellschaft, Munich, 1962: many comparisons between the Council and Pfitzner's second act.

SFORZA PALLAVICINI, *Geschichte des tridentinischer Konzil*, German translation Augsburg, 1835.

LUDWIG PASTOR, *History of the Popes*, Vols. XV and XVI, English translation by Ralph Francis Kerr, Kegan Paul, London, 1928.

LEOPOLD VON RANKE, *History of the Popes*, English translation by Sarah Austen, John Murray, London, 1851.

PAOLO SOAVE (i.e. Sarpi), *The Historie of the Councel of Trent*, English translation London, 1620.

KARL WEINMANN, *Das Konzil von Trent und die Kirchenmusik*, Leipzig, 1919.

Index
of Hans Pfitzner's Works

General Index

Abdisu, Patriarch of Assyria, 266
Abendroth, Walther, 33, 48, 83
Adamy, Bernhard, 10, 54, 124, 204n
Agazzari, Agostino, 220
Alsace, 47
Ambros, August Wilhelm, 30, 223
Amulius, 267
Andro, L., 33
Arcadelt, Jakob, 215
Arensen, Adolf, 80
Aristotle, 103
Assyria, Patriarch of, 266
atonality, 93-94
Aue, Hartmann von, 21
Augsburg, Diet of, 239, 240
Avosmediano, see Guadix, 269

Bach, Johann Sebastian
 B minor Mass, 124
 St Matthew Passion, 111, 197-98
Bacon, Francis, 77
Baini, Giuseppe, 221, 222
Bardi, Giovanni de', 225, 227
Bargagli, Girolamo, 229
Bavarian State Opera, 156n, 279
Beethoven, Ludwig van, 112, 118, 273
 influence, 21
 Missa Solemnis, 114
 String Quartet, Op. 131, 57

Bekker, Paul, 66, 91
Bender, Paul, 43
Berg, Alban, 92, 93, 115, 122, 276
Berlin, 20, 22, 44, 59
Berlioz, Hector
 Benvenuto Cellini, 73-74
 La Damnation de Faust, 75n
 Les Troyens, 123
Blois, 261
Böhm, Karl, 56
Boito, Arrigo, 30
Bologna, 235, 237
Borgia, Cesare, 255
Borromeo, Federigo, 259
Borromeo, Carlo, 220, 249, 251, 255, 256 *et seq.*, 281
Borromini, Francesco, 256n
Brahms, Johannes, 48n
 influence, 21
 Piano Quintet, Op. 34 22
Brandenburg, Margrave of, 238
Braus, Dorothea, 54
Brecht, Berthold, 77
Brian, Havergal, 112, 273
 Symphony No. 4 (*Das Siegeslied*), 75n
Brockeler, John, 156n
Brodersen, Friedrich, 43
Bruch, Max, 114
Bruckner, Anton, 171, 274
Brumel, Antoine de, 166n
Budoja, Bishop of, 268
Budva, 268
Bülow, Hans von, 20
Busch, Fritz, 66
Busoni, Ferruccio, 66, 87,